THE
SUPER BOWL

THE FIRST FIFTY YEARS OF AMERICA'S GREATEST GAME

DAVID FISCHER

FOREWORD BY FRANCO HARRIS

SP
SPORTS
PUBLISHING

Sports Publishing books may be purchased in bulk at special discounts for sales promotion, corporate gifts, fund-raising, or educational purposes. Special editions can also be created to specifications. For details, contact the Special Sales Department, Sports Publishing, 307 West 36th Street, 11th Floor, New York, NY 10018 or sportspubbooks@ skyhorsepublishing.com.

Sports Publishing® is a registered trademark of Skyhorse Publishing, Inc.®, a Delaware corporation.

Visit our website at www.sportspubbooks.com.

10 9 8 7 6 5 4 3 2

Library of Congress Cataloging-in-Publication Data is available on file.

Cover design by Tom Lau
Cover photo credits: Associated Press

Table of Contents photo credits: top, middle (AP Photos), bottom (Wikimedia Commons/Kristi Machado)

ISBN: 978-1-61321-896-9
Ebook ISBN: 978-1-61321-897-6

Printed in China

To Michael, my brother, thanks for fifty years of love, encouragement, and support.

CONTENTS ||||||||||||||||||||||||

FOREWORD

Every NFL player chases the dream of playing in the Super Bowl. I would never have imagined that my dream would come true four times. Yes, I've played in four Super Bowls with the Pittsburgh Steelers. And we won them all—in 1975, 1976, 1979, and 1980—becoming the first team in NFL history to win four Super Bowls. There is no doubt that you measure a team's success by whether or not it's won a Super Bowl. For those of us who've done it, there is a feeling that you have accomplished it all!

The great majority of NFL players will never play in a Super Bowl game. Only a small number have experienced the thrill of winning one. So many legends have passed through the NFL without participating in what we call America's Greatest Game. For some of these players, it made their NFL experience incomplete.

The 1974 season was a tough one for us. There were so many challenges that year, including a quarterback controversy. No one was expecting us to make it to the AFC Championship game against the Oakland Raiders. To top it off, the Raiders had shut us out 17-0 in the third game of the regular season. But when we took the field in Oakland on December 29, all of the challenges were behind us and our total focus was on this one game. In the NFL it is all about "Team." You win because of "Team," and we had an incredible team effort during this conference championship game. We were down 10-3 at the end of the third quarter. But we

scored three touchdowns in the fourth quarter and held the Raiders to one field goal and 29 rushing yards overall. We took care of business, beating the Raiders 24-13. The win sent us to the first Super Bowl in Pittsburgh Steeler history.

The second the game was over we started celebrating. We were totally overwhelmed. There was a lot of excitement, hugging, and smiling. What an unbelievable feeling. We'd made it.

A week later, we were headed to New Orleans to play the Minnesota Vikings in Super Bowl IX. What a high it was, landing in the Super Bowl city. I loved that our first Super Bowl was in New Orleans. It's a great place for the Super Bowl, which must be why the game has been held there ten different times since 1967. There was dancing and music in the streets. You felt like there was a continuous party going on. And the food? Incredible. The first few nights, Chuck Noll allowed us to enjoy it all, and we did. Back then, the size and number of big corporate parties and events were nothing like they are now. But for the players, one thing has remained constant: the excitement, fun, and importance of the game are what it is all about.

On game day, I couldn't help being a bit nervous as I headed out onto the field. But the overwhelming feeling was one of excitement. I'd played in big games before, but never one in which the whole world was watching. When the whistle blew, the nervousness melted away and it was all football. The game was a tough defensive battle. The Vikings had the third-ranked defense in the league. But *our* defense was incredible, holding Minnesota to just 17 rushing yards in the game. In the second half, our offense started to click and we scored two touchdowns. That was all we needed. We, the Pittsburgh Steelers, won our first Super Bowl by the score of 16-6. We did it. It was so unbelievable. A truly memorable moment was when team captain Andy Russell, who had been there through the bad years, had the chance to hand the game ball to owner Art Rooney, the Chief.

With just a handful of winning seasons over the decades, Art Rooney knew better than anyone how special it is to reach the highest pinnacle of your sport. And we did it four times in six years. Each of those Super Bowls was special and we never got tired of winning and being the best.

The hoopla surrounding America's Greatest Game has grown over time. Rules have been updated, players change teams more often, there is more money involved, and fans are treated to more spectacular halftime shows and parties. But come game time, football is still football. And winning is the only thing. In the end, people want to watch football. There is something great about that.

The first fifty years have been amazing in terms of how far this game has come. This book, *The Super Bowl*, gives you great information on the game and its players. There will always be debates on who had the best team, or which was the greatest Super Bowl. If you need to know, it all comes together in David Fischer's *The Super Bowl*.

But, I do have my opinion.

FRANCO HARRIS

PREFACE

A word about how this book is organized. Certain teams—like the Green Bay Packers in the 1960s and the Pittsburgh Steelers in the 1970s, to name but two—dominated their respective decades. These teams, along with teams like the San Francisco 49ers of the 1980s and the Dallas Cowboys of the 1990s, earn inclusion in the "Ring of Honor" chapter. The team's leaders are highlighted in profiles I call "The Best Who Never Lost." Players and coaches who experienced both Super Bowl victory and defeat are highlighted in profiles titled "A Pantheon of Heroes." In a volume of this size, just as on the sports pages, these dynastic teams can crowd out other Super Bowl-winning teams of the same decade. And so to enhance the variety of teams and athletes covered here, I've opted to highlight an important game or memorable athletic performance by selecting that game or athlete for inclusion in other ways. Compelling athletes are featured in the section called "One Shot at Glory" (for winners and losers). The chapter titled "Game Action" includes a selection of the shocking upsets, the seesaw battles, and the beat downs. Finally, the chapter "Power Plays and Mind Games" will bring to light a few plays that turned the game and analyze some of the coaching decisions that turned the game.

I've attempted to choose these top Super Bowl games and personalities by accepting three premises: that news value is primary; that some events and personalities become more compelling when viewed with hindsight; and that the world of professional football cannot be interpreted apart from the era in which it exists. Much internal debate went into making the choices. With certain concessions for balance and pace, I have chosen for inclusion in this book what in my judgment are the most important or compelling Super Bowls and big-game performers. The selection process and methodology is a little like choosing the best-tasting gourmet meal. There is an "eye of the beholder" factor. I can only go with my gut, and doubtless some will disagree with some of my choices.

But that's one of the reasons why the Super Bowl is such a great event. It provides endless fodder for spirited conversation and debate.

INTRODUCTION

THE FIRST FIFTY YEARS OF AMERICA'S GREATEST GAME

Writing in the *Los Angeles Times,* in 2011, Joe Flint made this observation about America's premier sporting event. "The Fourth of July, Thanksgiving and New Year's Day have nothing on the Super Bowl. Without being an official holiday, the gonzo game has flags, food, friends and drink aplenty—and can claim the largest national TV audiences ever."

It seems as if the Super Bowl has been around for as long as there has been football. But that's not the case. The NFL was started in 1920 as the American Professional Football Association and played its own championship games. (It became the NFL in 1922.) A new league, the American Football League, began play in 1960, and it had its own separate championship games.

The two leagues became fierce rivals. They battled for players, fans, and television viewers. In the spring of 1966, the two leagues decided that instead of fighting each other, they would join together to make pro football bigger than

Plenty of seats were available in the Los Angeles Coliseum for Super Bowl I. (AP Photo)

(AP Photo/Bill Waugh)

ever. They agreed to combine for the start of the 1970 season. They also decided that beginning in January 1967, they would play an annual world championship game between the two league champions. That game soon became known as the Super Bowl—and it was the start of something big.

But the first game was not Super Bowl I. The date was January 15, 1967. The place was the Los Angeles Memorial Coliseum. The teams were the Green Bay Packers of the NFL and the Kansas City Chiefs of the AFL. It was called the AFL-NFL World Championship Game. The game didn't officially become the "Super Bowl" until 1969. That's also when the games were given Roman numerals. The 1969 game became Super Bowl III.

Lamar Hunt, the owner of the Kansas City Chiefs and one of the founders of the AFL, liked the idea of an AFL-NFL World Championship Game. But Hunt wanted a catchier name. He wanted it to be some kind of a bowl—such as college football's Cotton Bowl, Orange Bowl, or Rose Bowl, which were already very popular. One day, during the summer of 1966, Hunt saw his daughter playing with a new toy: a ball that could bounce very high. She told him it was called a "Super Ball." When Hunt heard that, he knew *super* was just the word he had been looking for. Hunt began calling the AFL-NFL Championship Game the "Super Bowl." Despite his doubts that the name would catch on, mainstream publications like the *New York Times* began using it in news stories as early as 1966.

In some ways, the event got off to an awkward start. In Super Bowl I (as it came to be called), each team used its own official league ball when it was on offense. The referees had to remember to keep making the switch throughout the game. The game was also televised over two networks: CBS (the

(AP Photo/Doug Mills)

network that broadcasted NFL games) and NBC (the network that broadcasted AFL games). Each network paid $1 million for broadcast rights and charged advertisers premium rates at the time: $85,000 per minute for CBS and $70,000 per minute for NBC. The total television audience was 51.1 million viewers.

In 1967, only 61,946 fans attended the Super Bowl at the enormous L.A. Coliseum. That meant more than 30,000 seats were empty. But at least the tickets were cheap. The face value cost of the most expensive ticket to Super Bowl I was $12. Frugal fans could get a seat for $6 or $10.

In 2015, Super Bowl XLIX between the New England Patriots and Seattle Seahawks dwarfed all of these numbers. As is true of all modern Super Bowls, tickets (at the 63,400-seat University of Phoenix Stadium) quickly sold out. As for broadcast rights, The Game is now rotated among NBC, CBS, and Fox as part of the NFL's TV contract, which is estimated to be $3 billion a season, on average. Worldwide viewership in 2015 was 114.4 million. Advertisers paid $4.5 million for each thirty-second ad. And in a thoroughly modern twist, CNN reported that more than 28 million tweets related to the game and halftime show were sent during the live telecast.

But one thing hasn't changed. Every year, millions and millions of fans stop what they're doing, turn on their TV sets, and watch a game: the Super Bowl.

CBS newsman Bob Schieffer did Joe Flint one better when he said that "the truth is, the Super Bowl long ago became more than just a football game. It's part of our culture, like turkey at Thanksgiving and lights at Christmas."

This book celebrates that game—a game that didn't sell out in 1967 and that now dominates America's sporting landscape. My goal is to cover the action, the heroes, the strategy, and the records from half a century of championship football.

I only wish I could be the one to write the centennial edition.

(AP Photo/Roberto Borea)

FIRST QUARTER
RING OF HONOR

|||||||||||||||||||||||||||||||||||||||||||||||||

Whoever coined the phrase, "no pressure, no diamonds," could have been describing the experience of playing in the Super Bowl. To a man, players understand that practically the whole world is watching on Super Sunday. They also know that if they perform, they get a ring. If not, they go home empty-handed.

It's as simple as that. And as complicated. Why do some football players rise to the occasion, while others wilt under pressure? This chapter profiles the greatest players, coaches, and teams of Super Bowls from today and all time. These legends set the amazing records that today's stars are trying to break.

THE 1960s

Until the 1950s, most football players played both offense and defense. What's more, these players were called "60-Minute Men," which simply means they played the entire game. They played offense on one series, then turned around and played defense on the next. For example, during the 1940s, Sammy Baugh routinely set records in passing, punting, and interceptions. The "free substitution" rule totally changed the way a player played. Adopted in 1950,

the rule eventually led to the development of the game we know today. Teams were divided into offensive and defensive units. The two-way players began to specialize in one position only, such as passer, receiver, blocker, or kicker.

As professional football entered the Sixties, the defense was reasserting itself, and high-scoring games, the norm in the Fifties, would become a thing of the past. During this decade, most defenses had figured out how to bottle up the run and shut down the long pass. Bigger, faster defensive specialists, focusing solely on ways to counter an offensive threat, no longer waited for the offensive play to develop and then react. Instead, defensive coaches decided that defenses should go on offense, swarming from sideline to sideline, trying to ruin whatever play the offense happened to be running before it developed. To offensive players like Tom Fears, a Hall of Fame receiver, the field seemed to shrink. "We've run out of room. The quick defensive backs and linebackers have filled up the field. There's not much space out there any more." Defenses played with an aggressive attitude. They read plays so well and reacted so fast that they snapped shut on offensive plays like a Venus flytrap. For the first time, defenders went after running backs believing they had an equal right to the ball. These football-grabbing defenses had ball carriers worried as much about holding onto the football as about gaining yards.

Green Bay Packers, Super Bowls I and II

The Green Bay Packers won three NFL championships before the first Super Bowl was played, then took home the title in Super Bowls I and II. So their dynasty essentially bridged the

Chiefs quarterback Len Dawson looks down field against the Packers in Super Bowl I. (AP Photo)

two eras. This powerful, efficient machine of a football team used no tricks to steamroll its opponents during the decade, winning title after title (to cap the 1961, 1962, 1965, 1966, and 1967 seasons). The Pack simply came right at the other team, daring the opponent to beat them.

What is most impressive about this team is the architect who built it. When coach Vince Lombardi took over the Green Bay Packers in 1959, the team was coming off the

worst record in their history, 1–10–1. On his first day as head coach he addressed his new team. "Let's get one thing straight," he declared. "I'm in complete command here. Gentlemen, I've never been associated with a losing team. I do not intend to start now."

In 1959, Bart Starr took over as quarterback. In Starr, Lombardi saw a quarterback with an accurate arm, great intelligence, and poise. The coach thought that Starr could be the key to Green Bay's rebuilding effort. Lombardi's "run to daylight" offensive strategy wasn't complicated. He liked to run the ball, and throw safe pass patterns. But he needed an intelligent quarterback to make it come together. In Starr's first season as the starter the Packers became contenders. The next year the Packers reached the 1960 championship but lost to the Philadelphia Eagles, despite outrushing them 401 yards to 296. It was the last time that Lombardi's Packers ever lost a championship playoff game.

Lombardi symbolized America's obsession with professional football during the 1960s. He once said, "Winning isn't everything; it's the only thing." And he lived by those words. He told his players: "You will make mistakes, but not very many if you want to play for the Green Bay Packers." In 1961, when the Packers won their first of five NFL titles in seven years, 14 of the 22 starters were the same players who'd been with the club during that awful 1958 season. Lombardi didn't clean house. He inspired those same players to greatness. He physically and mentally beat them up. He was a disciplinarian. A taskmaster. He was a demanding, no-nonsense coach. "When he tells me to sit down, I don't even look for a chair," defensive tackle Henry Jordan said.

Green Bay finished either first or second in rushing offense in the league six times during the decade. The Pack boasted a rushing attack led by hard-nosed fullback Jim Taylor and complemented with multi-talented halfbacks Paul Hornung, Elijah Pitts, and Donny Anderson. Lombardi's signature offensive play was the Packer Sweep, in which guards Jerry Kramer and Fuzzy Thurston pulled along the line of scrimmage and raced in tandem toward one sideline or the other before surging up field, blocking defenders, and providing an avenue for the runner behind them.

The Packer Sweep commonly ran to the right, because the Green Bay offensive line featured one of the greatest right sides in NFL history with right tackle Forrest Gregg playing alongside Kramer. Once described by Lombardi as "the finest player I've ever coached," Gregg won Super Bowls I and II with the Packers and Super Bowl VI as a member of the Dallas Cowboys. Gregg later coached the Cincinnati Bengals in Super Bowl XVI, a 26–21 loss to the San Francisco 49ers. He is the first person to play in a Super Bowl and coach a team to the Super Bowl.

With Paul Hornung and Jim Taylor carrying the ball behind Kramer, Thurston, and Gregg, the Packer Sweep was close to unstoppable, even though opponents often knew it was coming. "Football is a simple game of blocking, tackling, and running," said Lombardi. "The team that wins is the team that tackles better, blocks better, and runs to daylight."

The Packer accomplishments during the 1960s were remarkable. They were the first team in sixty years to win three NFL championships in a row. By winning the first two Super Bowls convincingly, the Packers maintained NFL dominance when the upstart AFL began challenging the old league.

A few days before Super Bowl I, when the Packers, of the forty-eight-year-old NFL, took on the Chiefs, of the seven-year-old AFL, Green Bay coach Lombardi was feeling the heat. He couldn't lose. Not to those upstarts. NFL patriarchs George Halas and Wellington Mara sent Lombardi a telegram saying, "We are proud of you and the Packers for representing us, the NFL, in this first game." Lombardi worried about the great expectations. He couldn't sleep that week leading up to the big game. He felt like the weight of the league was on his shoulders. The players felt the pressure, too. Green Bay safety

Tom Brown said, "We've just beaten Dallas for our second straight NFL championship. But you know something? If we lose this game, the season won't mean anything. If we lose, people will remember us as the NFL team that lost to Kansas City in the first game played between the leagues."

The Chiefs, by contrast, could afford to feel more relaxed, with a nothing-to-lose attitude. "We're the kids from across the tracks," said Jerry Mays, the Chiefs' defensive captain. "We're coming over to play the rich kids." Kansas City Chiefs cornerback Fred Williamson was an early proponent of trash talking. He was nicknamed "The Hammer" because he loved to knock down opposing ball carriers with hard forearm tackles to their head. Before Super Bowl I he told reporters that the Green Bay Packers weren't so tough and that any receiver who "catches a pass in my territory, they're going to pay the price."

It was fitting the Chiefs represented the AFL in the inaugural Super Bowl, since Kansas City owner Lamar Hunt was a founding father of the league and had come up with the Super Bowl moniker. In order to help bring about the merger of the two leagues, NFL commissioner Pete Rozelle negotiated some strange compromises. One of them concerned which ball to use for the first league championship game. The official ball of the NFL was made by Wilson. The AFL used a Spalding ball. Since the shapes of these balls were slightly different, both leagues wanted to use their own. So a compromise was arranged. During the first NFL-AFL World Championship a Wilson ball had to be used when the NFL played offense. When the AFL was on offense, the ball in play was a Spalding.

An estimated 50 million Americans watched that first game. CBS tried to lure viewers by preceding its Super Bowl coverage with an exhibition by the Harlem Globetrotters. It worked. The Nielsen Company reported that CBS won the ratings battle with a 22.6 rating, compared to 18.5 for NBC. Despite a TV blackout in the Los Angeles area, Super Bowl I was not a sellout. CBS announcer Frank Gifford interviewed Lombardi during the pregame show and said Lombardi was so nervous, "he held onto my arm and he was shaking like a leaf. It was incredible."

Prior to the inaugural Super Bowl, aging Packer veteran Max McGee told fellow receiver Boyd Dowler not to get hurt, because McGee, who'd been living it up well past curfew, was in no shape to play. When the game finally began, the Chiefs sacked Bart Starr twice on the first series. Soon after, of course, Dowler got hurt, forcing the thirty-four-year-old McGee to take the field. A few plays later, McGee made a one-handed, behind-the-back catch of a Bart Starr pass and took off 37 yards to score the first touchdown in Super Bowl history.

Kansas City hung tough, holding Green Bay to a 14–10 halftime lead. The first Super Bowl halftime show featured jazz trumpeter Al Hirt and the marching bands from the University of Arizona and Grambling State, along with 300 pigeons and 10,000 balloons. Fans marveled at the sight of two jetpack pilots blasting off and flying like Space Age supermen for a short trip around the stadium, landing at the 50-yard line and shaking hands.

With NBC and CBS both broadcasting the game, NBC missed the second half kickoff because Charlie Jones was interviewing entertainer Bob Hope, which caused NBC to fall behind in airing its commercials. At the start of the second half, while the NBC television audience was still watching commercials for McDonald's (introducing the Big

Mac), Green Bay kicked off to the Chiefs. Referees immediately threw their penalty flags and blew their whistles, signaling the ball from the first kickoff dead and ordering the Packers to kick off a second time, and this time NBC was back from break. According to reports, the on-field official who ordered the re-kick also asked CBS sideline reporter Pat Summerall to inform Lombardi what had happened. (Having played for the New York Giants when Lombardi was the team's offensive coordinator, Summerall was understandably reluctant to approach his old coach with a piece of bad news.) If this all seems like amateur hour, it's worth remembering that the age of television networks broadcasting major sporting events was still in its infancy in the late Sixties; for in a subsequent year, NBC inadvertently made TV history with the Heidi Game, when it cut away from a dramatic AFL postseason contest between the New York Jets and Oakland Raiders to show the movie about a pig-tailed Swiss girl.

The game-time temperature for the second-half kickoff (both of them!) reached 80 degrees. Some expected the Packers to melt in the heat of the Los Angeles Coliseum. And when Kansas City quarterback Len Dawson got the Chiefs to midfield early in the third quarter, the crowd moved to the edge of their seats. But then Green Bay safety Willie Wood intercepted a wobbly Dawson pass, running it 50 yards to the Chief's 5-yard line. Soon it was 21–10. Two drives later Starr found the hung-over McGee open again, and McGee made another dramatic juggling catch for the clinching touchdown. In all, it was quite a day (and one imagines quite a night) for Max McGee. He had caught four passes all season; against Kansas City's weak cornerbacks he caught seven passes

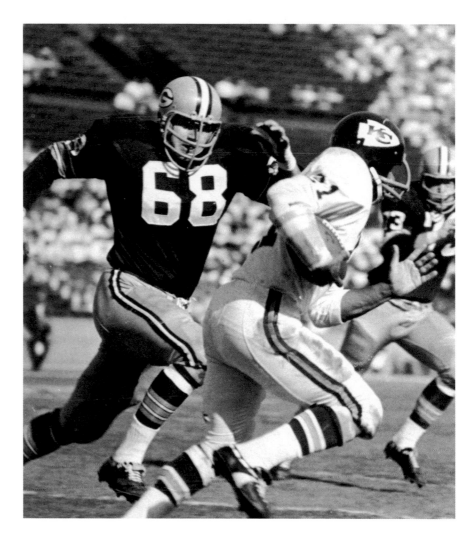

Mike Garrett carries the ball for the Chiefs as the Packers close in during Super Bowl I. (AP Photos)

for 138 yards and two touchdowns, his biggest game in years. "Green Bay picks out a weak spot and sticks with it better than anyone I've ever seen," said Chief running back Mike Garrett.

Bart Starr was the MVP of Super Bowl I. He completed 16 of 23 passes for 250 yards, including 37- and 13-yard touchdown strikes to receiver Max McGee, earning a 35–10 victory. Most impressive, on third down situations, Starr completed 10 of 13 passes to convert the first down. Remember the bulletin board material spewed by Fred "The Hammer" Williamson? As it turned out, it was The Hammer who was nailed by the Packers. In the fourth quarter, the Packers ran their power sweep around his end. When the pileup was untangled, The Hammer was at the bottom, knocked out cold with a broken arm.

So Green Bay won, and they won big, as they should have, and as everyone in the NFL hoped they would. "In my opinion, the Chiefs don't rate with the top teams in the NFL," said Lombardi. "They're a good football team, with fine speed, but I'd have to say NFL football is tougher." (Chiefs coach Hank Stram was stunned when he learned of Lombardi's comments. "He didn't say that, did he? Vince is a friend of mine. He wouldn't say that.")

The Green Bay Packers were each paid a $15,000 winners' share. The Chiefs were paid $7,500 each. Asked to design the Packers' 1967 Super Bowl ring, Lombardi had it emblazoned with the words "Love" and "Character." No known broadcast footage of this game exists. Neither network preserved a tape. All that survived of this broadcast is snippets of sideline footage shot by NFL Films. Somehow, this historic game has been lost to history.

Television did get its act together. Super Bowl II, televised by CBS, was the first sports broadcast to show images from a camera carried on a blimp, and the first to use slow-motion, instant replay. The live gate was $3 million and 60 million households had the game tuned in on TV. During the on-field pregame show, two thirty-foot tall figures made of paper-mache, with smoke pouring out of their noses, faced off at midfield. One resembled a Green Bay Packer and the other resembled an Oakland Raider, the two teams competing in the 1968 game.

Green Bay, setting out to defend its title, sent Oakland an early message at the start of Super Bowl II. On Oakland's first offensive play, Green Bay linebacker Ray Nitschke shot into the backfield and decked Hewritt Dixon with a bone-rattling tackle, upending the Raider running back, and setting the tone for what would become Lombardi's final championship with Green Bay. According to Bart Starr, Ray Nitschke was a "classic example of Dr. Jekyll and Mr. Hyde." Off the field he was a thoughtful and caring person. On the field, he was a ferocious middle linebacker who at times seemed to truly enjoy hitting and hurting people. "Linebackers, by the nature of their position, have to be aggressive. If you really love football, that's where you want to be," Nitschke said. "But you're not an animal. That's a sportscaster tag, and they say a lot of the wrong things."

The Pack scored on three of their first four possessions, with two Don Chandler field goals and a touchdown. By the half their lead was only 16–7. Lombardi, it was rumored, would be stepping down as coach after the game. In the locker room at halftime, Packers guard Jerry Kramer exhorted his teammates. "Let's play the last 30 minutes for the old man." The Packers seized control in the third quarter, scoring a touchdown and a field goal to go up 26–7. Cornerback Herb Adderley clinched the victory in the fourth quarter with a 60-yard interception return. Chandler kicked a Super Bowl record fourth field goal to give the Packers their second straight Super Bowl win, 33–14. Adderley, who was the Packers first African-American player, later played with

Before Super Bowl II, these giant figures met for a pre-game handshake. (AP Photos/Harold Valentine)

the Dallas Cowboys, appearing in four of the first six Super Bowl games, and winning three rings. Bart Starr again was picked as the game's most valuable player, completing 13 of 24 passes for 202 yards and one touchdown.

At game's end, Jerry Kramer and victorious teammates carried Lombardi off the field in one of the most indelible imagines in Super Bowl history. Kramer's diary of the 1967 Green Bay Packers season, the best-selling *Instant Replay*, written with sports journalist Dick Schaap, gave fans an unprecedented look into the locker room of one of the greatest teams in NFL history. Not only did the book chronicle the daily workings of a championship team, it gave everyone a warts-and-all look at coach Vince Lombardi, revealing a man who cared deeply for his players. "Many things have been said about Coach and he is not always understood by those who quote him," said Kramer. "The players understand. This is one beautiful man."

Indeed, following his second Super Bowl win, Lombardi did retire, but he missed the game. In 1969, he returned to coaching with the Washington Redskins, guiding them to their first winning season in 14 years. A few weeks before the 1970 season began, Lombardi died of cancer. The football world mourned. "It's like losing a father," said Starr. Lombardi was elected to the Pro Football Hall of Fame the year following his death. In an amazing 10-year coaching career he had a record of 105–35–6. No other coach in NFL history has a better win percentage. To honor his dedication to winning, the NFL renamed the Super Bowl trophy the Vince Lombardi Trophy. But sadly, Lombardi never saw the Super Bowl become the spectacle that it is today.

THE BEST WHO NEVER LOST

Bart Starr

Two rings in two consecutive Super Bowls with the Green Bay Packers; MVP of Super Bowls I and II

STARR QUALITY

Bart Starr was an intelligent quarterback who is considered one of the best ever at calling audibles, meaning changing a called play at the line of scrimmage after seeing how the defense lines up. In Super Bowl II, the Packers were leading 6–0 and had

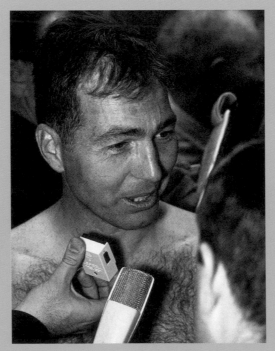

(AP Photo)

the ball on their own 38-yard line. On first down, rather than sticking with a simple running play call, Starr changed the play and threw over the heads of the Oakland defense for a 62-yard touchdown pass to Boyd Dowler. The score demoralized Oakland and boosted Green Bay to its second straight Super Bowl championship by a score of 33–14. The win bears the stamp of Starr's brainy play calls. He completed 13 of 24 passes for 202 yards and the one backbreaking touchdown. He was the Super Bowl MVP for a second straight time.

THE BEST WHO NEVER LOST

Vince Lombardi

Two rings in two consecutive Super Bowls coaching the Green Bay Packers

IN-VINCE-ABLE

Vince Lombardi worked his players until they were near exhaustion. After such workouts the games seemed easy by comparison. He stressed the team concept and punished any player who was late for practice. Players set their watches ahead ten minutes to what they called "Lombardi time." The coach was tough,

Vince Lombardi is carried off the field after his Green Bay Packers defeated the Oakland Raiders in Super Bowl II. Jerry Kramer is at right. (AP Photo)

but he was fair. "He treats us all the same," said defensive tackle Henry Jordan. "Like dogs."

When Green Bay won its fifth NFL title with Starr sneaking into the frozen end zone to beat Dallas in the 1967 championship game, known as "The Ice Bowl," Cowboys coach Tom Landry knew why his team had lost. "The discipline and conditioning programs they went through, the punishment and suffering, they all tend to develop character. And once you get character, you develop hope on all situations. Therefore, they never were out of a game. That is what beat us."

THE 1970s

The Pack's victories in the first two AFL-NFL championships confirmed what most folks believed: that the NFL was the superior league with the better teams. However, Joe Namath, quarterback for the AFL's New York Jets, changed their minds. Just before Super Bowl III, he guaranteed that his team would win, even though the experts predicted the NFL's Baltimore Colts would win by 17 points. Everyone laughed at Namath's guarantee until he led the Jets to a stunning 16–7 upset.

The following season, the AFL evened up the Super Bowl series at two games apiece, thanks to Kansas City quarterback Len Dawson. Praised by Chiefs coach Hank Stram as "the most accurate passer in pro football," Dawson was the team leader of Chiefs' teams that reached two of the first

Len Dawson hands off to Mike Garrett during Super Bowl IV. (AP Photo)

four Super Bowls. He is best remembered for his courageous MVP performance in leading the underdog Chiefs to a 23–7 upset of the Vikings in Super Bowl IV. The morning of the game, Dawson woke up with leg cramps and nausea, but he summoned the strength to take the field. He connected on 12 of 17 passes for 142 yards, and his 46-yard touchdown pass to flanker Otis Taylor wrapped up the surprise victory. "I asked the good Lord to give me strength and courage to play this one to the best of my ability," said Dawson.

After the dust of the league war had settled, the future seemed to be brighter in the football world. In 1976, the NFL had expanded to Tampa Bay and Seattle, and increased their regular season to sixteen games two years later. In the real world, the haze of the Vietnam War still lingered. As the nation moved into the "Me Decade" of the Seventies, when many people became self-absorbed and withdrew from public participation, interest and attendance at NFL games remained strong. In 1971, the NBC telecast of Super Bowl V was the top-rated one-day sports telecast ever to that point, with fans watching in nearly 40 million homes. By the end of the decade, interest in the Super Bowl grew exponentially, and by Super Bowl XIV, the big game attracted over 75 million Americans.

In the 1970s, two teams with devastating defensive units dominated the league. Miami's "No-Name Defense" led the Dolphins to two Super Bowl wins in three tries. And the Pittsburgh Steelers, by dropping their "Steel Curtain," won all four Super Bowl games in which they appeared.

Miami Dolphins, Super Bowls VI, VII, and VIII

For one season, the Dolphins were arguably the best team ever. In 1972, a year after losing Super Bowl VI to the Dallas Cowboys, the Dolphins became the only team in NFL history to have an unbeaten, untied season. It's amazing that it has happened only once in the ninety-six-year history of the NFL, but Miami, at 17–0–0 in 1972, is the only unblemished team of all time. Still, the Dolphins don't seem to get the respect they deserve because they didn't win games in dominant fashion. They didn't roll through the 1972 playoffs: they beat Cleveland by six, Pittsburgh by four, and Washington by seven. And they didn't sustain their greatness; they went 15–2 and won another Super Bowl the year after the perfect season, but then they went eight years without winning another playoff game. The World Football League sprang up in 1974 and stole three of Miami's premier weapons: fullback Larry Csonka, halfback Jim Kiick, and wide receiver Paul Warfield.

This was a classic team of role players. Bob Griese was certainly not the best quarterback of his day, but he was maddeningly accurate and had zero ego. The ground game churned perfectly behind the strongest and most technically perfect line of its era, with Csonka and Mercury Morris becoming the first pair of teammates to rush for 1,000 yards in the same season. A downfield threat, Warfield stretched defenses, although he caught but 29 balls in the perfect season. The defense, which had allowed just eighteen touchdowns in fourteen games, and whose very moniker—the "No-Name Defense"—bespoke a lack of star power, had a different standout every week. The star of Super Bowl VII, for instance, was the team's eleventh leading tackler, safety Jake Scott, who intercepted two Redskins passes. How fitting: Scott is now an almost forgotten figure, yet he was the MVP of the game that capped the only perfect season ever. "How in the world could you not pick us the best team of all time?" wonders coach Don Shula.

The 1972 Dolphins were very close to perfection as an offensive unit. They had perfect balance in the backfield: Csonka for muscle, Morris for flash, and Kiick for third-down receptions out of the backfield. Their middle three on the offensive line—guards Larry Little and Bob Kuechenberg and center Jim Langer—were the best of the decade. Their wideouts were the classic matching pair. Warfield deep and Howard Twilley as the possession receiver. They had the old Packer, Marv Fleming, as the blocking tight end and Jim Mandich as the pass catcher. And in Griese they had a mechanically precise quarterback who wouldn't let ego get in the way of the offense. Griese did not possess exceptional speed or a spectacular throwing arm, but his ability to read defenses, deliver passes with pin-point precision, and lead his team methodically down the field was unmatched in the Super Bowl era.

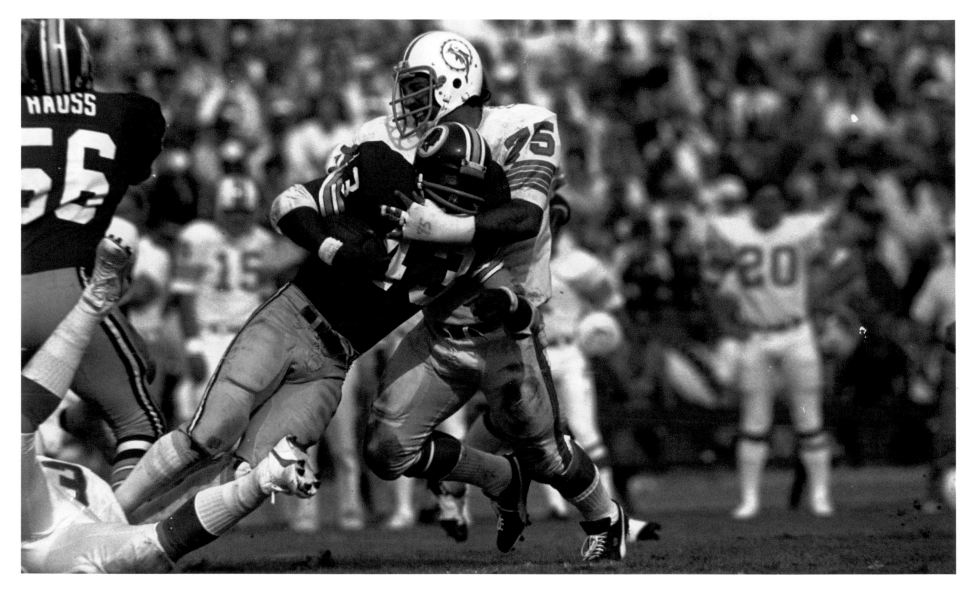

Washington running back Larry Brown is getting nowhere with Miami's Manny Fernandez in Super Bowl VII. (AP Photo)

During their heyday of the early 1970s, Miami relied on a strong rushing attack to wear down opponents. "Running puts the man in football," coach Don Shula was fond of saying. The Dolphins used a consistent, short-yardage passing game to keep opposing defenses from keying solely on the backfield, and in this offensive system Griese thrived, never caring about his own stats, so long as the team succeeded. In Super Bowl VII, for instance, only eleven of Miami's fifty plays were passes; but Griese's eight completions accounted for one touchdown and set up the second, as Miami manhandled Washington to complete their perfect season. The next year, in Super Bowl VIII against Minnesota, the Miami Ground Machine called fifty-three running plays, while Griese attempted only seven passes, completing six for 73 yards as the Dolphins pounded the Vikings for a second straight championship. "It was obvious from the beginning that our offense could overpower their defense," said center Jim Langer, who along with guards Larry Little and Bob Kuechenberg laid down the devastating, pulverizing blocks that Larry Csonka ran behind thirty-three times for 145 yards and two touchdowns en route to his MVP performance. "We were prepared to throw more," said Griese, who threw one pass in the second half, "but we also knew what we could do. We'd run straight at them, then around them, then a trap."

The possibility of the Dolphins achieving perfection was all the talk leading up to their Super Bowl VII matchup against coach George Allen's veteran Washington Redskins squad, known as the "Over The Hill Gang."

Oddly enough, considering the stakes, the Redskins took the field at the L.A. Coliseum and seemed to be flat on this Super Sunday. The Redskins put up very little fight. The final score was 14–7. The 21 total points made this the lowest scoring game in Super Bowl history. Despite the closeness reflected on the scoreboard, this was a one-sided affair in favor of Miami. On offense, the Redskins passed midfield only once in the first half, to the Miami 48, and QB Billy Kilmer threw an interception on the next play. The Dolphins led 14–0 at the half. Washington had gained 72 yards. The only thing that made the score close was Garo Yepremian's botched pass off a blocked field goal, but it came with 2:07 left.

Shula had sent in his kicker to try a 42-yard field goal to clinch the game. Yepremian, a former soccer player from

Cyprus, had never seen a pro football game in person until he played in one. Garo's kick was blocked and the ball bounced back toward him. He picked it up and tried to throw a pass to a teammate. Bad idea! The ball squirted from his fingers. Garo reached for it, but instead, he batted it to Mike Bass, the Redskins' cornerback.

"My mind went blank," said Garo afterward. Mike's didn't.

Bass grabbed the ball and sprinted down the sideline for a touchdown. Now the game—and the perfect season—was in jeopardy. The Dolphins, however, held on to win, 14–7, preserving their perfect season. "Now we laugh about it, but it wasn't funny then," said Miami linebacker Nick Buoniconti.

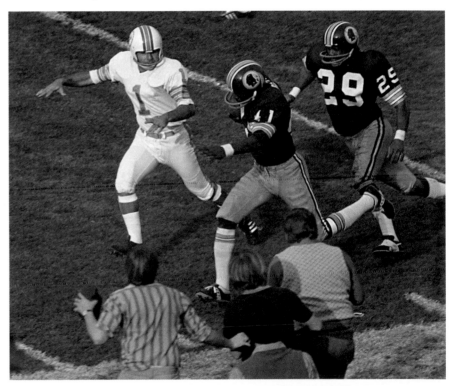

Mike Bass races down the sideline for Washington's only score in Super Bowl VII. Miami kicker Garo Yepremian is in pursuit after his field goal attempt was blocked. (AP Photo)

Allen, the losing coach, wasn't laughing, either. "It doesn't do any good to play in the Super Bowl unless you win."

While Jake Scott took home the car, the better choice for MVP would have been defensive left tackle Manny Fernandez, who helped keep the Washington rushing game in check. Over the course of the afternoon, Fernandez had 17 tackles, a sack, and numerous hurries of Redskins quarterback Billy Kilmer.

"It was the game of his life," said linebacker Nick Buoniconti. "In fact, it was the most dominant game by a defensive lineman in the history of the game, and he would never be given much credit for it. They should have given out two game balls and made Manny Fernandez the co-MVP with Jake Scott."

Said Fernandez: "Winning the [MVP] never entered my mind until I heard that Jake won it. I was happy for Jake, he played a helluva game for a guy who was healthy, but he had two bad shoulders."

Buoniconti was the inspirational middle linebacker who anchored the No-Name Defense. In Super Bowl VII he intercepted a Billy Kilmer pass in the second quarter, returning it 32 yards to set up Miami's eventual game-winning score. A fiery leader and relentless competitor, he once said, "Every play is like life or death. I can't think of anything except the play that is taking place at the moment."

The next year, the 1973 Dolphins repeated as champs, making it look easy, with a 24–7 win over the Minnesota Vikings in Super Bowl VIII, played at Rice Stadium, in Houston, on January 13, 1974. The first popular Super Bowl commercial was a 1974 ad for Noxzema featuring Super Bowl

legend Joe Namath. The New York Jets quarterback looks into the camera, grinning like a Cheshire cat, as he says, "I'm so excited. I'm going to get creamed!" before *Charlie's Angels* star Farrah Fawcett spreads shaving lotion across his face. The thirty-second spot cost $103,000. This raunchy bit is the only lasting memory of what to date is the most anonymous Super Bowl contest. Indeed, the Dolphins made quick work of the Vikes, disposing of them in 2 hours 29 minutes, the all-time record for shortest Super Bowl measured by length of time. Super Bowls today can last about 4 hours.

The 1973 Miami team might have been better than the unbeaten 1972 squad, mainly because the defense was better and Griese was healthy for the whole season. Larry Csonka ran like crazy during his MVP performance against the Vikings in Super Bowl VIII. He carried 33 times for 145 yards and two touchdowns. Csonka, who had rushed for 112 yards on 15 carries in Miami's Super Bowl VII victory over the Washington Redskins, became the first running back to rush for 100 or more yards in back-to-back Super Bowls, a feat since achieved by Denver's Terrell Davis and Dallas' Emmitt Smith. With the win, Csonka and the Dolphins became the second team to win back-to-back Super Bowl championships. (Green Bay had done it in Super Bowls I and II). Marv Fleming, a tight end who played on both clubs, said of these Dolphins: "This is the greatest team ever." Fleming was the first player in NFL history to appear in five Super Bowls, and he took home the winners' share four times, twice with the Packers in Super Bowls I and II, and twice with the Dolphins in Super Bowls VII and VIII. Before one Super Bowl, he famously said: "I get

A PANTHEON OF HEROES

Larry Csonka

Two rings in three consecutive Super Bowls with the Miami Dolphins; MVP of Super Bowl VIII

ZONK: LIKE BRONK

The second leading rusher in Super Bowl history, with 297 yards, Larry Csonka and power running became synonymous in the NFL of the 1970s. A tenacious and punishing fullback, the 6'3", 227-pound Zonk, as he was called, charged through the middle of defenses like a bulldozer and rarely, if ever, fumbled. Oddly enough, he had not fumbled once in 195 carries in the 1971 regular season. Early in Super Bowl VI, he fumbled a handoff from quarterback Bob Griese. The Cowboys recovered and kicked a field goal, their first score on the road to a 24–3 thrashing of the Dolphins.

The Dolphins triumphed in the next two Super Bowls. The ground game of Csonka and Jim Kiick, affectionately known as "Butch Cassidy and the Sundance Kid," pounded opponents inside for hard-fought yardage, and speedy Mercury Morris kept them off balance by running wide. Csonka thrived by grinding out the tough yards with straight-ahead runs, and he wasn't afraid to get dirty or bloodied. He broke his nose at least twelve times in his career. "He was always bleeding in the huddle," said Kiick. "He was a modern-day Bronko Nagurski," said coach Don Shula.

Larry Csonka plows through a huge opening made by his offensive line in Super Bowl VIII. (AP Photos)

A PANTHEON OF HEROES

Don Shula

Two rings in six Super Bowls coaching the Baltimore Colts and the Miami Dolphins

DOMINEERING AND DOMINATING

Only one other coach, Bill Belichick, has made six trips to the Super Bowl, but Belichick has done it all with one quarterback, Tom Brady. Shula, with an ability to change tactics to suit his team's personnel, was able to transition from the old style running game of the successful Baltimore and Miami teams of the 1970s to the new passing attack offense of the 1980s.

Shula won with Colts teams that had Johnny Unitas, who Shula said was "probably the toughest guy, mentally and physically, that's ever played the position," and Earl Morrall at quarterback; a team that is stunned in Super Bowl III by the Joe Namath Jets. Moving to Miami in 1970, he won with a Dolphins team that had QB Bob Griese ("a thinking man's quarterback") and fullback Larry Csonka, producing a perfect 17–0 record in 1972, then earning a second consecutive Super Bowl ring the next season to culminate a two-season span when

(AP Photo)

the Dolphins won 32 of 34 games. In 1982, he won with a no-name QB, David Woodley, who was no match for the Redskins in Super Bowl XVII. During the 1984 season, he won with a young QB, Dan Marino, who threw a record 48 touchdown passes before losing Super Bowl XIX to Joe Montana's 49ers.

"That's what makes Don the best coach," said Bill Walsh, whose 49er teams won three Super Bowls. "His ability to win with different teams in different eras. He's done it with passers like Unitas and Marino. He's done it with runners like Csonka, Jim Kiick, and Mercury Morris. He's even done it with a rollout quarterback like Woodley who really wasn't much of a passer. Don Shula is the best."

Shula's legacy stands alone in NFL history. He is the NFL's all-time winningest coach, with 347 career victories, and his 1972 undefeated season with the Dolphins is all the more remarkable with each passing season. The square-jawed Shula is famously demanding and gets results: in 33 seasons as coach of the Colts and Dolphins, his teams qualified for the postseason 19 times, appearing in six Super Bowls, and winning two championships.

up for the money. Most of these guys will be playing with pride as the main incentive, but, with me, it's money."

The two-time Super Bowl champion Dolphins, with most of their stars at prime age, had all the makings of a dynasty. That's what everyone thought after they crushed the Vikings—Miami was a dynasty to rival Green Bay's. Unfortunately, a new upstart league, named the World Football League, put an end to that, grabbing Csonka, Kiick, and Warfield by making them offers they couldn't refuse. It took

Miami nine years to get back to the Super Bowl. "The NFL couldn't stop us," said offensive lineman Bob Kuechenberg. "It took another league to do it."

Pittsburgh Steelers, Super Bowls IX, X, XIII, and XIV

When Chuck Noll became Pittsburgh's head coach in 1969, the Steelers hadn't won any kind of championship

Pittsburgh Steelers board chairman Art Rooney and coach Chuck Noll enjoy the winning moment after Super Bowl XIV. (AP Photos/Harry Cabluck)

in almost forty years. Ten years later, the Steelers were the Team of the Decade. Pittsburgh took home Super Bowl trophies in 1975, 1976, 1979, and 1980, becoming the first franchise to win four Super Bowl titles—and Noll was the first head coach to win four Super Bowls. When linebacker Jack Ham heard his coach was elected to the Hall of Fame, in 1993, he said: "I think [that] of all the people who were involved in the Steelers organization during our Super Bowl years, Chuck Noll is by far the most deserving to be inducted."

Noll's strategy was to build a winning team through the college draft. Every year he picked a potential superstar.

THE BEST WHO NEVER LOST

Franco Harris

Four rings in four Super Bowls with the Pittsburgh Steelers; MVP of Super Bowl IX

FRANKLY SPEAKING

Franco Harris was a durable ball carrier whose hard-hitting style of play was a perfect fit with teammates as well as with the lunch-pail mentality of the Steel City's football fans.

"A player should not be measured by statistics alone," Harris said. "He should be measured by something more special, such as the sharing of teammates and fans. Both the city of Pittsburgh and the Steelers team were building at the same time. It was a good feeling to be a part of it.

(AP Photo)

"Halfway through the 1970s, we realized that we had a great team and that we could do great things." After the first Super Bowl win in 1975, Harris and his teammates knew they'd be back. As he told the *New York Daily News* years later, "This is the way we felt. We enjoyed it so much that we said, 'we have to do this again,' and we kept saying that. That's what we did. We took time to enjoy it and that's what made it special. It did not get old. It was something that we wanted to be a part of all the time. And isn't it amazing that the same core of people made up the four Super Bowls? And I think the first Super Bowl might have been people that were all drafted by the Steelers, which was really unique."

Every year the team got better. "Mean" Joe Greene and L.C. Greenwood in 1969; Terry Bradshaw and cornerback Mel Blount in 1970; Jack Ham, Dwight White, Ernie Holmes, and Mike Wagner in 1971; Franco Harris in 1972; Lynn Swann, Jack Lambert, John Stallworth and Mike Webster in 1974. Greene, Bradshaw, Blount, Ham, Harris, Lambert, Stallworth, and Webster became Hall of Famers.

Franco Harris was one of the last building blocks coach Noll signed when he was putting together a winning team. With Greene, Ham, and Blount on defense, plus Bradshaw as quarterback, Noll needed a big-play running back. When the 6'2", 225-pounder from Penn State came on board in 1972, the Steelers almost magically transformed into a championship caliber team. Harris had a sensational rookie season in 1972, and that year the Steelers won the AFC central division. He was an immediate favorite of Pittsburgh fans, including a group known as "Franco's Italian Army," which supported Harris throughout his career with the Steelers and even recruited Frank Sinatra as a member. (Harris' father was African-American and his mother Italian.) Harris' "Immaculate Reception" against the Oakland Raiders in the 1972 AFC divisional playoff remains one of the most famous and controversial plays in NFL history.

During Harris' twelve years with Pittsburgh, the Steelers never had a losing record. They won eight division titles, four league championships, and four Super Bowls. Harris proved to be a workhorse, carrying 101 times for 354 yards—both records—and scoring four rushing touchdowns. Year after year, Harris' durable ground attack was a consistent factor the team could count on. "What Joe Greene meant to our defense—setting the tone—that's what Franco did for our offense," said Ham. "The constant factor became our running game."

The Steelers had a nose for drafting great talent. They scouted black colleges extensively, and came away with hidden gems like Greenwood in the 10th round, Holmes in the 8th round, and Stallworth in the 4th round. The decisions made by their scouting department all seemed to turn to Steelers gold. The city of Pittsburgh grew to love their team, and the feeling was mutual. "I still feel it to this day: It was like being in Camelot," said Art Rooney Jr., then the team's scouting director.

In 1973, the Steelers landed a wild card playoff berth, but in 1974, they went straight to the top, reaching the Super Bowl for the first time. Seven of the eleven defensive starters on that team had been acquired through the draft. Pittsburgh won its first AFC championship and advanced to face the Minnesota Vikings in Super Bowl IX, at Tulane Stadium. When the Steelers arrived in New Orleans, in January 1975, Noll told his players to enjoy Bourbon Street early in the week and get the partying out of their system. There were no curfews early in the week. Maybe that's why Noll's teams played loose and confident and were at their best in the biggest games.

Super Bowl IX was billed as a showcase of two great defensive units: Pittsburgh's Steel Curtain and Minnesota's Purple People Eaters. The score at the half was the lowest in Super Bowl history: 2–0 Pittsburgh. The Steelers scored those two points when Dwight White sacked Minnesota QB Fran Tarkenton in the end zone for the first safety in Super Bowl history. White, who was known as "Mad Dog," had spent the week of Super Bowl IX in the hospital with pneumonia and lost twenty pounds. He wasn't expected to play but did anyway.

Franco Harris set rushing records with 158 yards on 34 carries, and was selected as the game's MVP. Bradshaw's pass

Franco Harris looks for an opening against the Vikings in Super Bowl IX. On this day, he would find many. (AP)

to Larry Brown in the fourth quarter clinched the Steelers' first Super Bowl win, a 16–6 victory over the Vikes. The defensive star of the game was L.C. Greenwood, the 6'6", 245-pound left defensive end. Greenwood deflected three passes by Tarkenton. (Prompting Pete Rozelle's famous line at the next draft meeting, when Minnesota got its pick in late. "Minnesota passes—and L.C. Greenwood knocks it down.")

Greenwood, known for wearing golden high-top shoes, played in all four of the Steelers' Super Bowl victories in the 1970s. Lining up alongside "Mean" Joe Greene at left tackle, Ernie Holmes at right tackle, and Dwight White at right end, they formed one of the most oppressive defensive lines in NFL history. Greenwood was especially formidable in Super Bowl games. In Super Bowl X, he sacked Dallas QB Roger

Staubach three times in the Steelers' win. Three years later, in Super Bowl XIII, he sacked Staubach once more in another Steelers victory.

Led by Greenwood, Pittsburgh's defense held Minnesota to 17 yards rushing, a record low, and allowed Tarkenton to complete only 11 of 26 passes, while intercepting him three times. The Steelers were a young team on the rise. They would win the Super Bowl again the next year, and two more Super Bowls, three and four years later, with much of the same cast.

The Goodyear Blimp and the 80,187 spectators at Miami's Orange Bowl for Super Bowl X were used as "extras" in the movie *Black Sunday*. In that movie, terrorists in a blimp attack the Super Bowl. Two weeks before, Pittsburgh's wide receiver Lynn Swann suffered a concussion in the AFC championship game. Doctors told him not to play in Super Bowl X against the Dallas Cowboys. "I'm going to play," he announced. By the end of the game, it was Swann who had given the Cowboys a headache! In the first quarter, he and Dallas cornerback Mark Washington raced down the sideline, fighting for the ball. It looked as if Washington would intercept it. But Swann wrestled the ball away and came down with an acrobatic 32-yard gain.

His most spectacular catch happened near the end of the first half, when the Steelers were pinned on their six-yard line. Once again, quarterback Terry Bradshaw heaved the ball toward Swann, who leaped into the air and tipped the ball away from Washington. As both players fell to the ground, Swann caught the ball for a 53-yard gain. In all, he caught four passes for 161 yards and one touchdown, including an over-the-shoulder 64-yard grab on the dead run with Washington draped all over him in the fourth quarter. The man who was taking a chance by playing at all made his risk pay off: He led the Steelers to their second straight Super Bowl with a 21–17 victory, and became the first wide receiver to be named the Super Bowl's most valuable player. In four Super Bowl games, he caught 16 passes for a total of 364 yards.

From 1972 through 1979, the Steelers had a regular season record of 88–27–1. The Steelers were gunning for their third straight Super Bowl title in 1976. But with Bradshaw

One of Lynn Swann's more spectacular catches during Super Bowl X in Miami. (AP Photo)

THE BEST WHO NEVER LOST

Terry Bradshaw

Four rings in four Super Bowls with the Pittsburgh Steelers; MVP of Super Bowls XIII and XIV

TERRY TERRIFIC

Terry Bradshaw was tough as nails. In Super Bowl X against the Dallas Cowboys, a 64-yard pass to Lynn Swann won the game with 3:02 left. But Bradshaw didn't know this until after the game. Just as he released the ball a blitzing safety Cliff Harris knocked him unconscious. Bradshaw woke up after the game was over. Thanks to his pass, Pittsburgh had won, 21–17.

When the Steelers and Cowboys met again in Super Bowl XIII, Bradshaw beat Dallas almost single-handedly, with a 318-yard, 4 touchdown passing explosion. In Super Bowl XIV against the Rams, he passed the Steelers to their fourth championship victory with 309 aerial yards, a 47-yard scoring pass to Swann and a 73-yard bomb to John Stallworth.

Bradshaw was named the MVP in both Super Bowl XIII and XIV. In four Super Bowls, he passed for an impressive 932 yards and 9 touchdowns.

"As a player, it says everything about you if you made the Hall of Fame. But, then again, boy … there's something about winning a Super Bowl," said Bradshaw.

(AP Photo/Kathy Willens)

hurt, they started the season with a 1–4 record. Over the season's final nine games, their defense turned stifling, shutting out five opponents and yielding a total of 28 points. The offense scored 234. "How could you not win?" asked linebacker Andy Russell. "We had an all-star team." But the Steelers lost to the Raiders in the AFC title game that year; Harris and fullback Rocky Bleier had gotten hurt the week before and couldn't play. Still, Pittsburgh would win four Super Bowls in six years. The only team close to that record is San Francisco, but it took the 49ers nine years to win four. "What we had," said Bradshaw, "was an undeniable hatred of losing. We despised losing! Woe be to the fool who came into our stadium on Sunday. We had the fangs and the blood and the slobber! We loved it, Jack!"

Super Bowl XIII was one of the most anticipated games in years, because it matched the two best teams in the game. The Steelers ran up an NFL-best 14–2 record in the regular season, and then waltzed through two AFC playoff games by a combined score of 67–15. Dallas, the defending Super Bowl champs, had just crushed the Rams in Los Angeles 28–0 for the NFC title. There was some controversy leading up to the game. "Terry Bradshaw couldn't spell cat if you spotted him the *C* and the *A*," said Dallas linebacker Thomas "Hollywood" Henderson. He went on to call Pittsburgh linebacker Jack Lambert "a toothless chimpanzee."

The Hollywood hype helped build a huge television audience, foreshadowing the Super Bowl's commanding place in modern American life, which drove Norman Vincent Peale, the minister and author, to say in 1974, "If Jesus Christ were alive today, he'd be at the Super Bowl." This game still holds a TV record that probably will never be broken. Of all the TV sets turned on during this game, 74 percent were tuned to

NBC's telecast of the game. (Rating is a measure of the total audience members tuned into a program at a given time, while share is the percentage of people watching television tuned into a specific show at a certain time.) During the broadcast, Coca-Cola aired one of the most popular Super Bowl ads of all time. The ad features fearsome Pittsburgh lineman "Mean" Joe Greene, scowling as he limps through a stadium tunnel after a game. A young fan offers Greene his soda and "Mean" Joe responds by giving the boy the jersey off his back.

Following the pregame festivities, which featured the Dallas Cowboys Cheerleaders and several military bands, Bradshaw responded—as one sportswriter punned—purrfectly. He converted two third-and-long situations on Pittsburgh's first series, and then hit John Stallworth with a 28-yard touchdown strike. He again linked up with Stallworth, this time for a 75-yard score in the second quarter, and then, just before the half, he unexpectedly put the Steelers in position to score again with two long passes to Swann. A rollout, off-balance seven-yard touchdown throw to Rocky Bleier with 26 seconds left in the half gave Pittsburgh a 21–14 lead. In the second half Bradshaw threw his fourth TD pass of the day, to Swann, giving Pittsburgh a 35–17 lead. But Dallas wouldn't die. Despite the Cowboys QB Roger Staubach's two late scoring passes, Pittsburgh held on to win 35–31.

"Ask Thomas Henderson if I can spell now!" Bradshaw howled as the final seconds ticked off the clock. We may never know about c-a-t, but we know Bradshaw could spell v-i-c-t-o-r-y.

Stallworth and Swann gave Pittsburgh a dynamic duo at the wide receiver position. Swann was already a superstar, and now it was Stallworth's turn to step forward. In Super Bowl

XIII against the Cowboys, Stallworth caught three passes for 115 yards and scored the first two Pittsburgh touchdowns. The next season, in Super Bowl XIV against the Rams, he caught three passes for 121 yards in a 31–19 win. His fourth quarter 73-yard touchdown catch put the Steelers ahead for good. Stallworth holds the career record for most yards per catch in Super Bowl history (24.4 yards) and highest single-game average (40.3 yards) in Super Bowl XIV.

The one neglected element of these great Steeler teams was the offensive line. Everyone else got a share of the publicity—the Steel Curtain defense, running backs Franco Harris and Rocky Bleier, quarterback Terry Bradshaw, and receivers Lynn Swann and John Stallworth. But those agile, mobile blockers who executed coach Chuck Noll's trap-block running game to perfection were almost unknown. Only the center, Mike Webster, eventually got some acclaim, but that came later in his career.

Webster, the undersized 6'1", 255-pound center, was a pivotal player on these standout Steelers teams. Considered by many to be the best center in NFL history, he anchored an offensive line that paved the way for running back Franco Harris and provided protection for quarterback Terry Bradshaw. "I couldn't have been the player I was without him," said Bradshaw. "He was so smart, so prepared for everything we would face in a game. We all worked hard, but none as hard as Mike did."

"Iron Mike" played in 150 consecutive games with bare arms, even in freezing weather, to keep opponents from grabbing the sleeves of his jersey. "Mike was a symbol of our team," said defensive tackle Joe Greene. "When you saw that Pittsburgh offense, he was the first one you saw running up to the line, fists pumping. They knew what they had to deal with right off with Mike."

The Steelers dynasty of the Seventies was truly a total team effort. In fact, there were an amazing twenty-two players who were on all four Pittsburgh Super Bowl teams during the decade.

Dallas Cowboys, Super Bowls V, VI, X, XII, and XIII

The Dallas Cowboys have been called "America's Team." And one man played a great role in shaping the Cowboys' reputation and winning tradition: Tom Landry. Spanning three decades, from their first game in 1960 through the 1988 season, Landry was the Cowboys' only head coach. Just one other coach, Green Bay's Curly Lambeau, has coached one team for more consecutive years. With his steely stare, arms folded, holding a laminated play sheet in his right hand, and wearing his trademark fedora hat, Landry became one of the most recognizable people in football.

Landry had twenty consecutive winning seasons, an NFL record. During that span, Dallas won thirteen division titles, made eighteen playoff appearances, and won two Super Bowls in five appearances. Despite all his success, one of the raps on Landry's Cowboy teams was that they "couldn't win the big one." Entering the 1971 season, the Cowboys had lost in the playoffs for five straight years, often in demoralizing ways. The most painful defeat occurred in the 1967 NFL championship game played against the Green Bay Packers, literally on the frozen tundra at Lambeau Field. This legendary game, known as the Ice Bowl, was contested in frigid game-time temperatures that registered between 13 and 18

Running back Duane Thomas goes low against a Colts defender during Super Bowl V. (AP Photo)

degrees below zero. The Cowboys led 17–14 and were just a few ticks on the clock away from a victory that would propel them to Super Bowl II. The Packers had the ball on the goal line, but with no timeouts. The Cowboy defense needed only to make one last stop. In a courageous play call, Green Bay's Bart Starr scored a touchdown on a quarterback keeper as time expired, and the Cowboys lost in heartbreaking fashion, 21–17.

Three years later, the Cowboys finally did reach the Promised Land, where they would meet the great Johnny Unitas and the Baltimore Colts in Super Bowl V, at the Orange Bowl, in Miami, Florida. In the week leading up

Jim O'Brien's game-winning field goal in Super Bowl V. (AP Photo)

to Super Sunday, in one of the first mass interviews, a reporter looking to hype the contest asked the Cowboys' enigmatic rookie running back Duane Thomas if this was the ultimate game. "If it's the ultimate game, would they play it again next year?" (NFL commissioner Pete Rozelle once said it was his "all-time favorite quote.") As it turned out, the Dallas Cowboys played an awful game in Super Bowl V. One of the main culprits was starting quarterback Craig Morton. Moments before the kickoff, Morton knew something didn't feel right. "I'm looking out at the field, and I see this gigantic, inflatable Johnny Unitas," Morton recalled. "I say to myself, 'What the heck am I doing playing against this guy?' I mean, it was only a few years earlier I was watching the guy win the greatest championship game ever [the Baltimore Colts' 1958 NFL title game against the New York Giants]. Now, I'm about to go toe-to-toe with him. It was tough to get my head around that."

Morton and the Cowboys played Unitas and the Colts tough, but the game wasn't an offensive masterpiece. Known as the "Stupor Bowl" for its sloppy play, this game featured a missed extra point, penalties, and turnovers galore. The teams committed a Super Bowl record of eleven combined turnovers, and the Colts' seven turnovers is the most ever by a Super Bowl winning team. In addition to committing four turnovers—including a first-and-goal fumble by Thomas near the Baltimore goal line—Dallas produced ten penalties for 133 yards.

But it was Dallas's last turnover that hurt the most. With less than two minutes left and the score tied, 13–13, Morton threw an interception—his third of the fourth quarter! With nine seconds remaining and no timeouts, Baltimore decided to attempt a 32-yard, Super Bowl-winning field goal. Out trotted rookie kicker Jim O'Brien, who had made just 19-of-34 field goals during the regular season. Talk about pressure! In the final dramatic seconds, as O'Brien came onto the field, one of his teammates told him not to worry. "Just kick the ball," Jim was told. He did. As the ball sailed between the uprights, Jim and the rest of the Colts celebrated the 16–13 win. Dallas lineman Bob Lilly threw his helmet forty yards in a rage. "If we were beaten by 40 points, you could just say we were whipped. But we had every opportunity to win," said Lilly.

Super Bowl V was the only time a Super Bowl most valuable player award was presented to a member of the losing team. Dallas linebacker Chuck Howley intercepted two passes and sacked thirty-seven-year-old QB Johnny Unitas. Howley earned the honor, but refused to accept the award because his team had lost.

The season after suffering a narrow loss to the Baltimore Colts in Super Bowl V, the Cowboys set out to change the perception they were a great team that would always choke at the end. But halfway through the 1971 season, the Cowboys had every reason to worry. A quarterback controversy was brewing between Craig Morton and Roger Staubach. A contract dispute caused star running back Duane Thomas to take a vow of silence. With a 4–3 record after seven weeks, Landry named Staubach the team's starter, and Dallas didn't lose another game that season. With Staubach firmly at the controls, the Cowboys stormed through the rest of the regular season and the playoffs.

The Cowboys met the Miami Dolphins in Super Bowl VI, at Tulane Stadium, in New Orleans, on January 16, 1972. A

A PANTHEON OF HEROES

Tom Landry

Two rings in five Super Bowls coaching the Dallas Cowboys

GOD'S COACH

Tom Landry was a winner. During his twenty-nine seasons at the helm of the Dallas Cowboys, Landry's teams won 250 games, more games than every other coach except Don Shula and George Halas. Sixteen times his teams won 10 or more games—when the NFL regular-season schedule lasted 14 games. But Landry was also an innovator. He created the now-popular 4–3 Defense, which featured four down linemen and three linebackers. Previously, a down lineman was placed over the center. But Landry had this player stand up and moved him back several yards. This created the middle linebacker position, and revolutionized defenses. "It opened the door for all the variations of zones and man-to-man coverage, which are used in conjunction with it today," said Sam Huff, a Hall of Fame middle linebacker.

Landry later refined the 4–3 Defense by moving any two of the four down linemen off the line of scrimmage one or two yards, depending on which direction he thought the opposing offense

(AP Photo)

might run. This change he called the Flex Defense, and the purpose of the flexed linemen was to improve pursuit angles to stop the run. In essence, the Flex Defense was a kind of zone defense against the run. Each lineman was responsible for covering a gap and stayed there until he knew for sure where the ball carrier was going.

In addition to being a great defensive coach, Landry also was an innovator on offense. In the 1970s, he began sending a wide receiver as a "man in motion." The motion was used as deception to give the defense a different looking alignment prior to the snap of the ball, hopefully too late for the defense to make an adjustment. The most significant innovation Landry installed was the Shotgun Formation, which is now as much a part of the game as the hash marks. Landry thought if an opponent had a terrific pass rush, then his quarterback should take the snap about seven yards deep rather than from under center.

This, he reasoned, would not only give his quarterback more time to spot receivers downfield, but also would cause the defense's timing to be thrown off. He was right on both accounts. According to Mel Renfo, a Hall of Fame defensive back who played fourteen seasons under Landry: "They don't make coaches like Tom Landry anymore. He was right there with Lombardi as one of the greatest of all time."

few days before the game, the President of the United States called Miami Dolphins coach Don Shula. President Richard M. Nixon was a big football fan and a former player at Whittier College. He suggested a play for Shula to use in Super Bowl VI against the Dallas Cowboys. It was a pass pattern for wide receiver Paul Warfield. The pattern called for Warfield to run straight and then slant down the field, a play Shula assured the president was already in the game plan. "Warfield was a great receiver, one of our biggest threats," Shula explained, "so I'm sure we game-planned him to be a big part of what we were trying to do offensively." The Dolphins ran the play on their eighth snap of the first quarter. The result? Cowboys' cornerback Mel Renfro batted the ball away, resulting in an incomplete pass. "Nixon's a great strategist, isn't he?" joked Dallas' Cliff Harris. The following season, after Shula earned his 100th career coaching victory, Nixon sent a congratulatory letter, which said, "This new milestone is convincing proof of your superior coaching ability and, therefore, I will do my very best to resist suggesting any more plays should you get through the playoffs and into the Super Bowl again."

Super Bowl VI's kickoff temperature of 39 degrees is the coldest in Super Bowl history. But the Cowboys and Dolphins were hot teams. Seventeen future Hall of Famers participated in Super Bowl VI. One of them, Larry Csonka, running back for the Miami Dolphins, had not fumbled once in 195 carries in the 1971 regular season. Early in Super Bowl VI, he fumbled a handoff from quarterback Bob Griese. Dallas linebacker Chuck Howley recovered and the Cowboys kicked a field goal for the first score of the game. Howley also returned an interception 41 yards to set up his team's final touchdown in the fourth

quarter. Dallas' defensive tackle Bob Lilly was unstoppable whether crunching a running back or chasing down a scrambling quarterback. Lilly had seven tackles in the game, with the most memorable defensive highlight being when he chased Miami quarterback Bob Griese practically out of Tulane Stadium for the longest sack in Super Bowl history, a loss of 29 yards. "There isn't any use arguing with him if he gets hold of your jersey," said Griese. "You just fall wherever Lilly wants." Lilly and the rest of the "Doomsday Defense" limited Miami to just 185 total yards. Dallas did not permit Miami to score a touchdown, the only time in Super Bowl history that a team did not reach the end zone.

Super Bowl VI was the defining game for the Doomsday Defense, which was the backbone of the Cowboys' dynasty which won two Super Bowls (VI and XII) and played in three more (V, X, and XIII) during the team's heyday from 1966 to 1982. Often recognized as two generations—the Original Doomsday Defense from 1966 to 1975 and Doomsday II from 1976 to 1982—there is no fixed or agreed-upon definition of exactly which players comprised which group. However, there are four defensive players from the Doomsday Defense who appeared in all five of Dallas' Super Bowl games during that span. They are: Larry Cole (defensive line); D.D. Lewis (linebacker); Cliff Harris and Charlie Waters (defensive back). Offensive lineman Rayfield Wright also played in five Super Bowls for the Cowboys.

While the Doomsday Defense was taking its bows, the offense was also getting the job done. Dallas gained 352 total yards. The Cowboys rushed for 252 yards, with 95 coming from Duane Thomas and 74 from Walt Garrison. Roger Staubach was named the Super Bowl MVP. He completed

A PANTHEON OF HEROES

Roger Staubach

Two rings in five Super Bowls with the Dallas Cowboys; MVP of Super Bowl VI

(AP Photo)

A SCRAMBLING SAILOR

The Heisman Trophy winner from the U.S. Naval Academy joined the Dallas Cowboys as a 27-year-old rookie quarterback and never made it off the sideline at Super Bowl V. Instead, he watched the Cowboys lose as Craig Morton played with a sore right shoulder. The next season, Roger Staubach won the starting job and led the Cowboys to Super Bowl VI, where Dallas blew away the

Miami Dolphins, 24–3. It was the storied franchise's first Super Bowl title.

During the eight full years Roger Staubach was the starting quarterback for Dallas—from 1972 to 1979—the Cowboys enjoyed their greatest success. They won 85 games and lost 32, for a .726 win percentage. Staubach led Dallas to the playoffs each season but one. He was the Cowboys' winning quarterback in four NFC championship games and in Super Bowls VI and XII. Both of Staubach's losses as a starting Super Bowl quarterback came against his nemesis, the Pittsburgh Steelers. Both times the Cowboys lost by four points. And both times Staubach staged furious late rallies that fell maddeningly short. In Super Bowl X, trailing by 11 points in the fourth quarter, Staubach reduced the lead to four with a touchdown pass to Percy Howard—his only NFL catch! The Cowboys soon got the ball back and were driving for the winning score when Staubach was picked off in the end zone by Glenn Edwards as time expired with a 21–17 Steelers win. In Super Bowl XIII, the first-ever Super Bowl rematch, the Cowboys were trailing 35–17 with less than seven minutes to go. Some of the Steelers players began to celebrate, but Staubach's Cowboys refused to give up. Staubach threw two touchdown passes in the final minutes of the game, cutting the lead to 35–31 with just 22 seconds left in the game. But the Dallas onside kick attempt was unsuccessful and the Steelers were able to run out the clock and win the game. The Cowboys ended up being the first losing Super Bowl team to break the 30-point scoring barrier.

Staubach was one of the greatest "two-minute-drill" quarterbacks in football history. "Captain Comeback" had an uncanny ability to come up with some kind of daring play in the last minutes of a game.

Staubach was responsible for one of football's most famous terms to describe a play. He coined it after some typical last-minute heroics in the 1975 NFC playoffs. The Cowboys were trailing the Minnesota Vikings, 14–10. With 52 seconds to play, Dallas had the ball on the Vikings 32-yard line. On second down, Staubach took the snap, faked to his left, then turned to his right and fired a pass to wide receiver Drew Pearson. Vikings cornerback Nate Wright was also right under Staubach's pass. Pearson cut inside Wright—causing him to lose his balance and fall—and grabbed the ball. Hugging the ball to his hip, Pearson ran the remaining five yards for the winning touchdown. No one could believe what Staubach had done. Even Staubach, playing with bruised ribs, doubted his chances to pull out a victory. "It was just a Hail Mary pass," Staubach said. "You throw it up and pray he catches it." Ever since, the term *Hail Mary pass* has been used to describe a last-second heave into the end zone.

12 of his 19 throws for 119 passing yards and two touchdowns, to Lance Alworth and Mike Ditka. Staubach engineered two long touchdown drives of 76 and 71 yards. The series that the Dolphins said settled this game was the Cowboys' 71-yard drive that started the second half. The eight-play drive, all but one a running play, consumed over five minutes off the clock, and opened a 17–3 lead for Dallas. "That drive killed us," said Miami defensive end Bill Stanfill. "They drove the ball right down our throats."

Dallas entirely dominated Super Bowl VI from start to finish. The Cowboys were never threatened. Dallas won in a rout, 24–3, to win the first Super Bowl—and first championship—in franchise history. The Cowboys and Landry had finally shaken their runners-up identity. "I can't describe how we feel," said Cowboys coach Tom Landry. "We fought so hard [and] had come so close so many times."

The big game moved indoors for the first time, into the Louisiana Superdome, for Super Bowl XII, on January 15, 1978. This was also the first game played in prime time. Nearly 79 million viewers tuned in to CBS to listen as Pat Summerall and Tom Brookshier described the action. The game pitted the Cowboys against the Denver Broncos, who were led by Craig Morton, formerly the Dallas quarterback whose three interceptions made him the scapegoat in the Cowboys' Super Bowl V loss. The Cowboys advanced to their fourth Super Bowl after posting a 12–2 regular season record and playoff victories over the Chicago Bears and Minnesota Vikings. In a match-up of future Hall of Famers, Rayfield Wright, the 6'6" and 255-pound right tackle known as the "Big Cat," got the best of Minnesota's defensive end Carl Eller. "An all-day fight with Rayfield Wright definitely is not my idea of a pleasant Sunday afternoon," said Eller.

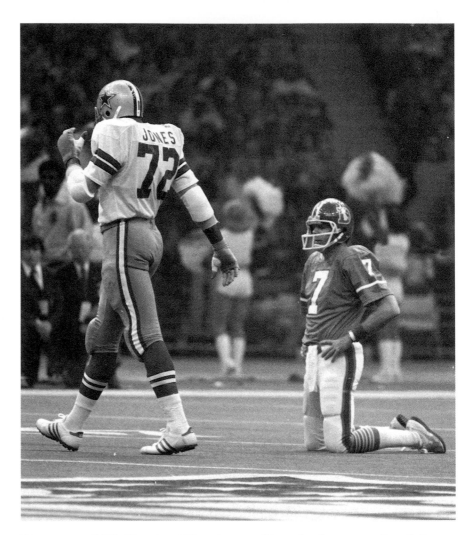

Denver QB Craig Morton after being sacked by "Too Tall" Jones in Super Bowl XII. (AP Photo)

The Broncos, also 12–2, won playoff games against the Pittsburgh Steelers and Oakland Raiders. The orange-jerseyed Denver Broncos defense in Super Bowl XII was called the "Orange Crush," which used a 3–4 formation anchored by the outstanding linebackers Tom Jackson and Randy Gradishar. The backbone of the line was defensive end Lyle Alzado, while the secondary boasted four superb defensive backs, including Louis Wright and Billy Thompson. The

Broncos defense had given up an average of just 10.6 points per game, third fewest in the NFL.

Too bad the Orange Crush personnel couldn't play on offense, too. The Broncos committed a staggering seven turnovers in the first half. You had to feel sorry for Morton, who no doubt hoped to play well against his former team. But turnovers did him and Denver in. Before getting benched in the third quarter, Morton lost three fumbles and threw four interceptions. He completed just 4 of 15 passes for 39 yards. It was a lousy day. It was also a lousy game, featuring a total of 10 fumbles, four interceptions, a Super Bowl record 20 penalties, and three missed field goals. The Broncos never stood a chance. Their longest play of the game was a Morton pass 21 yards to receiver Haven Moses, on the opening drive of the game.

The Cowboys unveiled a new offensive weapon: the rookie running back Tony Dorsett. He didn't become a starter until the tenth game of the season, but he led the team with 1,007 rushing yards and scored 13 touchdowns. Tony Dorsett lived up to his initials in a big way, scoring 91 touchdowns in his eleven-year career. Against Denver, he carried the ball 15 times for 66 yards and a touchdown.

Roger Staubach completed 17 of 25 passes for 183 yards and one touchdown, with no interceptions. Wide receiver Butch Johnson provided an offensive spark by making a diving catch in the end zone for a 45-yard touchdown play. The Cowboys put the game out of reach in the fourth quarter when Landry, showing his affection for flimflammery, called upon fullback Robert Newhouse to throw a 29-yard touchdown pass on a halfback option play to receiver Golden Richards. The score gave the Cowboys a 27–10 lead and crushed Denver's hopes for its first championship. Newhouse became

the first running back in Super Bowl history to complete a touchdown pass.

Morton had the dubious distinction of starting at quarterback on the losing side of two different Super Bowl teams. Atrociously poor play forced him to take his lumps on both occasions. In his two Super Bowl starts, Morton threw seven interceptions in 41 pass attempts, with just 16 completions for 166 yards and 1 touchdown.

For the first and only time in Super Bowl history, two players shared the most valuable player award: defensive tackle Randy White and defensive end Harvey Martin. The voters actually wanted to name the entire 11-man starting defensive unit for Dallas as co-MVPs, but the league would not allow it. A Hall of Fame performer, White was one of the best defensive linemen ever to take a three-point stance. He recorded four sacks in three Super Bowl games, including two in Super Bowl X against Pittsburgh.

Oakland Raiders, Super Bowl XI

During the first twenty years of Super Bowl competition, the Oakland/Los Angeles Raiders came one win away from playing in the Super Bowl an astonishing eleven times. Four of those AFC or AFL championship games resulted in appearances on Super Sunday; and on three occasions the Raiders celebrated a world championship. What makes the Raider franchise so special is that they won in different eras, with different coaches, with contrasting quarterbacks and rushing styles, in Oakland and Los Angeles, and with a different cast of characters that the nation's fans could truly love, or love to hate. Al Davis had a lot to do with that. His whole life, all Al Davis ever wanted to do was win, period. "Just win, baby," was his slogan. For a generation, that's practically all the Raiders did. Davis never played a pro football game, but his determination to win at any cost helped create the AFL-NFL merger, and his fierce independence led to a historic lawsuit against the NFL. When Davis, as the Oakland Raiders owner, wanted to move the team to Los Angeles, the NFL said no. Davis felt he could move his team to any city he wanted, and the courts agreed.

Before Davis joined the Raiders, Oakland had won nine of its last 33 games. His first year, the Raiders went 10–4 and Davis was named AFL coach of the year. From 1963 to 1991, the Raiders compiled a .670 win percentage—the best record of any pro sports team in that period. The American Baby Boomer generation grew up watching the Raiders win on Sundays, year in and year out. The Raiders went 198–70–7 in the 19 seasons from 1967 to 1985, and during that span the team had only one losing season.

In 1967, the franchise started winning with quarterback Daryle Lamonica, a strong-armed passer who threw 64 touchdown passes in his first two seasons with the Raiders under head coach John Rauch. In a 1969 game against the Buffalo Bills, he threw a record six touchdown passes—*in the first half!* That's when Howard Cosell dubbed him "The Mad Bomber." The Raiders' owner, Al Davis, wanted his team to look for the deep pass first, and Lamonica was the perfect quarterback for that system. "Attack, fear, pressure," Davis once said summing up his philosophy on offense. "Don't take what they give you. You're going deep, and they're not going to stop you by design or location. They say they can stop us? Prove it."

In Lamonica's first year he took the Raiders to Super Bowl II against the Green Bay Packers. However, they lost

33–14. In 1973, Lamonica was benched in favor of Ken Stabler, a fourth year backup quarterback from the University of Alabama with the breezy, easy demeanor of a gunslinger. Stabler earned a reputation as a ladies' man, partying until the wee hours, and then going out on Sunday afternoon to throw that pigskin around for 200 yards and a touchdown or two. His image is similar to that of Joe Namath, another quarterback who led his team to a Super Bowl victory, had a cool nickname, won a player of the year award, and made headlines off the field. They also played for the same college, and their pro careers overlapped for eight seasons.

In 1976, Ken "The Snake" Stabler led all NFL quarterbacks with 27 touchdown passes (in twelve games) and a 66.7 completion percentage. His career completion rate was nearly 60 percent, particularly impressive considering the rules of the day allowed defensive backs downfield to "bump-and-run" with receivers. The Snake would wait as long as possible for his receivers to flash open, uncoil, and deliver the ball with precise timing nary a nanosecond before taking a hit. And clutch? That he was. "When we were behind in the fourth quarter, with our backs to our end zone, no matter how he had played up to that point, we could look in his eyes and you knew, you knew, he was going to win it for us. That was an amazing feeling," said Hall of Fame teammate Gene Upshaw.

That season, the Raiders and their boisterous young coach John Madden thundered into Super Bowl XI with a 15–1 record, winner of 12 games in a row. They beat the New England Patriots and defending Super Bowl champion Pittsburgh Steelers in the playoffs. Madden's Raiders likely kept the Steelers from being hailed as the best team of all time; the Silver and Black kayoed Pittsburgh in the

Fred Biletnikoff and Ken Stabler show who's number one after Super Bowl XI. (AP Photo)

1973 and 1976 playoffs, bookending two of the Steelers' four Super Bowl seasons. These Raiders won with one of the meanest defenses the league has ever seen. Linebacker Matt Millen once said, "The Raider defense is based on the three P's—pointing, pushing, and punching." Scroll down the roster and you'll find a squad full of players with forceful personalities, especially on the defensive side of the ball. The bone jarring tackling from safeties George Atkinson and Jack Tatum epitomizes Oakland's style of intimidation in the Seventies.

The defense also boasted two mobile linebackers, Ted Hendricks and Phil Villapiano, and two mammoth defensive ends, Otis Sistrunk and John Matuszak. At 6'5" and 265 pounds, Sistrunk was a man-child. He was one of the few football players who did not attend college, going directly from high school to the United States Marine Corps. After leaving the military, the twenty-one-year-old began playing semipro football. In 1972, a Raiders scout discovered Sistrunk and signed him for the team. During a *Monday Night Football* telecast that next season, a cameraman caught a shot of Sistrunk sitting on the bench, with steam emanating from the top of his shaved head. That, and the fact that the game program listed Sistrunk's alma mater as "U.S. Mars" (an abbreviation for U.S. Marines), prompted the ABC announcer and former NFL great, Alex Karras, to suggest that the extraterrestrial-looking Sistrunk was from the "University of Mars."

The Raiders met the Minnesota Vikings in Super Bowl XI, at the Rose Bowl, in Pasadena, California. The Vikings were making their fourth Super Bowl appearance, and were still seeking their first championship. This was the Raiders second Super Bowl appearance after losing Super Bowl II.

The key matchups on this Super Sunday didn't look good for the Vikings. Their defensive line was getting old; three of the four were thirty-one or older. The matchup that threatened to be a disaster for Minnesota was thirty-nine-year-old right end Jim Marshall, a 240-pounder, against 300-pound Raider tackle Art Shell, nicknamed the "Big Brahma." Shell was the best tackle in the game. On the other side of the ball, Oakland's 6'7", 271-pound nose guard Dave Rowe was up against 240-pound center Mick Tingelhoff, still hanging on at age thirty-six. "We knew by Wednesday we were going to win," said linebacker Phil Villapiano. "The only hard part from then on was waiting for the game."

After a scoreless first quarter, the Raiders scored on three straight possessions to take a 16–0 lead at the half. In the second half, it was all Raiders. Oakland gained a Super Bowl record 429 yards, including a record 288 in the first half. Even the defense contributed to the scoring, with two fourth quarter interceptions, including thirty-six-year-old cornerback Willie Brown's 75-yard return for Oakland's final touchdown. According to Brown, one of four Raiders holdovers from their Super Bowl II loss to the Packers, winning Super Bowl XI "made up for the other Raiders who came before and didn't have a chance to participate on a winning Super Bowl team. This victory meant not only a lot to me, it meant a lot to the entire Raider organization."

Oakland wide receiver Fred Biletnikoff, who had four catches for 79 yards that set up three Raider touchdowns, was named the Super Bowl's most valuable player. Among the wide receivers who have won the award, he is the only one who did not gain 100 receiving yards. Stabler was 12 for 19 for 180 yards and one touchdown. But it was the Raiders' rushing attack that overran the Vikings'

THE BEST WHO NEVER LOST

Ted Hendricks

Four rings in four Super Bowls with the Baltimore Colts and the Oakland Raiders

THE MAD STORK

The roster of the 1977 Oakland Raiders is a role call of some of the most party-crazed players in NFL history. For some, their off-field stories are more interesting than their exploits on the field. "Most Raiders loved to party," said quarterback Ken Stabler, "but Ted Hendricks was a party all by himself." Among all those outsized Raider personalities, Hendricks may have been the goofiest of them all. Ted Hendricks was called "The Mad Stork." What else would you call a 6'7", 230-pound linebacker with skinny legs and long arms? When his fifteen-year NFL career was over, he owned four Super Bowl rings and a spot in the Pro Football Hall of Fame.

The Baltimore Colts drafted Hendricks in 1969. He played linebacker on the Colts team that defeated the Dallas Cowboys in Super Bowl V when Jim O'Brien kicked a field goal with five seconds left in the game. He joined the Oakland Raiders in 1975. On the first day of practice, he showed up in full uniform wearing a German-style spiked war helmet and charged onto the field riding a horse, with a traffic cone for a lance. This was not the only time he wore a costume. At Halloween he showed up for practice wearing a pumpkin he carved in the shape of a helmet, complete with face bar. There is also the famous sideline shot of him from *Monday Night Football* with a Joker mask covering part of his face. He used to also put on shows for onlookers at the Raiders practices by lifting a barbell on the sideline with weights marked 500 pounds on each side. The weights were actually hollow—Hendricks hated to work out. As he liked to remind anyone who'd listen: "They never say, 'You work football.' They say, 'You play football.'"

Hendricks played his final NFL game in Super Bowl XVIII with two pulled abdominal muscles. Despite pain, he started at his usual spot, left outside linebacker, and contributed to the Raiders' 38–9 trouncing of the Washington Redskins. "My rings are the greatest things I have left from football," Hendricks says. "My rings and my memories. My rings possess me. I am possessed by them. They are in my will. I rub them. I call them, 'my precious.'"

famous but aging "Purple People Eaters" front four. The Raiders set a Super Bowl rushing record with 266 yards. Clarence Davis gained 137 yards on just 16 carries and Mark van Eeghen added 73 tough yards on the ground. Pete Banaszak, a bronco-busting fullback who was one of four Raider holdovers from the Super Bowl II loss to the Packers, rushed for two short touchdowns. Time and again, gaping holes were opened on the left side of the field by Oakland's offensive left guard Gene Upshaw and left tackle Art Shell. Shell was one of the best tackles to ever

John Madden is carried from the field after Super Bowl XI. (AP Photos)

strap on shoulder pads. In this game, he faced off opposite Jim Marshall and shut him down; Marshall did not record a single tackle in the game.

Oakland's first Super Bowl triumph extended the frustration of the Vikings, who lost their fourth Super Bowl in eight seasons. The final score, 32–14, actually belied the complete whipping the Raiders handed the Vikings. At game's end, linebacker Ted Hendricks (6'7", 220 pounds), along with John Matuszak (6'8", 272 pounds) and Charles Philyaw (6'9", 276 pounds), lifted stout coach John Madden onto their shoulders and carried him off the field. "Madden really wasn't that heavy," said Hendricks. "Tooz could've carried him all by himself." Oakland's crushing victory in Super Bowl XI would turn out to be coach John Madden's lone title. He later became a beloved television network game analyst. "Super Bowl XI was ours and ten years from now or twenty years from now Super Bowl XI will still be ours," he said. "I'll never take off the Super Bowl ring. It's something I will always cherish."

THE 1980s

An original AFL team, the Raiders moved from Oakland to Los Angeles prior to the 1982 season. It was the first relocation of an existing franchise since the Dallas Texans moved to Kansas City ahead of the 1963 season. Before the Raiders could actually play a home game in Los Angeles, however, the players went on strike following the Week Two games of September 19, 1982. Ultimately, the league lost seven weeks of games due to the players' strike. Another players' strike occurred in 1987, again following Week Two games. The league cancelled the Week Three games, and played the next

The Raiders' Al Davis hoists the Lombardi Trophy after Super Bowl XV, a 27–10 victory over the Eagles. (AP Photo/Paul Sakuma)

THE BEST WHO NEVER LOST

Jim Plunkett

Two rings in two Super Bowls with the Oakland/Los Angeles Raiders; MVP of Super Bowl XV

THE COMEBACK KID

Through forty-nine Super Bowls there have been eleven quarterbacks who have won more than one Big Game. Seven are in the Hall of Fame and three—Eli Manning, Ben Roethlisberger, and Tom Brady—are still active. And then there's the underappreciated and always underestimated Jim Plunkett.

A recap of Jim Plunkett's football career has all the ups and downs of a rollercoaster. The 1970 Heisman Trophy winner from Stanford was the No. 1 overall pick in the NFL draft by the New England Patriots, in 1971. An outstanding NFL rookie season with the Pats was followed by numerous injuries and a descent to the ranks of mediocrity. He was traded to the San Francisco 49ers and released after two ordinary seasons. He joined the Raiders in 1978 and spent two seasons on the bench, throwing no passes in 1978 and just 15 passes in 1979. Finally, he got a chance to play in 1980 subbing for an injured Dan Pastorini.

The Raiders had a 2–3 record in 1980 when thirty-three-year-old Plunkett took control. He passed for 18 touchdowns and 2,299 yards during the remainder of the season, guiding the Raiders to nine victories in their last eleven games and a wild-card spot in the playoffs. The NFL's Comeback Player of the Year then led four postseason wins, the first three on the

(AP Photo)

road. He completed 14 of 18 passes for 261 yards and two touchdowns in the AFC championship game victory over San Diego. Then in the Super Bowl he completed 13 of 21 passes for 261 yards (again) and three touchdown passes, two to Cliff Branch and an 80-yarder to Kenny King.

Oakland beat the Philadelphia Eagles, 27–10, in Super Bowl XV, to become the first wild-card team to win the Super Bowl. Plunkett was named the game's MVP. "I'm proud of that game," said Plunkett. "Many people felt I was washed up, and I wasn't sure they were wrong. After ten years and struggling with New England and San Francisco, that first one meant a lot to me."

Three years later, Plunkett helped the Raiders to another Super Bowl triumph, this one over the Washington Redskins. The second title came after yet more struggles in Los Angeles, after losing his starting job to Marc Wilson and then regaining it after Wilson was injured. In Super Bowl XVIII, in 1984, Plunkett, now thirty-six, passed for 172 yards and one touchdown in the Raiders' 38–9 rout of Washington, to that point the biggest Super Bowl victory margin. "He has to be one of the great comeback stories of our time," said Raiders owner Al Davis.

Over the next three seasons, Plunkett made only 17 more starts, mostly because of injury. He sat out all of 1987 with a shoulder injury. His NFL career ended at the age of forty when the Raiders released him during the 1988 preseason.

three weeks with replacement players until the labor dispute was resolved.

The 1980s saw as many football battles in the courtroom as it did on the gridiron. Football was prosperous and that was the problem. By 1981, the number of fans attending NFL games had increased four seasons in a row. That same year three major television networks had signed new five-year contracts to broadcast games. Football's pot of gold was overflowing and others tried to carve out a slice of the money pie. In 1983, football's prosperity enticed another league, the United States Football League, to take to the gridiron during the NFL off-season, from March to July. The USFL signed lots of stars, including Steve Young, Jim Kelly, and Reggie White. The new league eventually lost its better players to NFL teams and in July 1986, the USFL folded.

America during the decade of the Eighties was characterized by narcissism and self-indulgence, individualism and overt commercialism. All of this was reflected in professional football. Jim McMahon, the Chicago Bears' quarterback, liked to wear a headband under his helmet. During the 1985 playoffs, he was fined by NFL commissioner Pete Rozelle for wearing one with a corporate logo, a violation of the league policy. McMahon switched to one that said R-O-Z-E-L-L-E for the NFC championship game. For Super Bowl XX, McMahon prepared a bunch of headbands with the names of different charitable causes and kept switching them during the game.

After absorbing the USFL's top performers, many NFL teams were better than ever, and so was the action on the field. All the rules the NFL had adopted in the 1970s to increase the passing game were working. By the 1980s, more passes for more yards were being thrown per game than ever before. Bill Walsh's San Francisco 49ers were the passing team of the Eighties. With quarterback Joe Montana throwing short, quick passes to speedy, elusive receivers, San Francisco won four Super Bowls between 1981 and 1989. With more action to see, the fans headed back to the stands, setting another new attendance mark of nearly 17.5 million in 1986.

Oakland/Los Angeles Raiders, Super Bowls XV and XVIII

After ten consecutive winning seasons and one Super Bowl championship, John Madden left the Raiders (and coaching) in 1979 to pursue a career as a television football commentator. His replacement was Tom Flores, the first Hispanic head coach in NFL history. Flores had already won championship rings as a Raiders' assistant coach under Madden (Super Bowl XI) and as a player for the Kansas City Chiefs backing up quarterback Len Dawson (Super Bowl IV). The Raiders did not make the playoffs in Flores' first season, in 1979. The following year, the entire organization was distracted during a season marked by turmoil and uncertainty caused by Al Davis' unsuccessful attempts to move the team to Los Angeles.

Davis wanted to move his Raiders from Oakland to Los Angeles to play their home games in the Los Angeles Coliseum. He even signed an agreement to do so. Pete Rozelle,

the NFL's commissioner, was vehemently against Davis' relocation plan, and worked behind the scenes to quash it, angering Davis to no end. The move, which required a three-fourths approval by league owners, was defeated 22–0 (with five owners abstaining). Davis filed an injunction against the league and sued the NFL for antitrust violation. The first case was declared a mistrial, but the second jury sided with Davis, clearing the way for the move. Davis finally did move his Raiders to L.A. for the 1982 season. That year, the L.A. Raiders had the best record in the AFC, but lost in the second round of the playoffs to the New York Jets.

In 1980, the Raiders finished 11–5 and qualified for the playoffs as a "wild-card" team. The Raiders then advanced to Super Bowl XV with playoff victories over the Houston Oilers, Cleveland Browns (in a thriller), and San Diego Chargers to become the first wild-card team to win three postseason rounds since the NFL expanded to a 10-team playoff format in 1978.

The throng of 76,135 people who arrived in New Orleans for Super Bowl XV was treated to an amazing sight. An 80-foot by 30-foot bow of yellow ribbon was hung above the door of the Louisiana Superdome. This was to honor the 52 Americans who, just five days earlier, had been released by Iran's fanatical leader, the Ayatollah Khomeini, after 444 days in captivity. The Raiders' opponent in Super Bowl XV, the Philadelphia Eagles, were heavily favored, and for good reason. Philadelphia owned the No. 1 defense in the league, and had already defeated the Raiders, 10–7, two months earlier, pounding Jim Plunkett to the turf eight times by quarterback sack. But on Super Sunday, Plunkett and the Raiders were superb. With plenty of time in the pocket to search for downfield receivers, Plunkett threw three touchdown passes. One of his passes on a broken pattern turned into an 80-yard scoring play to running back Kenny King, setting a Super Bowl record. The other two touchdown strikes went to Cliff Branch on passes covering 2 and 29 yards. "I knew we could pass on them," coach Flores said. "At our quarterback meeting Saturday night I told Jim Plunkett that we weren't going to be conservative. I told him to go right after them."

Plunkett did just that. He played aggressively, and came out firing. He ended up completing 13 of 21 passes for 261 yards, three touchdowns, and not a single interception. He was named the Super Bowl most valuable player, capping one of the great personal comeback stories in sports history. By contrast, the Eagles quarterback Ron Jaworski felt the pressure all game. The punishing Oakland defense, led by defensive end John Matuszak and a trio of great linebackers in Ted Hendricks, rookie Matt Millen, and Rod Martin, flustered "Jaws" all day. Although he wasn't sacked, Jaworski was only 18 for 38 for 291 yards, and he threw three interceptions—all into the arms of Martin, whose three picks set a Super Bowl single-game record.

While Martin grabbed interceptions and the defensive headlines, another Raider defender, cornerback Lester Hayes, made a name for himself, too. One of the best man-to-man, lockdown-coverage corners of all time, Hayes had his best season in 1980, intercepting 13 passes during the regular season, and five more in the postseason. Hayes was known for his bump-and-run coverage style and generous use of Stickum, a gooey substance he lathered on his hands to enhance the potential for sure-handedness. "I could catch a football behind my back on one knee," he said. "It was

tremendous stuff." Hayes used so much Stickum even his teammates thought he went overboard. "You practically had to pry the ball loose from him whenever he got his hands on it," said Raiders linebacker Ted Hendricks.

In Super Bowl XV, Hayes didn't intercept a pass, but he limited his man to just two receptions in the Raiders' 27–10 victory. "The sole focus of our team was to win consistently," said Hayes. "Whether it was a mental or a physical advantage, we were going to do whatever was necessary to win. Our attitude was that if we could get away with something, we were going to do it."

The Raiders became the first wild card playoff team to win a Super Bowl—and the first team ever required to win four postseason games to earn a ring. Flores became the first man to win Super Bowl rings as a player and a head coach. (Mike Ditka and Tony Dungy would, too.)

As the giddy and triumphant Raiders celebrated their unlikely victory, the only Super Bowl drama that remained was the locker room meeting between NFL commissioner Pete Rozelle and Al Davis, when Rozelle was duty-bound to present the Vince Lombardi Trophy to Davis, his longtime rival and nemesis, who had been denied a move to Los Angeles and was suing the NFL. But with a national television audience of an estimated 68 million viewers looking on, the two combatants remained professional. "This is our finest hour," Davis said, sounding like a Brooklyn-born Winston Churchill. "This is the finest hour in the history of the Oakland Raiders."

Tom Flores and the Raiders won with quarterback Jim Plunkett in Oakland, and in the years after moving to Los Angeles, they won together there, too. Once again, Plunkett had to overcome great odds to earn a championship. The Raiders went 12–4 during the 1983 season, the franchise's second season in Los Angeles since moving from Oakland. The team's most impactful offensive player was second-year running back Marcus Allen, who led the team in rushing yards and total yards from scrimmage, while ranking second on the team in receptions and touchdowns. Allen emerged as the team's new star during the playoff run, leading the Raiders to convincing victories against the Pittsburgh Steelers and Seattle Seahawks while gaining a total of 375 combined yards and scoring three touchdowns.

On defense, linebacker Matt Millen was the Raiders' stalwart. The Raiders drafted Millen in the second round in 1980. They moved him from defensive tackle, which he had played at Penn State, to linebacker. In Millen's rookie season they had won the Super Bowl. (Millen, who later

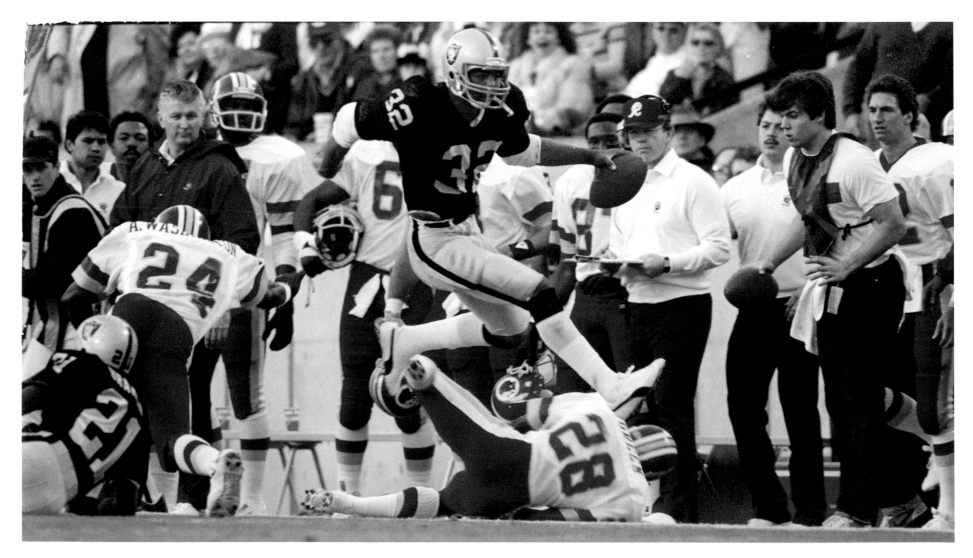

Marcus Allen hurdles Washington's Todd Bowles during Super Bowl XVIII in Tampa. (AP Photo)

played with the San Francisco 49ers and the Washington Redskins, holds the distinction of being the only player to win Super Bowl rings with three different teams.) The next season the Raiders' second-round pick was Howie Long, a power defensive end out of Villanova. Now they were back in the Super Bowl.

Over 77 million viewers saw CBS's telecast of Super Bowl XVIII. Barry Manilow sang the national anthem. Bronko Nagurski, who was one of the toughest players in football history and the man who came out of retirement to score the go-ahead touchdown in the 1943 NFL championship game for the Chicago Bears, handled the ceremonial coin toss. The broadcast of this game included the debut of one of the most famous television commercials ever: Apple Computer's "Think Different" ad introducing the Macintosh. Inspired by author George Orwell's dystopian novel *1984*, the commercial's impact on the game's huge television audience inaugurated a new era of sophisticated Super Bowl advertising. And some not so sophisticated. In later years, in what was called the Bud Bowl, bottles of Budweiser took the field against bottles of Bud Light in a stop-motion-animation classic that turned the Super Bowl on its head for a few years.

On the field, the Raiders' Super Bowl XVIII matchup would be a showdown against the defending Super Bowl champion Washington Redskins, who entered as big favorites, understandable with their league-best 14–2 record and regular season win over the Raiders, 37–35. But it was quickly apparent that the Skins were overmatched. Five minutes into the game, the Raiders blocked a punt and recovered the ball in the end zone for a touchdown. The Raiders scored early and often and in a variety of ways. During the first half, the Raiders scored touchdowns on offense, defense, and special teams. Meanwhile, the Redskins offense was struggling.

Washington's offense produced the most points in a single season in 1983, but it had just three points to show for itself as halftime approached. Pinned at their own 12-yard line with 12 seconds to go, and trailing 14–3, Washington's coach Joe Gibbs opted not to run out the clock. Instead, he called for a dangerous swing pass to halfback Joe Washington in the flat. The ball never reached Washington. When quarterback Joe Theismann threw the ball, little known Oakland linebacker Jack Squirek, anticipating a screen pass, read the play perfectly. He leaped in front of Washington at the five-yard line, picked off the pass and trotted into the end zone for a touchdown. "We were in zone, they told us to anticipate the screen and that's what we did," said Squirek. "I was surprised when they threw it. I was even more surprised when I caught it." The Redskins players were devastated. On the other sideline, ecstatic players galloped into the Raiders dressing room with a 21–3 lead. Gibbs later explained his decision. "You have two choices," he said. "You can either fall on the ball or try to get something. I wanted to run something safe. I was hoping we'd get 20 or 30 yards and maybe get a field goal. I didn't like the idea of falling on the ball."

Super Bowl XVIII was a game of big plays for the Raiders. None was bigger than the one provided by Marcus Allen. At the University of Southern California, Allen became the first college running back to top the 2,000-yard mark in a season, rushing for what was then a record 2,342 yards in his senior year. He won the Heisman Trophy as the nation's top collegiate player. In 1982, as a Los Angeles rookie, Allen led the NFL in scoring and was named the rookie of the year. Three years later, he again topped the league in scoring. Allen didn't have the greatest speed, but his ability to find the goal line and his unique running style made him a treat to watch. In 1985, his 2,314 total yards from scrimmage set an NFL record. He once rushed for 100 yards in 11 straight games.

Marcus Allen's greatest performance was in Super Bowl XVIII, in 1984. On one play, Marcus took the hand-off and tried to run a sweep toward the left sideline. No good. Washington Redskin tacklers grabbed at him from all sides. He reversed field and ran toward the right sideline. By avoiding five would be tacklers, he ran for 74 yards and scored the touchdown that put the game away for the Raiders, on a jaw-dropping, reverse-the-field, scoring play that still flashes in the mind as one of the truly great plays in Super Bowl history. In all, Allen rushed for a then-Super Bowl record 191 yards. (Timmy Smith of the Washington Redskins rushed for 204 yards in Super Bowl XXII, in 1988). For his efforts, Marcus Allen was named the game's most valuable player. Allen joined Plunkett and Dallas Cowboys quarterback Roger Staubach as players who have won the Heisman Trophy and then gone on to win the Super Bowl MVP award. (Green Bay Packers kick returner Desmond Howard would also accomplish this rare double feat.)

The Raiders' 38–9 win set then-Super Bowl records with most points and biggest margin of victory. For the second time in four years, Jim Plunkett's Raiders had once again overcome great odds to earn a championship. Plunkett's story of resurrection and redemption in two Super Bowls is now part of NFL lore. The stories about intimidation, the Silver and Black, the Commitment to Excellence, and Al Davis' "Just win, baby!" mantra usually meant that Raider games were billed as a clash between good and evil. Morali-ty-play aspects aside, the Raiders under the leadership of Jim Plunkett were a very courageous team. There's nothing evil about that.

San Francisco 49ers, Super Bowls XVI, XIX, XXIII, XXIV, and XXIX

The San Francisco 49ers had gone through five coaches in the four seasons before hiring Bill Walsh in 1979. In the third round of his first draft, Walsh took Joe Montana from Notre Dame, and the Niners were on the fast track to greatness.

"The minute I saw Joe move, there was no question in my mind that he was the best I'd seen," Walsh said, referring to Montana's pre-draft workout. "I knew with the offense I planned to run, Joe would be great."

Montana wasn't the biggest quarterback and he didn't have the strongest arm, but he was the perfect QB to execute Walsh's "run-and-shoot" offensive system: accurate, mobile, calm, and smart. Many teams used the "run-and-shoot" passing attack. Each team had its own name for variations on this innovative and popular offensive strategy. Walsh's creative system was called the West Coast offense, and his added wrinkles to the short-passing offense proved so effective he earned the nickname "The Genius." Basically, it consisted of the quarterback throwing a quick pass to one of four receivers. After the ball was snapped, each receiver would use a different running pattern to get downfield. Which pattern he used depended on how he was being covered by the opposition's defense. It was the quarterback's job to decide where, when, and how to deliver the football to a streaking receiver—a skill Montana executed to perfection. Montana was drafted by San Francisco in 1979, and in just

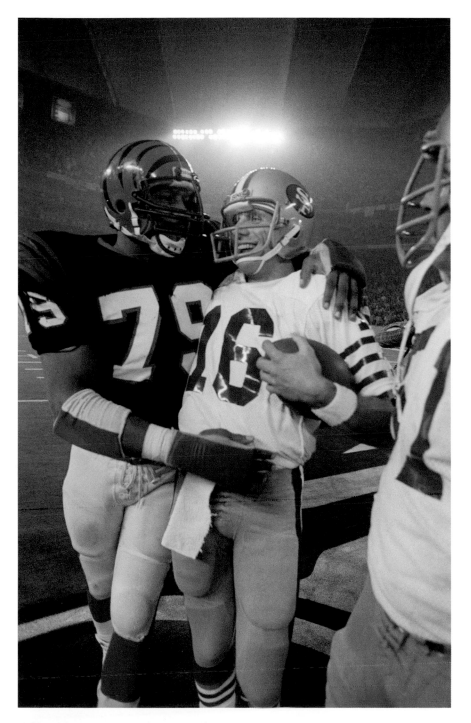

The Bengals' Ross Browner congratulates Joe Montana following the 49ers 26–21 win in Super Bowl XVI. (AP Photo)

three years, he was leading the 49ers to their first Super Bowl appearance, against the Cincinnati Bengals in Super Bowl XVI, to be played in the Silverdome, an indoor stadium in a suburb of Detroit.

The fertile mind of Bill Walsh would regularly script the first ten to fifteen offensive plays before the start of each game. In preparation for his first Super Bowl, Walsh had cooked up all sorts of imaginative schemes for the big game. A pass play to fullback Earl Cooper they hadn't used in two years was put back into the playbook. (This time they got a touchdown out of it.) Walsh also came up with the idea of Ray Wersching squibbing his kickoffs, getting them to bounce and slide on the artificial carpet. (Three Bengal kick-off returns failed to reach the 20-yard line.) "We played here the opening game of the season [against the Detroit Lions] and we saw how kickoffs could bounce on this turf. So we worked on this all the past week," said Walsh. He also had his defensive coordinator, George Seifert, concoct an exotic blitz to free up Fred Dean and allow him to rush the quarterback. (It forced a sack that killed a first quarter Cincinnati drive.) Walsh was tinkering right up to kickoff time. "Our bus was delayed coming into the stadium," Montana said. "If it would have been out there another hour, Walsh would have put in a whole new offense." Vice President George Bush attended Super Bowl XVI in Pontiac, Michigan, and his presence caused such a traffic tie-up that half of the 49ers arrived just half an hour before their warm-ups. Coach Bill Walsh kept his team laughing on the bus. "I've got the radio on and we're leading 7–0," he told his players. "The trainer is calling the plays."

Super Bowl XVI included the first Super Bowl musical performance by a major recording industry superstar:

San Francisco 49ers coach Bill Walsh is carried off the field after the Niners' 38–16 win over Miami in Super Bowl XIX. (AP Photo)

Motown legend Diana Ross performed the national anthem, kicking off a new era in elaborately produced pregame and halftime entertainment. Once the actual game started, the supremely confident Niners jumped out in front, 14–0. Following the second touchdown came a squib kick by Wersching that pinned Cincinnati deep in its own territory. After San Francisco forced a punt, Montana led another scoring drive that resulted in a field goal. With just 15 seconds left in the half, Wersching kicked another squibber that was mishandled by Archie Griffin, who was surprised that the 49ers would try a squib kick. "I used to have a theory on that kind of kick, that the first two bounces would be funny and the next bounce would be high. Today they all were funny." Wersching's two field goals within the space of 13 seconds set a Super Bowl record. The 49ers took a 20–0 lead into the intermission, the largest halftime lead in Super Bowl history to date.

While the halftime show featured Up With People presenting a "Salute to the 1960s and Motown," players in the Cincinnati locker room were feeling a sense of urgency. "We knew we had our backs against the wall," said tight end Dan Ross, whose 11 catches broke George Sauer Jr.'s record of 8 for the Jets in Super Bowl III. "We decided," said Ken Anderson, "that we had to get down to business." The Bengals began to rally in the second half with Anderson's 5-yard touchdown run and a 4-yard touchdown pass, but a courageous goal line stand by the 49ers defense and two more Wersching field goals ultimately put the game out of reach. (The four FGs equal the Super Bowl single-game record set by Green Bay's Don Chandler in Super Bowl II.) Cincinnati managed to score their final touchdown with 16 seconds left in the game, which

ended when Dwight Clark recovered the onside kick and Joe Montana took a knee. The final score was 26–21. The Bengals scored all of their points in the second half, but they came up five points short. The goal-line stand cost Cincinnati more than five minutes on the clock before they could get close.

Montana completed 14 of 22 passes for 157 yards with 1 touchdown passing and 1 rushing touchdown. In recognition of his performance he won his first Super Bowl MVP award. "Joe Montana is not human," Bengals wide receiver Cris Collinsworth said after the game. "I don't want to call him a god, but he's definitely somewhere in between." Collinsworth caught 5 passes for 107 yards, an average of 21.4 yards per catch. He and tight end Dan Ross became the second pair of teammates to each have 100 yards receiving in a Super Bowl. (Pittsburgh's Swann and Stallworth, in XIII, were the first.) Ross had 11 catches for 104 yards and 2 touchdowns, the most touchdowns ever by a tight end in a Super Bowl. The 11 receptions remained the Super Bowl record until Demaryius Thomas grabbed 13 balls for the Broncos in Super Bowl XLVIII.

Bill Walsh's coaching talents were not immediately discernible in his first season in San Francisco. For the second consecutive season, the team finished with a 2–14 record. Nobody expected the team to do much after going 6–10 in 1980. So Walsh decided to rebuild the defense through the 1981 draft and with trades and free-agent signings. The team really came together defensively with three rookie defensive backs—Ronnie Lott, Eric Wright and Carlton Williamson—and a pair of imports, linebacker Jack "Hacksaw" Reynolds (from the Los Angeles Rams) and pass-rush specialist Fred Dean (from the San

Diego Chargers). In his second season, Dwight Hicks, only twenty-five years old, was thrust into the role of the veteran leader of the young ball-hawking 49ers secondary affectionately called "Dwight Hicks and His Hot Licks." Despite a lack of experience, the 49ers defense ranked among the best in the league. Lott quickly earned a reputation as a hard-hitting intimidator, but he was also an excellent pass coverage defender.

The influx of new talent helped transform the Niners from a 6–10 team in 1980 into a 13–3 team in 1981, the best record in the NFL. "Reynolds was the veteran who steadied our young defense," said coach Walsh. "If there's one key factor or individual we can point to for our success in 1981, it's Reynolds. Jack made more difference than anyone. His experience brought us together." An outstanding run-stopping linebacker with great football instincts, Hacksaw played 11 seasons with the Los Angeles Rams and was a linchpin of one of the most feared and imposing defenses in any era in NFL history. (His famous nickname was earned in 1969 at the University of Tennessee following a tough loss to rival Mississippi, which prompted him to cut a 1953 Chevrolet in half using a hacksaw.) After a Super Bowl XIV loss to the Steelers, the thirty-three-year-old moved north to San Francisco, bringing his tough-nosed style of play to a young 49ers team, and helping them win two Super Bowl rings (XVI, XIX).

The defending Super Bowl winners could not repeat as champs in 1983. San Francisco's title hopes ended with a bitter defeat to the Redskins in the NFC title game on a Mark Moseley last-minute field goal set up by controversial pass interference and holding penalties by the 49ers secondary. A crestfallen Dwight Hicks, the defensive captain, delivered an impassioned speech to his teammates, asking them to "Remember this feeling, because we don't ever want to feel this way again. Don't forget it. We will play Washington again next year, and we will beat them, and we will begin building toward a trip to Super Bowl XIX. We can do it. We *will* do it!" Hicks' emotional speech touched everyone, and buoyed by his message of future redemption, that loss drove the Niners from the start of training camp all the way through the next season. They went 15–1 (the first team to win 15 regular-season games) and then dominated during the playoffs, leaving no doubt this time that their first Super Bowl title was no fluke.

Both the Niners (17–1) and the Miami Dolphins (16–2) crushed opponents throughout the 1984 regular season and in the playoffs. At 33–3, the combined record for the two teams is the best in Super Bowl history. This Super Bowl was unique in that the host site, Stanford Stadium, is thirty miles from San Francisco, giving this a home game feel for the Niners. In addition to being a master strategist, Walsh was also a brilliant psychologist. He knew how to read the personality of his teams, and he could sense when the players needed to be stroked, or bullied, or amused. He was a willing prankster. To break the tension players may be feeling on the morning of the Super Bowl, Walsh arrived early at the team's hotel, disguised himself as a bellman, and met the team bus to carry his players' bags.

Over 100 million viewers tuned in to watch Super Bowl XIX, which produced network television's first $1 million minute. In all, thirty-six advertisers spent a combined $30 million for 52 minutes of commercials spread out over six hours of pre- and postgame broadcast coverage. Advertisers were now willing to front the cost because Super Bowl

Dan Marino sees Super Bowl XIX slipping away. (AP Photo)

commercials were beginning to become a cultural phenomenon unto themselves—and ad exposure resonated far beyond television viewership on game day.

The gamc was billed as the quarterbacking battle of the century. Miami's record-setting, second-year quarterback, Dan Marino, was coming off the greatest passing season in NFL history, throwing for 5,084 yards and 48 touchdowns.

Dan Marino vs. Joe Montana gave this Super Bowl its greatest QB matchup, and for one quarter, it lived up to the hype. Marino came firing out of the gate and looked ready to break every passing record in existence. He completed 9 of his 10 passes for 103 yards and a touchdown in the quarter, leading the Dolphins to a 10–7 lead. But in the second quarter, Montana took advantage of Miami's poor punting on three separate occasions to turn excellent field position into three touchdown drives, giving San Francisco a 28–16 lead at the half. "All we heard all week long was Miami's offense: 'How you going to stop them?'" said Montana. "Deep inside we knew we had a great offense, too. Nobody was thinking about how to stop us."

For all of Marino's success at the start, it all came to a resounding halt after the 49ers' defensive coordinator, George Seifert, made a wise adjustment at halftime. The Niners broke from their normal defensive alignments and deployed five defensive backs, called a nickel defense. "We knew all week, among us in the secondary, that we would be the key to beating those guys," said Wright. The four Pro Bowlers—Wright, Lott, Hicks, and Williamson—were now as elite a quartet as any secondary in NFL history. Their play won the day, as they completely shut out Miami and rattled Marino in the second half, sacking him four times and intercepting him twice.

So while the 1984 season belonged to Marino, Super Bowl XIX belonged to Montana. "Super Joe" threw for 331 yards and three touchdowns and also ran for 59 yards and a score, leading the Niners to a 38–16 victory. Montana, who ran for more than double the yardage of Miami (59 to 25), won his second Super Bowl and second Super Bowl MVP award. "Montana is the greatest quarterback in this league, maybe of all time. This was his year," said coach Bill Walsh. "He hurt us in every way," said Miami coach Don Shula. So did Roger Craig. He rushed for 58 yards, caught a team-high 7 passes for 77 yards and scored touchdowns on a 2-yard run and on passes of 8 and 16 yards, becoming the first player to score three touchdowns in a Super Bowl game. After the game, President Reagan was on the phone, telling San Francisco

THE BEST WHO NEVER LOST

Joe Montana

Four rings in four Super Bowls with the San Francisco 49ers; MVP of Super Bowls XVI, XIX, and XXIV

NO ORDINARY JOE

Joe Montana may not be considered by many to be the most talented quarterback who ever lived. He didn't throw the ball as hard, or as deep, as many of his NFL peers. But who has ever played the position better when the game is on the line? Montana stands alone for incredibly consistent greatness. And his greatness in critical situations was just as wondrous. He will surely go down as the greatest clutch performer in the star-studded history of the NFL.

Where to start? How about the throw on the play that became known as "The Catch." That's when a scrambling Montana, with three Cowboys closing in for the kill, lofted the ball in the end zone to Dwight Clark. The six-yard touchdown pass, with 51 seconds left, gave the 49ers a 28–27 victory over Dallas for the 1981 NFC championship. And then there was the dramatic 92-yard drive in the final minutes of Super Bowl XXIII to come from behind and beat Cincinnati. That was probably his defining moment as "Joe Cool." Trailing by three points with as many minutes to go, Montana strolled onto the field, looked into the crowd, and happened to spot the late comedic actor, John Candy, in the stadium. Montana said to tackle Harris Barton, "Hey, look over

(AP Photo)

there, in the stands, standing near the exit ramp. Isn't that John Candy?" Montana's crack broke the tension. "Some of the guys seemed tense, especially Harris Barton, a great offensive tackle who has a tendency to get nervous," said Montana. "Everybody kind of smiled, and even Harris relaxed, and then we all concentrated on the job we had to do." Montana then led his team on a 92-yard drive in just 11 plays, completing 8 of 9 passes on the march. He hit receiver John Taylor with the winning TD pass with just thirty-four seconds remaining for a dramatic 20–16 victory over the Bengals. Even though this was the only Super Bowl game in which he played that he was *not* the MVP, Montana still completed 23 of 36 passes for 357 yards, 2 touchdowns, and no interceptions. Not too shabby.

With Montana in the lineup, the rest of the 49ers always knew they had a chance to win—and they usually did. In all, Montana led the Niners to four Super Bowl victories in the 1980s, and he also became the first player ever to be named MVP of the Super Bowl three times. (The feat has since been matched by Tom Brady.) In four Super Bowls, Montana completed 83 passes in 122 attempts for a 68 percent completion rate, totaling 1,142 yards, with 11 touchdowns, and 0—*zero!*—pass interceptions. His passer rating of 127.8 is the highest of any Super Bowl quarterback with at least 40 pass attempts.

"There have been, and will be, much better arms and legs and much better bodies on quarterbacks in the NFL," said former 49er teammate Randy Cross, "but if you have to win a game or score a touchdown or win a championship, the only guy to get is Joe Montana."

coach Bill Walsh: "I guess, as a coach, you couldn't have asked for anything greater than what they gave you tonight." And Walsh responded: "It's the greatest football team I've ever been around."

A Super Bowl appearance in only his second NFL season was supposed to be the first of many for Dan Marino. Nobody thought at the time this would be Marino's only trip to the Super Bowl. It's truly shocking that during his seventeen years with Miami, Marino never hoisted a Super Bowl trophy, especially when you consider all of his other accomplishments. Speaking at his Hall of Fame induction, in 2005, he told coach Don Shula, "We didn't win a Super Bowl together and that's something I will always regret, not knowing what that feels like."

The Niners' 1985 season marked the appearance of newly acquired rookie Jerry Rice. Thus began the franchise's careful personnel planning, which paid off as capable new players came aboard when veteran stars retired or moved on. Over the next few years, the 49ers would retool, rebuild, change on the fly, and continue to contend for championships, adding Rice, linebacker Charles Haley, and quarterback Steve Young. But in 1988, the 49ers struggled to find their team chemistry. At one point, they were 6–5 and in danger of missing the playoffs, but eventually finished the season at 10–6. In the first round playoff game, they crushed Minnesota, 34–9, and then thrashed Chicago, 28–3, in the NFC championship game. The upset win over the Bears sent the 49ers to their third Super Bowl of the decade, where they met the Cincinnati Bengals in Super Bowl XXIII, in Miami.

But then a simmering powder keg was ignited, erupting into mayhem. Three days of rioting leading up to Super Sunday underscored the growing tension between Miami's black and Latino communities. Rioters set fires and looted stores and one person was shot dead in widespread gunfire as 700 police officers poured into two black neighborhoods, arresting hundreds of people in an attempt to halt three days of violence. The riots, which began on Monday, six days before the game, began in the Overtown section following the shooting death of a black motorcyclist by a Latino police officer there, and spread to the Liberty City neighborhood on Tuesday. All hell broke loose as Miami made final preparations for the Super Bowl. Rumors swirled that the Super Bowl might be moved to Tampa (it wasn't). To the 49ers, sequestered at the Miami Hilton, eight miles from the turmoil, the riots were just images on the evening news. But the Bengals were staying in a downtown hotel, just six blocks away. They could see the fires from their hotel room windows. NFL security told them to stay in their rooms. "I feel like I'm being held hostage," said Bengals QB Boomer Esiason. "What's going on out there is life. It makes you wonder, what does football really matter?"

The Bengals in particular prepared for Super Bowl XXIII under almost impossible conditions. To make matters worse, on the morning of the game, the Bengals backup fullback and short-yardage specialist, Stanley Wilson, was suspended from the game because of a drug violation. Then on the Niners' second series of the game, the Bengals were hit by another blow. All-Pro nose guard Tim Krumrie, the heart and soul of the Cincinnati defense, suffered a grotesquely broken ankle. Players on both sides stood around for ten minutes until the cart took him off. Everything pointed to a Cincy fold, but the game was 3–3 at the half, the first time in Super Bowl history the game was tied at intermission. (Only Super Bowl IX between Pittsburgh and Minnesota had a lower halftime score: 2–0.)

In the third quarter, the 49ers took the lead when an interception by rookie linebacker Bill Romanowski set up a San Francisco field goal. After the teams traded third-quarter field goals, the Bengals jumped ahead 13–6 on Stanford Jennings's 93-yard kickoff return for a touchdown with 34 seconds remaining in the quarter. It was the Bengals' only touchdown of the game.

The day before, Jennings's wife had given birth to a baby girl. That night, Stanford later told reporters, he dreamed of running back a kick for a touchdown in the Super Bowl as a birthday present for his new daughter. Jennings joined Miami's Fulton Walker as the only other player at the time to return a kickoff for a touchdown in the Super Bowl. (It's been done eight more times since.) Montana & Company didn't waste any time coming back as they responded quickly with a four-play, 85-yard drive that ended with Montana's 14-yard scoring pass to Jerry Rice 57 seconds into the fourth quarter. With the score tied, 13–13, Cincinnati took a 16–13 lead on Jim Breech's 40-yard field goal with 3:20 remaining. It was Breech's third field goal of the day, following earlier successes from 34 and 43 yards.

The heroic effort by the Bengals was lost in the excitement of watching Joe Montana lead the 49ers on a stirring, last minute touchdown drive. Pro football historians might record this game as the official start of the Joe Cool legend in the NFL. Down by three points with 3:20 to play, he took the Niners 92 yards for the winning touchdown—102 yards if you count a penalty. Montana showed poise under pressure. With a minute and a half to go he was in serious physical distress. He was hyperventilating. He couldn't catch his breath. He tried to motion to Walsh that he needed a time out, but he couldn't catch his coach's attention, either. Montana

stayed cool. He threw a pass away, purposely incomplete, buying extra time to get himself together and clear his head. (It was the only incompletion of the nine passes thrown by Montana on the drive.) Then suddenly he was okay again. "No one else could have gotten himself together as quickly as Joe did," said Walsh. "It was like a soldier taking two in the belly and still finishing the charge."

Three passes later, Montana had his touchdown, on a 10-yard seam pass to John Taylor, the secondary receiver, with 34 seconds to play. Taylor achieved what little kids can only dream about: scoring the winning touchdown in a Super Bowl. Incredibly, it was his only catch of the game. San Francisco won, 20–16, and the Montana legend was born. It was the first time that a team had come from behind to win the Super Bowl at the end.

Rice, who was named the Super Bowl MVP, caught 11 passes for a Super Bowl record 215 yards and 1 touchdown. Running back Roger Craig finished the game with 71 yards rushing and 8 receptions for 101 receiving yards. He was the first running back in Super Bowl history to gain over 100 receiving yards. One of the most versatile running backs to ever grace the gridiron, Craig's 410 combined rushing and receiving yards in Super Bowl play ranks third best all-time. In addition to the winning catch, Taylor finished the game with a Super Bowl record 56 punt return yards, including a record-long return of 45 yards. His 18.7 yards per return is the highest average in Super Bowl history. Taylor is also the career leader with 94 punt return yards and a 15.7 average.

The Cincinnati Bengals upheld the AFC's honor in Super Bowl XXIII, after four straight NFC blowouts. The Bengals played tough, but were outplayed by a master. Walsh, at the

The Niners' Jerry Rice dives into the end zone for a third-quarter touchdown in Super Bowl XXIII. (AP Photo/Phil Sandlin)

very peak of his career, stepped down a few weeks after the game. His record: ten years as an NFL head coach, three Super Bowl titles. He left an indelible mark on the nation's most popular sport. For Montana, though, the fun was just beginning.

Joe Montana took the 49ers to even greater heights in 1989 under new coach George Seifert, Walsh's handpicked successor. The 49ers had a 14–2 regular season record, best in the NFL. Their two losses were by a combined margin of five points. "It's always hard to compare teams," Montana said. "But it would be hard to take any team above this one. It's tough to say any team is better than this one." In the postseason San Francisco drilled their opponents, too. The 49ers won three playoff games by a margin of 28, 27, and 45 points—outscoring their opponents by a combined 100 points. "Each victory is sweeter," said Joe.

Super Bowl XXIV was the icing on the cake. The first Super Bowl of the Nineties set records for most points scored and most lopsided game. The final score was 55–10. That sound you heard was 74 million people clicking off their TVs. CBS's ratings sank as the score soared. Perhaps a spate of blowouts was what caused competing networks to aggressively counterprogram against the Super Bowl, rather than give in to the national pastime. Fox aired a live performance of its widely popular comedy *In Living Color* during halftime of Super Bowl XXIV, which featured a show starring Gloria Estefan. The Fox special episode drew 22 million viewers; Nielsen estimated that CBS lost 10 ratings points at halftime as a result of the Fox show. So perhaps we have the Denver Broncos to thank for bringing us the annual Puppy Bowl, or the Lingerie Bowl, which is so popular there's now a Lingerie Football League. *This one's for you, John!*

Diehard viewers who stuck around witnessed the 49ers totally obliterate the Denver Broncos. Montana completed 22 of 29 passes for 297 yards and set a Super Bowl record by throwing five touchdowns. At one point, Montana connected with his intended receiver 13 straight times, breaking Phil Simms's mark of 10 completions in a row in Super Bowl XXI, also against Denver. Montana hit on 17 of his last 19 passes before Seifert gave him the hook with 11 minutes left in the game. "Joe had a great game; he was on key," said Jerry Rice. He caught seven balls for 148 yards and three touchdowns. Nobody noticed.

The 49ers became the first (and are still the only) team to win back-to-back Super Bowls under different heads coaches. George Seifert became the first rookie head coach to win a championship since Don McCafferty of the Baltimore Colts in Super Bowl V. According to Seifert: "Putting my stamp on the team wasn't one of my goals. My goal was one of continuity." Mission accomplished.

The San Francisco 49ers won big in the Walsh-Montana era, and might have accomplished even more but for an inexcusable fumble. Running out the clock with a 13–12 lead in the 1990 NFC title game against the New York Giants, Roger Craig inexplicably fumbled, and the Giants won on a last-play field goal. The Seifert-Young era also enjoyed success, but might have gone further but for the Dallas Cowboys. After cruising through the 1992 season 14–2 with Steve Young now under center, the 49ers were beaten by a hungry up-and-coming Dallas team in the NFC title game. After two Dallas Super Bowl victories, the 49ers returned to the big game following the 1994 season. By then, only seven players were carry-overs from Bill Walsh's tenure, including quarterback Young.

A PANTHEON OF HEROES

Jerry Rice

Three rings in four Super Bowls with the San Francisco 49ers and the Oakland Raiders; MVP of Super Bowl XXIII

RIGHT ON, RICE!

Jerry Rice's otherworldly skill with his hands came from working with his father, who was a bricklayer. When he was a kid, Jerry would climb a scaffold and catch the bricks tossed up by his five brothers as they helped their father on the job during the summers. The training paid off for Jerry when he won a scholarship to Mississippi Valley State. The college was not well known for football, but NFL scouts heard about Jerry's performance. During his four years there, he set 18 NCAA Division I-AA records. "I got used to hard work early," he said. "It made my hands rough, but it made me strong."

Rice was chosen by the 49ers in the first round of the NFL draft, in 1985. In his rookie year, he caught 49 passes for 927 yards, and was named NFC rookie of the year. In 1987, he led the NFL in scoring with 138 points on 23 touchdowns. It was the most points ever scored by a wide receiver. Although Rice didn't possess great speed, teammate Ronnie Lott once said, "Nobody outruns Jerry in a game." During Super Bowl XXIII, in 1989, Rice gained 215 receiving yards (a record) on 11 catches and was named MVP. In January 1995, at Super Bowl XXIX, in Miami, Florida, Rice helped the 49ers beat the San Diego Chargers, 49–26.

Despite suffering a slightly separated shoulder in the first half, Rice caught 10 passes for 149 yards, including touchdown passes of 44, 15, and 7 yards. The three touchdowns equaled his record set in the 1990 Super Bowl (San Francisco's Roger Craig and Ricky Watters and Denver's Terrell Davis now also share the mark.) Rice holds five career Super Bowl records. He has the most Super Bowl receptions (33); most points (48); most touchdowns (8); most receiving touchdowns (8); and most receiving yards (589).

By the time he retired after finishing his 20-year career with Oakland (as a member of the Raiders team that lost to Tampa Bay in Super Bowl XXXVII) and Seattle, he was the most prolific wide receiver in NFL history, owning virtually every significant receiving record, including career records for most receptions (1,549); most consecutive games with a reception (274); most receiving yards (22,895 yards); most 1,000-yard receiving seasons (14); total touchdowns (208); and most consecutive games with a receiving touchdown (13).

"I wasn't the most physical or the fastest receiver in the NFL, but they never clocked me on the way to the end zone. The reason nobody caught me from behind is because I ran scared. It's hard to go into every game with a red X on your chest, and I could feel the hair rise on the back of my neck when people chased me," Rice said in his Hall of Fame enshrinement speech. "People are always surprised how insecure I was. … But I was always in search of that perfect game, and I never got it. Even if I caught ten or twelve passes, or two or three touchdowns in the Super Bowl, I would dwell on the one pass I dropped."

A member of two Super Bowl winning teams as a backup to Joe Montana (Super Bowls XXIII and XXIV), Steve Young made Super Bowl XXIX a personal crusade for his first Super Bowl ring as a starting quarterback. Three plays into the game, he connected with Jerry Rice for a 44-yard TD pass. Only 1:24 had ticked off the clock, making Rice's score the fastest touchdown in Super Bowl history. Four minutes later, Young made it 14–0 by hitting Ricky Watters on a 51-yard catch-and-run, and the blowout was on. By the end of the first half, Young already had four touchdown passes and a 28–10 lead. The only remaining drama was whether Young could break Montana's Super Bowl record of five touchdown passes in a game. Young did, with 1:11 remaining *in the third quarter*. San Francisco blew out the San Diego Chargers, 49–26. The teams' 75 total points is a Super Bowl record. Young's line: he completed 24 of 36 passes for 325 yards and a Super Bowl record six touchdowns. He also leads all rushers with 49 yards on five carries.

At the end of the game, with the 49ers about to wrap up their victory, Young acknowledged the pressure he was feeling by turning toward his teammates and joyfully yelling: "Somebody please pull this monkey off my back!" Linebacker Gary Plummer obliged, yanking away the imaginary weight. Young then raised his arms in glory—and relief. "I really want to give George credit for what he has done this year," Young said of his coach. "He let the reins go and let the horses run." Said Seifert: "I honestly felt that if I tried to impose too much of myself on that team and be too restrictive, the whole thing would have crumbled."

From 1981 to 1994, the 49ers won five Super Bowl titles. Nobody stayed around for all five, but six players earned four rings during their careers in San Francisco.

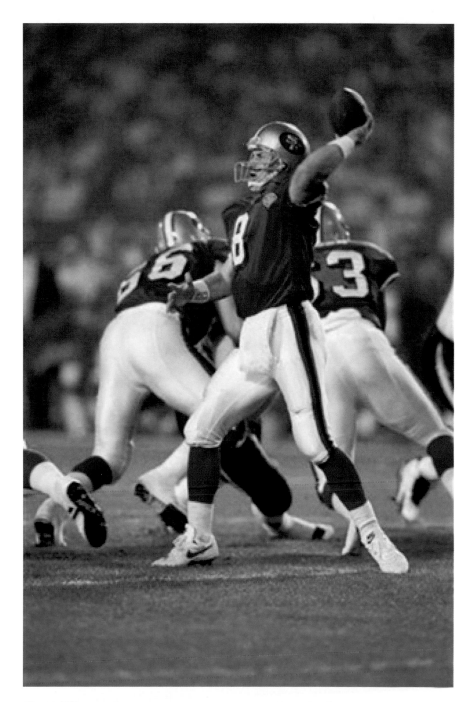

San Francisco 49ers quarterback Steve Young throws downfield during Super Bowl XXIX against the San Diego Chargers. (AP Photo/ Susan Walsh)

They are: Joe Montana (quarterback); Mike Wilson (receiver); Jesse Sapolu (offensive line); Ronnie Lott and Eric Wright (defensive back); and Keena Turner (linebacker).

THE 1990s

In the 1990s, professional football was inundated with great athletes flourishing on defense, as linebackers like Lawrence Taylor and Charles Haley and Cornelius Bennett defied double-teams and found ways to slip through and smash quarterbacks. This trend became pronounced as a means to lessen the impact of the behemoth offensive lines that were common in the previous decade. For example, in the 1970s, the average offensive lineman weighed 255 pounds. In the 1990s, the average lineman tipped the scales at over 300 pounds. So NFL draft boards were inundated with speedy pass rushers who could gain the edge against their stronger but slower rivals across the scrimmage line. Bigger players running faster and hitting harder was all the rage. It was smash mouth football once again. And the fans loved it.

The success of counterprogramming prompted the NFL to take steps to prevent the further loss of viewers at halftime during future games. Beginning at Super Bowl XXVII, the league began to invite major pop music performers to perform during the halftime show. The first of these, featuring Michael Jackson, led to a dramatic increase in viewership between halves—the first in the game's history. This practice continued until 2004, when an incident involving Justin Timberlake and Janet Jackson during the halftime show of Super Bowl XXXVIII caused a titillating controversy that ruled the water cooler conversation of the American workforce for weeks to come.

TV coverage expanded to feed the fans' insatiable appetite for their favorite game. By the middle of the decade, we started to see weekly games on Sunday, Monday, and Thursday nights. The revenues were just too enormous for the league to ignore, particularly with owners unable to keep a cap on salaries. Sunday afternoons don't contain the best football anymore. The real marquee games happen in prime time, almost exclusively.

In 1995, the league expanded for the first time since the Tampa Bay Buccaneers and Seattle Seahawks had joined the league in 1976, with the addition of the Carolina Panthers and the Jacksonville Jaguars. Not all fans were giddy, however. In a two-month span in 1995, both of Los Angeles' NFL teams fled the nation's second largest city for new locations. The Rams moved to St. Louis, while the Raiders returned to their original home of Oakland. Baltimore, who lost their beloved Colts to Indianapolis in 1984, said hello to a new team, called the Ravens, in 1996. The Ravens are actually the former Cleveland Browns. In 1995, Browns owner Art Modell announced plans to move the Cleveland Browns to Baltimore for the 1996 season. The NFL, Modell, and the city of Cleveland reached an agreement whereby the Browns franchise and history would remain in Cleveland to be resurrected in 1999. And prior to the 1997 season, the Oilers left Houston and moved to Tennessee.

The annual Super Bowl had become late Twentieth Century America's single greatest televised sporting event— indeed, its single greatest television event, period, with workplace water cooler talk the following Monday as likely to concern the new advertisements debuted in 30-second, $1 million advertising slots as on the game itself.

Dallas Cowboys, Super Bowls XXVII, XXVIII, and XXX

Tom Landry was looking forward to using the No. 1 pick in the 1989 draft to take UCLA quarterback Troy Aikman, but he was fired by new Cowboys owner Jerry Jones before he got the chance. As the man with the difficult task of replacing the only coach the Dallas Cowboys had ever known since its inception in 1960, Jones, an Arkansas oilman, picked his old buddy, former football teammate and roommate from the University of Arkansas, Jimmy Johnson, fresh off his winning a national collegiate championship at the University of Miami. Johnson followed through with Landry's plan, and took Aikman with the No. 1 pick.

As a rookie, Aikman started at quarterback for a woeful Dallas team that finishes with an NFL-worst 1–15 record. Despite the shaky start, Aikman quickly improved and the Cowboys, helped by Johnson's astute drafting and shrewd trades, improve along with him. The selection of Florida running back Emmitt Smith in the first round of the 1990 draft ultimately gave the Cowboys a trio of Aikman, Smith, and wide receiver Michael Irvin, that led the franchise back to prominence.

With three young studs featured on the offensive side of the ball, Dallas beefed up its defense before the start of the 1992 season. The main addition was defensive end-linebacker hybrid Charles Haley, a two-time Super Bowl champion with the San Francisco 49ers. Darren Woodson, a linebacker converted to safety, was drafted in the second round out of Arizona State and became a Pro Bowler, too. With all the pieces in place on both sides of the ball there was no stopping the Cowboys. Their 13 regular-season wins set a club

Troy Aikman celebrates a touchdown by Emmitt Smith during Super Bowl XXVIII against Buffalo. (AP Photo/Doug Mills)

THE BEST WHO NEVER LOST

Troy Aikman

Three rings in three Super Bowls with the Dallas Cowboys; MVP of Super Bowl XXVII

Troy Aikman and Michael Irvin celebrate a Cowboys victory in Super Bowl XXX over the Steelers. (AP Photo/Elaine Thompson)

THE WRITE STUFF

Dallas Cowboys quarterback Troy Aikman was almost as good at signing autographs as he was at throwing a football. That's because he started working on his penmanship almost as long ago as he began throwing footballs! "As a kid, I used to practice my signature," he said. "I'd say to myself, 'One day people will want my autograph.'"

Aikman quickly made that statement come true. Football fans started asking for his autograph after the Cowboys made him the number one pick in the 1989 NFL draft. But the demand for Aikman's signature skyrocketed in January 1993, after Super Bowl XXVII. In that game, he completed 22 of 30 passes for 273 yards and threw four touchdown passes. The Cowboys squashed the Buffalo Bills, 52–17, and Aikman was named the most valuable player.

"This team has meant everything to me," he said. "It's a tremendous weight off my shoulders. No matter what happens in my career from here on, I've taken a team to the Super Bowl and won it. Not a lot of people can say that. It's as great a feeling as I've ever had in my life. I wish every player could experience it."

He may have performed like a calm, cool pro in that game, but he was actually very nervous. "I was hyperventilating until the second quarter," he said.

Before long, though, it was the fans who were breathless—from watching Aikman. His accurate passing helped the Cowboys beat the Bills again to become only the fifth team to win the Super Bowl two years in a row. He was his usual efficient self in that game, completing 19 of 27 passes for 207 yards. Aikman's pinpoint passing accuracy continued in Super Bowl XXX, a 27–17 win over Pittsburgh. He completed 15 of 23 passes for 209 yards and one touchdown, becoming the first quarterback in NFL history to lead his team to three Super Bowl victories before the age of 30. In his Super Bowl career, Aikman completed 56 of 80 passes for a Super Bowl record 70 percent completion rate, to go along with 689 passing yards and five touchdowns.

Three NFL championships assured Aikman's place in the Hall of Fame but this Dallas championship run was over after winning the Super Bowl three out of four years, an NFL record. Aikman continued to play at a high level, but after two productive seasons in 1996 and 1997, injuries would take its tool. He missed five games in 1998, two games in 1999, and then decided to retire after the 2000 season due to several concussions sustained over the years.

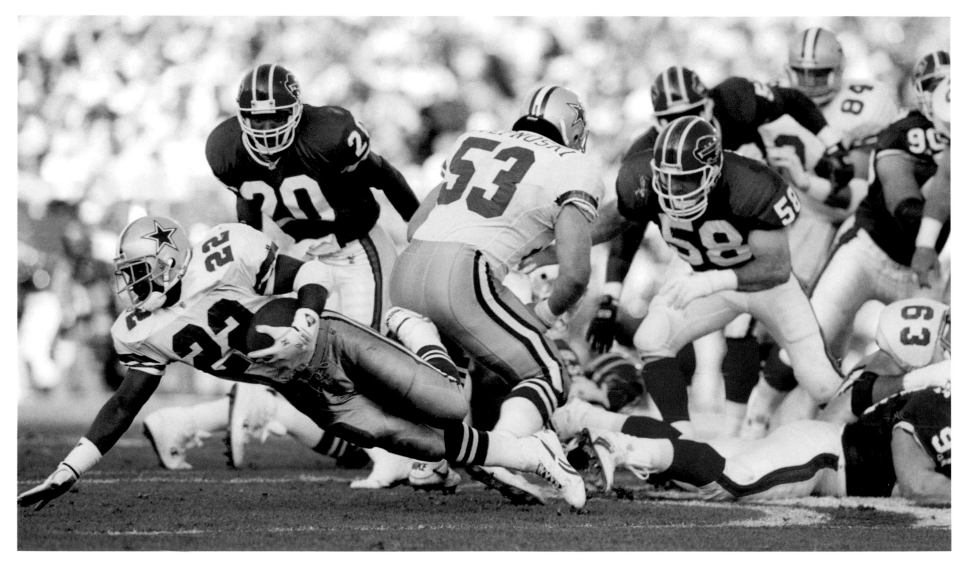

Emmitt Smith stretches out a run during first-quarter action in Super Bowl XXVII. (AP Photo/Rick Bowmer)

record. Coincidentally, the Super Bowl was being played in the Rose Bowl, in Pasadena, California—the home stadium of Aikman's alma mater. But to get back to Pasadena, Aikman's Cowboys would first need to get past the San Francisco 49ers, who had a league best 14–2 record. The teams hadn't met in a title game since the 1981 tilt won by the 49ers that ended famously with The Catch. This year's title game was considered by many to be Aikman's first step to elite status. He carved up the 49ers defense, throwing two game-changing touchdown passes, to lift the Cowboys to a resounding 30–20 win. The game is remembered not so much for the final score but for Cowboys coach Jimmy Johnson's jubilant

"How 'bout them Cowboys!" postgame speech to celebrate Dallas' first Super Bowl appearance in fifteen years.

Super Bowl XXVII wasn't much of a contest, but the game was high on theatrics. The game was originally scheduled to be played at Sun Devil Stadium, in Tempe, Arizona. But a controversy over the state's refusal to recognize the newly created national holiday to honor the slain civil rights activist Martin Luther King, Jr., prompted the NFL to move the game to the Rose Bowl, in California. The game was broadcast to 125 countries around the world. In the United States, about 91 million viewers tuned in to watch NBC's broadcast. Dallas jumped out to an 18-point lead at halftime, and the show at intermission proved to be the highlight of the evening.

Michael Jackson performed the halftime show of Super Bowl XXVII. The singer's popularity caused TV audience numbers to rise during the show, the first time that had ever happened during the Super Bowl. The King of Pop sure used more pyrotechnics than Up With People ever did! Jackson was literally catapulted on stage amid a flash of light and smoke. Then he stood dramatically still for 90 seconds in one of his "Dangerous" poses while the 98,374 spectators at the Rose Bowl cheered like crazy. NFL and television network officials decided that all halftime shows must also have the top pop stars to boost future viewership and interest from non-football fans, too.

In the end, the Cowboys routed the Bills, 52–17. Dallas forced a Super Bowl record nine turnovers—four interceptions and five lost fumbles—en route to their win over Buffalo. Thirty-five of the Cowboys' points came off of those turnovers, including three first half touchdowns. "I felt like we had the best football team," said coach Jimmy Johnson, who was becoming well known for his shiny, perfectly freeze-dried coif. "When you turn the ball over as many times as they did, you'll have trouble. Sometimes it snowballs."

In Super Bowl XXVII, Dallas quarterback Troy Aikman earned the MVP accolades with a near-spotless performance: 22 for 30, 273 yards, four touchdowns, and no interceptions. But he could have shared the trophy with running back Emmitt Smith for his 108 rushing yards and wide receiver Michael Irvin for his 114 receiving yards and two touchdowns. No one suggested that Aikman didn't deserve the honor, but the defense scored two touchdowns on its own. Charles Haley caused a Jim Kelly fumble that turned into a Jimmie Jones touchdown and Ken Norton Jr.'s nine-yard run with a fumble completed the scoring. Ken Norton, Jr. is the son of former heavyweight champion Ken Norton, who is one of the few boxers to ever beat Muhammad Ali. Norton Jr. played thirteen years in the NFL with the Dallas Cowboys and San Francisco 49ers, winning three Super Bowl titles as a linebacker on those teams. He is the only player in NFL history to win three straight Super Bowls, playing on championship teams in Dallas in Super Bowls XXVII and XXVIII before winning it all again the following season with the 49ers.

Charles Haley also holds a Super Bowl record that may stand up as an unbreakable feat. A devastating pass rusher, Haley is the only player in NFL history to win five Super Bowl rings. He began his career at linebacker in San Francisco, where he was a member of two 49ers' championship teams (Super Bowls XXIII and XXIV). He was shifted to defensive end and continued to excel at pressuring quarterbacks after a trade to Dallas, where he earned three more

THE BEST WHO NEVER LOST

Emmitt Smith

Three rings in three Super Bowls with the Dallas Cowboys; MVP of Super Bowl XXVIII

SUPER COWBOYS STAR

Many pro football scouts didn't think Emmitt Smith would make it in the NFL because of his height (he's only 5 feet 9 inches tall, which is short for the pros) and average speed. When sixteen NFL teams passed on him in the 1990 draft, Dallas traded up to No. 17 to nab him. With the Cowboys, he scored an all-time record 164 rushing touchdowns and high-stepped his way past the NFL's all-time rushing record

held by his idol, Walter Payton, and finished with 18,355 yards. He won four rushing titles, three Super Bowl rings, and the admiration of all those who thought he lacked the speed and size to play in the big leagues. "Emmitt Smith's about durability," said Dallas owner Jerry Jones. "He's about dependability. He's got the heart of a champion."

Smith had been on a fast track ever since coming into the league as a rookie in 1990 and earning Offensive Rookie of the Year honors and the first of eight career Pro Bowl nods. Smith carried the load for the Cowboys dynasty that won a

record three Super Bowls in four years from 1993 to 1996. During those years he became the first running back to win a rushing title and play in the Super Bowl in the same season. He also was the first running back to win a rushing title, the regular season Most Valuable Player award, and the Super Bowl MVP trophy, all in the same season!

In his first Super Bowl appearance, Smith rushed for 108 yards on 22 carries, becoming the first Cowboys player ever to rush for more than 100 yards in a Super Bowl. But he was at his best the next year in Super Bowl XXXVII against the Buffalo Bills. He rushed for 132 yards to become just the second player in Super Bowl history to run for 100 yards in back-to-back Super Bowls (Larry Csonka, VII and VIII). His final statistical line reads 30 carries for 132 yards and two touchdowns, but he gained 91 of those yards and both scores in the second half. In his third and final Super Bowl game, Smith ran for two touchdowns, including the game-clinching score with 3:43 left, in a 27–17 win over the Pittsburgh Steelers. In Super Bowl play, Smith is second on the all-time list with 70 career carries and third on the list with 289 rushing yards. His five career rushing touchdowns are the most in Super Bowl history.

Super Bowl rings. If you're counting, that gives Haley five championship rings in eight years. "Charles was the difference maker for us," said Cowboys' owner Jerry Jones. "He put the 1990s Cowboys over the top."

The Cowboys won with a defense that kept relentless pressure on Buffalo's ball handlers, and by forcing mistakes, making big plays, and handing the ball over to an offense that scored in waves. They got a pair of scores in a 15-second stretch in the first quarter, two more scores in an 18-second stretch of the second quarter, and three more scores during a 2:33 span of the fourth quarter. Jimmy Johnson proved his coaching mettle, not just in the myriad trades that he engineered to pull the Cowboys out of the cellar, but also by proving he could win at every level. He was the first man to play for a national college champion (Arkansas, 1964), coach a college champion (Miami, 1987), and coach a Super Bowl champion. During the exuberant celebration, during which Johnson was showered with the first of many Gatorade baths, he joked: "They messed up my hair a little bit. I felt we had the best football team. We said all year that the best game we were going to play was the last game. And we saved the best for last." President Bill Clinton telephoned the winning locker room to offer congratulations. "I think you understand how much we put into this thing," Johnson told the president. "It's a great feeling for all of our team. You know a little bit about perseverance yourself, so I know you understand."

Troy Aikman, Michael Irvin, and Emmitt Smith became known as "The Triplets" and they fueled a high-powered offense that opponents found nearly impossible to contain. The Triplets were three individuals but the sum of their parts made the Cowboys an amazing whole. "All three of us stepped up," said Smith. "We all pushed one another." In just

three short years the Cowboys had gone from worst to first in the NFL, and they also had youth on their side. Dallas' main contributors were in their prime and America's Team was back on top again.

The Cowboys reached the Super Bowl again the next year, and déjà vu, the Bills stood in the way again. Buffalo fought mightily to avoid its fourth straight Super Bowl defeat. The Bills defense played a gutsy and gritty first half, allowing Emmitt Smith just 41 yards on 10 carries. The Bills went into the locker room leading 13–6 at halftime. "Our guys were determined they were going to win," said coach Jimmy Johnson. "We felt once we caught up, we'd be fine. I hated to go in at halftime behind, but I thought we'd be okay."

Quarterback Troy Aikman said: "At halftime, we knew we had to get the running game going. We'd gotten away from it. We were too one-dimensional." The Cowboys were a different team in the second half. A non-existent running game sprang to life when the offense went back to basics, which meant giving Emmitt Smith the rock. "After scoring a touchdown to tie it, Emmitt was running hard and the line was wearing them down," Aikman said. "We stuck with it. Once we got ahead, we could pick and choose what we wanted to do."

The Cowboys went ahead by choosing to rely on Smith, the regular season MVP and league's leading rusher. Midway through the third quarter, the Cowboys executed a game-changing, 64-yard, eight-play drive. Smith got the ball on seven of the eight plays and got 61 of the 64 yards as the Cowboys again and again pulled left guard Nate Newton to the right and opened up huge holes. This was smash-mouth football at its gut-busting, nose-snot-flying finest. On third down and three at the Buffalo 15-yard line, Smith broke a jarring tackle, kept his legs churning, and then sprinted untouched into the end zone, giving the Cowboys their first lead of the game. After gaining 41 yards in the entire first half, Smith reeled off 61 yards on Dallas's first possession of the second half. His second touchdown came on a fourth-and-goal from just inches out, giving the Cowboys a 17 point lead with less than 10 minutes left in the fourth quarter.

That locked up the game along with the MVP trophy for Smith. At game's end the new Super Bowl MVP was mobbed by his teammates. "Our mission is completed," Smith said. "We came into this season with the idea of doing this. It's been a super year for me as well as my teammates. Being MVP of the league and this game, too, you can't ask for anything more."

As time ran out in the 30–13 victory, Gatorade was dumped on Jimmy Johnson and Smith mussed Johnson's never-a-follicle-out-of-place hairdo. Johnson and team owner Jerry Jones had begun feuding over control of the team. Whatever tension existed between coach and owner evaporated as Johnson and Jones shared a celebratory hug. Their club had just joined Green Bay, Miami, Pittsburgh, and San Francisco as the only back-to-back Super Bowl winners, and the franchise joined Pittsburgh and San Francisco as the only four-time winners. "Last year's Super Bowl was one of disbelief, a bunch of young, bright-eyed guys caught up it in all," Aikman said. "This is one of satisfaction because the expectations were so much higher."

Two months after the Dallas Cowboys had won a second straight Super Bowl title, it became evident the divide between Johnson and Jones had grown too wide. Johnson and Jones both wanted credit for the Cowboys' amazing revival. At a press conference on March 30, 1994, Johnson and Jones announced they were going separate ways. It was an amicable divorce, although the two had just split up after building a two-time Super Bowl champion everyone knew was poised to make a run at several more. No coach has ever won three Super Bowl titles in a row, but the team Johnson left behind was strong enough to win a Super Bowl two seasons later under new coach Barry Switzer.

The self-described "Bootlegger's Boy" had been out of coaching since resigning from the University of Oklahoma in 1988, had never worked in the NFL, and had long been Johnson's adversary during their college coaching days. Now he was being handed custody of the two-time defending champions. "Nothing is going to change," he crowed the day he was hired. "Get ready to watch the Dallas Cowboys be the best in the NFL. We got a job to do and we're going to do it, baby!"

The Switzer hire may have been Jones' way of demonstrating that the Cowboys were bigger than any one person. He had said as much during the off-season, suggesting there were "500 coaches who could have taken Dallas to the Super Bowl."

Barry Switzer's first season as Cowboys coach was watched with intense anticipation and scrutiny. In the 1994 regular season, the Cowboys, playing with a swagger and confidence to match the personality of their new coach, rolled to a 12–4 record, best in the NFC. But the team's chances of a three-peat was thwarted by a shocking loss in the NFC championship game to the 49ers, the eventual Super Bowl champs. In Switzer's second season the Cowboys posted another 12–4 record, and this time the team advanced all the way to Tempe, Arizona, to play the Pittsburgh Steelers in Super Bowl XXX.

Jerry Jones showed up in the Grand Canyon State ready to plan the victory party. Days before the game, he sought a waiver to the Arizona law requiring bars to stop serving alcohol at 1:00 a.m. When the game kicked off the Cowboys were sharp enough. A highlight of the first quarter was a 47-yard pass from Aikman to Deion Sanders—a defender playing offense—as the Cowboys marched 75 yards for a touchdown and an early 10–0 lead. One of the best all-around athletes to ever play in the NFL, Sanders started at right cornerback for the San Francisco 49ers in their 49–26 victory over the San Diego Chargers in Super Bowl XXIX the previous year. A two-sport star that liked to be called "Prime Time," Deion is the only person to have played in an NFL Super Bowl game and an MLB World Series game. He batted .333 and stole four bases for the Atlanta Braves during the 1992 World Series.

Dallas scored on its first three possessions but Pittsburgh only trailed 13–7 at the half. The halftime performance by Diana Ross featured an amazing four different wardrobe changes during the 12-minute show. Then the biggest diva at the Super Bowl (apart from Deion "Prime Time" Sanders) left the stage and exited the stadium by helicopter. A third quarter interception by Larry Brown set up a touchdown that put Dallas ahead 20–7. Pittsburgh clawed back to within 20–17 and was moving up the field midway through the fourth quarter when Brown intercepted another pass to kill the drive. Emmitt Smith scored soon after and the Steelers were out of answers. After winning Super Bowl XXX, Switzer exclaimed to Jerry Jones on the sideline: "We did it our way, baby!" Now Switzer had joined Jimmy Johnson as the only coaches to win a college national championship and a Super Bowl. (Pete Carroll would follow.)

The 27–17 Dallas Cowboys victory was the franchise's fifth Super Bowl championship, matching the mark set by the rival San Francisco 49ers just one year earlier. In addition, the Super Bowl XXX victory all but clinched for the Cowboys the title of Team of the Nineties with the bonus that it came against Pittsburgh, the franchise that had prevented Dallas from being the Team of the Seventies. It was the Steelers first loss in five Super Bowl trips. Charles Haley became the first player to win five Super Bowl rings, and Aikman's three put him in a group that included only Joe Montana and Terry Bradshaw among quarterbacks. Smith was three for three on turning regular season rushing titles into Super Bowl titles. In four years the Cowboys had three titles—more than they won in 29 years under Tom Landry.

"You can put the other two [Super Bowls] together and they equal this one," Irvin said. "Every time somebody counted us out this year . . . I saw my boys to my right and my boys to my left and we squeezed down and got a little bit tighter. Bottom line is, we got it done."

Denver Broncos, Super Bowls XXXII and XXXIII

It used to be cool to dis the Denver Broncos and call them chokers. During their first thirty-six years in the league, the Broncos always lost the big games. Take their Super Bowl record. Bronco fans watched their team lose four Super Bowls by a combined score of 163 to 50. The worst loss came at Super Bowl XXIV, in 1990. The San Francisco 49ers clobbered Denver, 55–10. To this day, it is still the most lopsided Super Bowl game ever played. Talk about embarrassment.

John Elway does "The Helicopter" in Super Bowl XXXII. (AP Photo/Elise Amendola)

So when the Broncos reached Super Bowl XXXII, eight years later, against the defending Super Bowl champions, the Green Bay Packers, it looked to be another bust for the Denver Broncos. An AFC team hadn't won a Super Bowl in its previous thirteen tries, and Denver was responsible for three of those defeats. Many people counted them out. But not Denver coach Mike Shanahan. "We're going to win the game," he said. "Our guys are pretty determined."

Nobody was more determined than John Elway. As a young quarterback, Elway had led the Broncos to the Super Bowl following the 1986, 1987, and 1989 seasons, but suffered through blowout losses each time—and each ending worse

Terrell Davis fought off a migraine to take home MVP honors in Super Bowl XXXII. (AP Photos/Lenny Ignelzi)

than the previous: 39–20 to the New York Giants, 42–10 to the Washington Redskins, and a crushing 55–10 to the San Francisco 49ers. Of the three Super Bowl losses, the most painful might have been the one to Washington. For one quarter, the Broncos looked like they were going to dominate the game. Denver jumped out to a 10–0 lead in the first quarter, but then the wheels fell off the wagon and the wagon caught on fire. The Redskins scored five touchdowns in the second quarter and Washington scored 35 total points as the Redskins turned the game into a rout. "Momentum swings in a Super Bowl are five times what they are in a normal game, it's so much bigger," Elway said. "When things go against you, it's like a wave."

Eight years after being trampled by the 49ers, Elway and the Broncos reached the Super Bowl again, this time against the defending champion Green Bay Packers. You couldn't blame football fans for feeling sorry for Elway, a great player who was gaining a reputation for getting clobbered in the biggest games. Leading up to Super Bowl XXXII, everyone knew the story, everyone knew the stakes: This was quite possibly Elway's last chance at winning a Super Bowl. "I'm going to tell a little secret that my mom and I had," said Elway. "It was when we were going to Super Bowl XXXII against the Packers. My mom sat in my house and offered these heartfelt words of encouragement, words only a mother could say to her son: 'Do we really have to go back to the Super Bowl?' I knew right then that we'd better win that one or she'd never go back."

Elway seized his chance for Super Bowl redemption in a big way. With the score tied, 17–17, Elway began to march his team the length of the field. The Broncos reached the Green Bay 12-yard line, and were facing a third down, when Elway took off on a keeper. He ran eight yards up the field, and making a desperate diving lunge for the first down, he was tackled so hard by two Packer defenders that Elway spun sideways through the air like a whirligig in what is now referred to as The Helicopter. "The way John Elway plays exemplifies what he is," Shanahan marveled. "He's going to throw his body on the line every time he plays."

Elway's gutsy run earned a first down and jazzed up his team. "It energized us beyond belief," said Broncos defensive lineman Mike Lodish. That play inspired the Broncos, who scored two plays later, and rode that energy to a 31–24 victory, leading the Broncos to an upset over the Packers. Though Elway completed only 13 of 22 passes (he did, however, have one rushing touchdown), it was his toughness and moxie that will always be endeared by Broncos fans for bringing the Vince Lombardi Trophy home to Denver for the first time in thirty-eight years. For Elway, after suffering three humiliating Super Bowl losses, this long awaited first Super Bowl triumph was reason to celebrate. "There's only four words: This one's for John!" Broncos owner Pat Bowlen exclaimed while holding the Vince Lombardi Trophy in the air during the postgame victory party, referring to Elway's long quest for a Super Bowl victory now finally complete.

Elway, thirty-seven, the oldest winning Super Bowl quarterback, was the sentimental hero, and Denver's triumph in Super Bowl XXXII finally gave him reason to rejoice. But the star of the game was running back Terrell Davis, who pounded Green Bay's stout defense with patented cutback runs. "I can't think of anything Terrell can't do," said Broncos coach Mike Shanahan. The best thing Terrell did was tear through NFL defenses. In 1995, his rookie season, he ran for 1,117 yards. The next year he was even better, leading the AFC with 1,538 yards. Davis was not the fastest back in football. Nor was he the biggest. So why was he so good? His teammate, lineman Mark Schlereth, thought he had the answer. "All great backs have great vision," he said. "With Terrell, he has eyes all over everything."

Davis was all over everything in 1997. He exploded for 1,750 yards and 15 touchdowns. In the Super Bowl against

John Elway stiff arms the Falcons Cornelius Bennett on his way to an MVP performance in Super Bowl XXXIII. (AP Photo/Doug Mills)

the Packers, Davis had a bad migraine headache. He didn't play in the second quarter. "My vision was blurred for a minute or so," he said. "I took some medication and the long halftime helped." Davis returned to finish off the Pack with 157 yards and 3 touchdowns, becoming the first player in Super Bowl history to score three rushing touchdowns in a game. He was named the game's most valuable player.

As the 1998 season NFL season began, fans wondered: Could the Denver Broncos repeat as Super Bowl champions? The answer: Yes! The Broncos had a nearly perfect season, losing only two regular-season games. They were heavy favorites when they arrived in Miami, Florida, to play the Atlanta Falcons (led by Elway's longtime coach Dan Reeves) in Super Bowl XXXIII. And from the moment the Broncos

A PANTHEON OF HEROES

John Elway

Two rings in five Super Bowls with the Denver Broncos; MVP of Super Bowl XXXIII

(AP Photo/John Gaps III)

Super Bowl Soap Opera

John Elway developed as a young quarterback in Denver under the tutelage of Dan Reeves, an NFL icon as both a player and coach. In 1981, Reeves took over as head coach in Denver; Elway arrived two years later. Together, the pair took Denver to the heights of the AFC, winning three league titles.

In the 1987 AFC championship game against the Cleveland Browns, Elway's miracle-working skills produced an amazing comeback in the clutch. In a span of five minutes, Elway led his team 98 yards in 15 plays to tie the game with 37 seconds left in regulation. Denver won the game in overtime with a field goal, 23–20. Elway's thrilling march nearly the entire length of the field will forever be known as "The Drive." The Broncos reached the Super Bowl three times in four years (1987, 1988, and 1990), but lost all three games by a combined score of 136 to 40. In fact, Super Bowl XXIV against the San Francisco 49ers was the most lopsided Super Bowl in NFL history

Reeves coached Elway for ten years, but their relationship soured after those three Super Bowl losses. Elway, who possessed one of the strongest throwing arms in NFL history, said he felt inhibited in Reeves' offensive system. Reeves began to think that Elway and offensive coordinator Mike Shanahan were plotting against him, scripting plays behind his back. Reeves fired Shanahan for insubordination after the 1991 season. Instead of derailing Shanahan's coaching career, though, the firing rejuvenated it. The San Francisco 49ers hired him as their offensive coordinator and then he became head coach of the Broncos in 1995, two years after Reeves was fired. Shanahan formed a vital partnership with Elway, helping him finally win a Super Bowl after suffering three humiliating losses earlier in his career. Said Elway: "When we were on the podium after we won our first Super Bowl, we looked at each other and said, 'We did it.' I'd been waiting fifteen years for that moment."

Reeves went on to New York to coach the Giants for four seasons, got fired again, and then joined Atlanta and turned the Falcons franchise around in just two years time. Late in the 1998 regular season, Reeves, who had the Falcons on the brink of the best record in franchise history, had quadruple bypass heart surgery and missed the last two regular season games. Reeves managed to return to the sidelines for the playoffs, leading the Falcons to their first NFC championship. In Super Bowl XXXIII, Reeves' Falcons would face off against his former team, Shanahan's Broncos, and John Elway, playing in his final season.

Elway summed up the story perfectly. "It is pretty ironic, all of this coming together," said Elway, who started his first game for Reeves in 1983. "The relationship with Dan, for both me and Mike, just didn't work out. Now, we're all going to play each other. That is strange. I think you will see two guys in the Super Bowl who will really want to beat each other to a pulp." Shanahan and Reeves could never forgive and forget. Both men had something to prove in this most personal of rivalries. "They watch each other, and if one messes up, the other loves it," said an assistant coach who worked with both men. "There is no question that Mike is working extra hard right now, because it would torment him forever to lose to Dan in the Super Bowl, and Dan is working extra hard for the same reason. That is how much they hate each other. They would rather fall off a mountain than lose the Super Bowl to each other."

Reeves and the Falcons lost to Shanahan, Elway, and the Broncos, 34–19, making Reeves one of four coaches in NFL history to lose four Super Bowls: Bud Grant, Marv Levy, and Don Shula are the others. In the Big Game, Reeves' four Super Bowl teams were outscored by a combined 170 to 59. Despite the losses, the first line of any Dan Reeves biography is that he has participated in more Super Bowls as player and coach than anyone else. "I was fortunate to participate in nine Super Bowls and only win two [as a player for the Dallas Cowboys]," Reeves said. "So I know what the agony of defeat is. To be that close is always difficult because that's the last game of the season and that's the one that you remember. You don't remember all the success you had to get you there. It's just a disappointment when you get that close, then all of a sudden, you lose."

Winning two Super Bowls also helped Elway come to appreciate his former coach over time. "Once I did that, it helped me feel different about things," said Elway. "I don't hold any grudges, any ill feelings toward him. The bottom line is we won a lot of football games when he was here. We didn't see eye to eye, but I still think he's a great football coach."

stepped onto the field at Pro Player Stadium, there was no doubt about who was in charge.

The Broncos were in top form—especially John Elway. The Atlanta Falcons seemed to have forgotten that he was one of the NFL's premier passers. During Super Bowl XXXIII, the Falcons decided that the best way to try to beat the Broncos was to make John Elway throw the ball. Had the Falcons lost their minds? Didn't they know that Elway was one of pro football's most dangerous quarterbacks over the previous sixteen seasons? Even though Elway missed three games because of injuries during the 1998 season, he still threw for 2,806 yards and 22 touchdowns. Denver won 11 of the 12 games that Elway started for them that season. And he had already quarterbacked his team to a Super Bowl win, in January 1998. The Falcons didn't seem to remember Elway or his stats. This fired up Elway. "All week long, all the Falcons talked about was stopping our running game. I knew they were saying, 'Make Elway beat us.' My thought was, Good, let's go. I was so motivated, it wasn't even funny."

The Falcons certainly weren't laughing at the end. Elway completed 18 of his 29 pass attempts for 336 yards and 1 touchdown. He even ran for a touchdown! But he didn't do it alone. Running back Terrell Davis rushed for 102 yards and gained 50 receiving yards. The defining moment of this game occurred with five minutes left in the first half. Elway faked a handoff to Davis and then fired a long-range missile over the middle to wide receiver Rod Smith, who burned Atlanta safety Eugene Robinson for an 80-yard touchdown to put Denver up by 14 points. Said Elway: "Although he had plenty of catches and touchdowns in his career, the only things that mattered to Rod were winning and competing for Super Bowls." Robinson getting torched by Smith on the game's biggest play capped an embarrassing 24 hours for the safety. The night before, he was arrested on a charge of soliciting prostitution from an undercover police officer. Ironically, the same day he received the Bart Starr Award, given by Athletes in Action to one NFL player a year for "outstanding character and leadership in the home, on the field and in the community." Later, Broncos cornerback Darrien Gordon got into the act. He intercepted two Atlanta passes in the end zone and returned them for a total of 108 yards, a Super Bowl record for a single game and the career record, as well. Gordon also played on losing Super Bowl teams with the San Diego Chargers (XXIX) and the Oakland Raiders (XXXVII).

During the regular season, the Falcon players had popularized an end zone dance they called The Dirty Bird. But their efforts were useless against Denver's tough defense, which held the Falcons without a touchdown until 2:04 left in the game. Atlanta quarterback Chris Chandler was sacked twice and threw three interceptions in the face of heavy pressure from Denver's blitzing defense. "The Dirty Bird is dead," Denver linebacker John Mobley said after Super Bowl XXXIII. "We plucked them turkeys."

The Broncos cruised to a 34–19 win and their second straight Super Bowl win. They became the seventh team to win back-to-back Super Bowls, putting a double exclamation mark at the end of Elway's Hall of Fame career. Playing in his final game, Elway, at thirty-eight, was the oldest player ever to be named Super Bowl MVP. "I never, ever thought I could be the Super Bowl MVP," he said. Obviously, neither did the Falcons. "They disrespected us all week," said Denver tight end Shannon Sharpe. "Everybody disrespected us. They never faced a running game like ours. They never faced a quarterback like ours. They never faced a coach who puts in a game plan like Mike Shanahan."

Shanahan is one of five coaches to win back-to-back Super Bowls; the others are Vince Lombardi, Don Shula, Chuck Noll, and Bill Belichick. At one time they were chumps, but the Broncos were now champs. For Elway, even though he was past his prime, the two late Super Bowl wins, at ages thirty-seven and thirty-eight, forever changed the conversation about his legacy.

The game ended with an emotional Elway walking victoriously to the sideline to celebrate with his adoring teammates as the final seconds ticked away. "That walk, I'll remember it for the rest of my life," said Elway. "That's the kind of walk you dream of as a kid."

THE 2000s

"The Super Bowl contains multitudes; it has always exemplified America at its best, America at its worst, and more than anything else, America at its most."
—Michael MacCambridge, author

In 2002, the NFL added a 32nd team, the Houston Texans. This addition allowed the league to correct some of the geographic confusion that occurred over the years as teams relocated and the league expanded. The NFL went to a four-team per division format. By adding a division, the top four seeds in the playoffs are now occupied by a division winner,

so that the top wild-card team no longer hosts a playoff game in the wild-card round, as had been the case from 1978 to 2001. Two teams now make the playoffs in each conference as a wild-card. Many accused the NFL of a money-grab by adding an additional round to the playoffs with these wild-card teams.

In the NFL's defense, who can blame them? The NFL playoffs draw a large audience of viewers. The top ten-rated sports events on TV in US history are Super Bowls. Eight of the top ten shows *ever* are Super Bowls. This record audience is obviously a big win for the television networks and the NFL, but it's also a big victory for many of the game's sponsors, like McDonald's and Budweiser, who will likely shell out $4.5 million per 30-second ad for this year's game.

The growing viewership results in increasingly higher prices for Super Bowl commercials. That's Economics 101. The average cost of a 30-second commercial, about $37,500 at the inaugural big game in 1967, broke the $1 million barrier for Super Bowl XXXIV between the St. Louis Rams and Tennessee Titans in 2000. The following year the price doubled to over $2 million, where it remained throughout the decade. Much like the irrational exuberance of stock market investors during the Dot-com bubble of the 1990s, the advertisers drawn to Super Bowl glory certainly will not recoup their investments.

At the dawn of a new millennium, counterprogramming was no longer limited to halftime. With a 30-second commercial costing $1.6 million in 1999, corporate advertisers began looking for more creative and cost-effective ways to lure eyeballs to their products. One company, Victoria's Secret, purchased cheaper TV ad time in the days before Super Bowl

XXXIII, in order to promote an upcoming show scheduled to compete head-to-head against the big game. Advertising for a web-only lingerie fashion show, scores of scantily clad models traipse in front of the camera. "The Broncos won't be there. The Falcons won't be there," reads the scrolling text. "You won't care." Victoria's Secret later claimed 1.2 million visitors to its website.

New England Patriots, Super Bowls XXXVI, XXXVIII, and XXXIX

The New England Patriots entered the twenty-first century never having won a Super Bowl. The Patriots played in two championship games—Super Bowl XX against the Chicago Bears and Super Bowl XXXI against the Green Bay Packers—and lost both times in games played in New Orleans against a highly decorated NFL franchise. In 2001, the Patriots began to rewrite the record book. They posted an 11–5 regular-season record and then defeated two storied AFC franchises, the Oakland Raiders and Pittsburgh Steelers, to earn their way back to New Orleans for Super Bowl XXXVI.

The Patriots nearly missed punching their ticket to the Crescent City. The first primetime NFL playoff game, contested in an unrelenting New England storm of snow and swirling wind, made for a dramatic setting. Players slipped and slid on a Foxboro Stadium field covered by a sheet of fresh white power. The Oakland Raiders built a lead, 13–3, as the game headed into the fourth quarter. That's when the Patriots' second-year quarterback Tom Brady, in his first NFL postseason start, introduced himself to a national audience. Brady announced himself as a Prime Time player by throwing nine complete passes in a row, and then scored

the first rushing touchdown of his career, scurrying six yards into the end zone, to slice the deficit to three points. It was a scintillating 67-yard drive in difficult conditions. "I saw [Brady] get up and spike the ball, then I saw him fall over," said teammate Troy Brown. "He looked [like] the young, clumsy quarterback he was at that time."

After two possessions, the Raiders could not run out the clock. The Patriots, still trailing 13–10, took over on their own 46-yard line with 2 minutes 6 seconds left and no time outs. Brady faded back to pass, pump-faked, and pulled the ball down in an attempt to tuck the ball back into his body. At that exact instant, he was hit and sacked by a blitzing Charles Woodson. The ball popped loose and was recovered by the Raiders. The teams reacted as if it was a fumble. Or so it appeared. Said Brady: "When Charles hit me on that play and I dropped the ball, I thought, 'Oh, man this is not looking good.'"

However, after reviewing the play, the referees ruled that Brady's arm was coming forward as he was hit. That made the play an incomplete pass, not a fumble. Had the play been ruled a fumble, the Raiders would have been able to run out the clock. Instead, the Patriots kept possession, continued driving, and kicked a game-tying field goal to force overtime in what is now called the Tuck Rule game. In the extra period, New England kicker Adam Vinatieri booted a 23-yard field goal, barely clearing the crossbar, to give the Patriots a 16–13 win in the final game ever played at Foxboro Stadium. "It was the worst loss I'd ever experienced," said Oakland fullback Jon Ritchie. "You know, I'd just as soon never talk about it again."

The Patriots went on to defeat the Steelers in the AFC title game, clinching a trip to New Orleans to face the St.

Louis Rams in Super Bowl XXXVI. The teams had already faced off during the regular season. The Rams wore down the Patriots and won, 24–17. The game was a physical battle. The Rams lost four defensive players to injury. The Patriots' toughness prompted Rams coach Mike Martz to say that the Patriots were "a Super Bowl–caliber team." After the loss, the Patriots dropped to 5–5, but did not lose again the rest of the season. The teams met again in the Super Bowl. The game was played at the Louisiana Superdome in New Orleans, on February 3, 2002. Following the September 11 attacks, the NFL postponed one week of the regular season and delayed its playoff schedule by a week. As a result, Super Bowl XXXVI was the first Super Bowl played in February. President George W. Bush showed up to flip a coin. Bush became the first US president to stand on the field and participate in a Super Bowl coin toss. (Ronald Reagan tossed a coin via satellite from the White House to kick off Super Bowl XIX, in 1985.)

The Super Bowl XXXVI halftime performance in the Superdome by the Irish rock group, U2, still stirs memories. The devastating horror of September 11, 2001, was still fresh as were the ruins in New York, Pennsylvania, and at the Pentagon. The performance was certainly the highlight of any halftime show before or since. As Bono hoarsely sang "Beautiful Day," a list of names of the September 11 casualties scrolled across the dome's ceiling. At one point, Bono revealed an American flag inside his jacket. The performance still causes tears.

The Rams had won a Super Bowl two years earlier, with a spectacular offense known as "The Greatest Show on Turf." Offensively, St. Louis still possessed an incredible amount of talent at nearly every skill position. Quarterback Kurt War-

Adam Vinatieri celebrates his 48-yard game-winning field goal in the final seconds of Super Bowl XXXVI against the St. Louis Rams. (AP Photo/Amy Sancetta)

A PANTHEON OF HEROES

Tom Brady

Four rings in six Super Bowls with the New England Patriots; MVP of Super Bowls XXXVI, XXXVIII, and XLIX

TOM TERRIFIC

The Patriots' chances for a Super Bowl appearance seemed bleak shortly after the 2001 season had begun. The Patriots lost their first two games. In the second loss, at home to the New York Jets, starting quarterback Drew Bledsoe suffered a sheared blood vessel on a hit by Jets linebacker Mo Lewis that would cause him to miss several weeks. His replacement was second-year quarterback Tom Brady—a sixth-round draft pick who had thrown only three passes during the 2000 season. The twenty-four-year-old Brady was an immediate success, leading New England to an 11–5 record. He completed nearly 64 percent of his passes and was selected to the Pro Bowl, a rare honor for a rookie quar-

(AP Photo/Dave Martin)

terback in the NFL. In Super Bowl XXXVI against the St. Louis Rams, Brady's heady exploits in leading his team to a dramatic Super Bowl victory changed the topic of discussion at game's end from the Rams' potential dynasty to the Patriots' manifest destiny.

At the outset of Brady's career, he and coach Bill Belichick combined to win three championships in a four-year span, in the 2002, 2004, and 2005 Super Bowls. Brady was the MVP in the first two of those. Following a decade-long title drought, after losses in the big games in 2008 and 2012, both times against the New York Giants, Brady and the Patriots captured their fourth Super Bowl crown, a 28–24 comeback victory over the defending champion Seattle Seahawks in Super Bowl XLIX. Brady completed 37 of 50 passes for 328 yards with four touchdown passes, each to a different receiver, including an 8-for-8 run of perfection on the drive that led to the go-ahead score with about two minutes left in the game. "Well, it's been a long journey. I've been at it for fifteen years and we've had a couple of tough losses in this game," Brady said. "This one came down to the end, and this time, we made the plays."

Tom Brady has rewritten the Super Bowl record book as the starting quarterback of the New England Patriots. He is the first quarterback to start in six Super Bowls, one more than John Elway's five with the Denver Broncos. So far, he has won four Super Bowl rings, equaling the mark of Terry Bradshaw and Joe Montana, his boyhood idol. A native of San Mateo, California, Brady grew up rooting for Montana and the San Francisco 49ers. His family owned season tickets at San Francisco's Candlestick Park. As a boy, Brady would wear a No. 16 jersey, just like Montana, and cheer for his favorite player's team.

In the days leading up to Super Bowl XLIX against Seattle, Brady grew nostalgic, using the occasion of Throwback Thursday to upload a photograph of himself as a kid posing in a replica Montana jersey. Then Brady did a fairly good impression of Joe Cool against Seattle, and joined Montana as the only players in NFL history to win the Super Bowl most valuable player award three times. "I haven't thought about that, I never put myself in those discussions," said Brady when asked about his place alongside Montana, considered the greatest clutch quarterback in NFL history. "That's not how I think. There's so many great players that have been on so many great teams and we've had some great teams that haven't won it and I think you've just got to enjoy the moment."

"Deflategate" notwithstanding, there is still time for Brady to add to his Super Bowl accomplishments and build onto his otherworldly legacy as an immortal player on Super Sunday. To date, Brady owns the Super Bowl career passing records for attempts (247), completions (164), passing yards (1,605), and touchdown passes (13).

"Tom Brady is so special because he's such a great leader and all the players can relate to him," said owner Robert Kraft. Indeed, Brady has earned the respect of his teammates, and when Brady speaks up, they all listen. Deion Branch, who won the Super Bowl XXXIX most valuable player award as a result of being on the receiving end of 11 Brady passes for 133 yards, may have summed up Brady best: "Tom thinks he's one of the boys. He can't be one of the boys. This guy is the face of the NFL."

ner won his second NFL most valuable player award after throwing for 4,830 yards and 36 touchdowns during the 2001 regular season. Running back Marshall Faulk was the NFL offensive player of the year for a third time in a row. He gained over 2,000 combined rushing and receiving yards for an unprecedented fourth consecutive season.

Coming into the game, the Rams were heavy favorites. However, after the Patriots took a 17–3 lead in the third quarter, it was the Rams who were in an unfavorable position. Though the Rams had dominated the game statistically, they had made three costly turnovers resulting in 17 New England points. Seven of those points came from Ty Law, one of the NFL's preeminent cornerbacks, who intercepted a Warner pass and returned it 47 yards for a touchdown in the second quarter to give the Patriots a 7–3 lead. Still, the Rams fought back, and by late in the fourth quarter, the Rams had the ball and were now just a touchdown behind. Warner needed to get the Rams offense back in gear. In the huddle, he called a play for wide receiver Ricky Proehl to streak down the field, creating a footrace that Proehl was sure to win. Warner took the snap and backpedaled into the pocket. The ball left Warner's fingertips just as a Patriot buried him. It zipped down the field. Proehl glanced back over his shoulder, realized what was happening, and adjusted his speed. At the last instant, Proehl plucked the ball out of the air for a clutch 26-yard touchdown to tie the game at 17–17.

That left 1 minute 30 seconds on the game clock. The Patriots had no timeouts. With the clock an adversary, and no way to stop it, most people—including TV announcer John Madden—suggested the Patriots may be shell shocked, and should merely run out the clock and take their chances in overtime. However, Tom Brady had other ideas. "I was plan-ning to go out there to win the game," he said with an edge. The entire season had come down to this one crucial drive. Starting on the Patriots' own 17-yard line, Brady marched his team 53 yards in eight plays, including three completed passes to J.R. Redmond, to the Rams' 30-yard line. Brady calmly spiked the ball to stop the clock with seven seconds to play. Miraculously, Brady had managed to move the ball into enemy territory, setting up an attempt for a potential game-winning kick on the far reaches of field goal range.

Adam Vinatieri had already converted two clutch kicks in the AFC divisional playoff victory over Oakland. He trotted onto the field once more with the balance of a big game hanging on his right foot. By the time Vinatieri's game-winning kick sailed through the uprights, time had expired, and the 14-point underdog Patriots had slain the NFL's version of Goliath for their first Super Bowl title. "A lot of bookies are mad at us right now, but we don't give a damn. We're the champs," said Ty Law.

When Vinatieri's kick split the uprights, long snapper Lonnie Paxton sprinted to the end zone, fell on his back and started to make imaginary snow angels—a reenactment of his celebration from the snowy overtime win against the Raiders in the AFC divisional round.

Kurt Warner finished the game with 28 completions in 44 pass attempts for 365 yards, one touchdown, and two costly interceptions. His 365 passing yards were the second best in Super Bowl history behind his own record of 414 yards set in Super Bowl XXXIV against the Tennessee Titans. Marshall Faulk gained 129 total yards, including 76 rushing yards on 17 carries. The Rams actually might have outplayed the Patriots, but not at crunch time, when it mattered most. The Rams outgained the Patriots 427 to 267.

They also ran 15 more plays than the Pats and held a 7-minute advantage in time of possession (33:30 to 26:30). "We shocked the world," said safety Lawyer Milloy. "This was a total team effort. We don't have any standout defensive players. On both sides of the ball, there's always somebody else coming through. It's so sweet."

The final few minutes of this game made it one of the most memorable Super Bowl matchups in history. The New England Patriots' upset over the St. Louis Rams in Super Bowl XXXVI was the first of three Super Bowl wins for Brady and Belichick during a four-year stretch. If coach Belichick opted for the safe route near the end of regulation, Brady's legend may not have been born on this night. To be sure, this game announced Tom Brady as a future icon. The Patriots' on-field celebration was a raucous love-fest, and deservedly so. But the Fox network postgame interviews took on a more somber tone. In the wake of the September 11 terrorist attacks of the past autumn, owner Robert Kraft's "We are all Patriots" message was one for the ages.

The nine-year-old Carolina Panthers franchise was a surprise guest on Super Sunday. Two years earlier, the Panthers won their first game of the regular season under coach George Seifert, previously a winner of two Super Bowls as coach of the San Francisco 49ers. But the Panthers then lost fifteen straight games to finish a league worst 1–15, in 2001. Seifert got fired; his coaching replacement, John Fox, led the team to a 7–9 finish, in 2002. The following season the Panthers were greatly improved and posted an 11–5 regular season record. Leading the charge was Jake Delhomme, a former quarterback in the NFL Europe league. His all-out, all-or-nothing playing style was equally effective as it was frustrating. During the 2003 season, the Panthers made a magical Cinderella run to the Super Bowl, where they faced the established Patriots, at 14–2 and seeking their second Super Bowl title in three years.

Super Bowl XXXVIII was a crazy game. The game was played exactly one year to the day after the Space Shuttle's *Columbia* disaster. Popular singer Josh Groban performed "You Raise Me Up" to commemorate the anniversary. A somber atmosphere quieted the 71,525 fans at Houston's Reliant Stadium. Once the game started, neither team provided much reason for excitement. The game had a schizophrenic scoring pattern. Both offensive units were held scoreless for 26 minutes 55 seconds, a Super Bowl record for scoring futility from the start of a game. At this point, the Patriots had outgained the Panthers 125 yards to -7 and Delhomme, playing very much like an NFL Europe quarterback, threw incompletions on eight of his first nine pass attempts. Three minutes before halftime, his Super Bowl stat line reads: 1 completed pass for 1 yard. So how did the teams then combine to score 24 points in the last three minutes of the second quarter? Who knows? It's crazy. Crazier yet, the third quarter was scoreless again. Crazier still, they scored five touchdowns in the fourth quarter.

The fast-and-furious action started about one minute into the fourth quarter, when both teams traded touchdowns, giving the Patriots the lead, 21–16. The Panthers had the ball but found themselves in trouble, backed up on their own 15-yard line; it was third down and long. Going for broke, quarterback Jake Delhommme made an unbelievable connection with his wide receiver, Muhsin Muhammad, the two hooking-up for an 85-yard touchdown pass—the longest play from scrimmage in Super Bowl history! In a flash, Carolina now had the lead for the first time, 22–21, after a failed two-point conversion. New England countered on its

David Givens (87) stretches for the goal line during fourth-quarter action in Super Bowl XXXVIII. (AP Photo/Michael Conroy)

next drive with bold strokes. With less than three minutes remaining, the Patriots faced a crucial third down and goal situation. New England's starting linebacker, Mike Vrabel, sprinted onto the field to join New England's offensive huddle, presumably as blocking reinforcement. He was already a defensive star of the night, having sacked Delhomme twice, once forcing a fumble. Nobody should have imagined Vrabel being an offensive star of the game, too. When the ball was snapped, Vrabel did a great acting job pretending to block for a running play. It was an Oscar-worthy performance, fooling the Panthers. He squeezed past two Carolina linemen, took one step into the end zone, turned his head at precisely the same moment Brady's touch pass arrived, and cradled the football like a loving parent holding an infant. Touchdown Patriots! New England was back in front, 27–22.

Early in Brady's career, Belichick occasionally used Vrabel on offense as an eligible receiver in goal line situations. Vrabel spent eight seasons with New England and scored 10 receiving touchdowns, but none bigger than this one. He was the first defensive player to score a Super Bowl touchdown on offense since William "Refrigerator" Perry rushed for a score for the Chicago Bears in Super Bowl XX, *against* the Patriots, in 1986. Vrabel's versatility and toughness made him popular among teammates. The Pats celebrated by mobbing him on the sidelines, slapping his helmeted head and padded shoulders. The party was still hopping when running back Kevin Faulk took a direct snap and ran into the end zone for a two-point conversion—the only points he would tally all season. That made the score 29–22 New England, with less than three minutes left in the game.

Delhomme needed to match Brady score for score. It took just seven plays. The Panthers capped an 80-yard drive with a 12-yard touchdown pass to receiver Ricky Proehl. Delhomme completed five of six passes for 73 yards during the drive. John Kasay's extra point tied the game, 29–29, with one minute and eight seconds to play. Proehl came oh, so close, to being a Super Bowl legend. Proehl scored the touchdown for St. Louis that tied Super Bowl XXXVI at 17–17 with ninety seconds to play. Now he scored another touchdown to tie a Super Bowl with sixty-eight seconds left. It's uncanny what Proehl achieved in Super Bowl games on two different occasions, playing for two different teams, with eerily similar results. In the final ninety seconds of two Super Bowls, with his team trailing by a touchdown, Proehl caught a touchdown pass to tie the score. But neither score ended up forcing the first overtime period in Super Bowl history. Super Bowl gods are fickle.

Meanwhile, Tom Brady and Jake Delhomme staged a classic fourth quarter Super Bowl duel. The final 15 minutes of the game were a pigskin version of "anything-you-can-do-I-can-do-better." Every time Brady led his team to a score, Delhomme had an answer. Thirty-seven of the game's 61 points were scored in a manic, back-and-forth, fourth quarter. The teams combined for 868 total yards, the second most in a Super Bowl, with both quarterbacks throwing for at least 300 yards. Such a spectacular feat of quarterbacking hadn't occurred on Super Sunday since Joe Montana and Dan Marino met twenty years earlier in Super Bowl XIX. Delhomme's performance was stirring, because he was an underdog, and maybe, just maybe, he was going to achieve this wild dream of winning a Super Bowl. He sure gave fans a lot to cheer about. He completed 9 of 14 passes for 211 yards and two touchdowns during the dramatic fourth quarter alone.

With the game score knotted, Tom Brady and the Patriots received the ensuing kickoff. They had one minute to maneuver into field goal range. For a quarterback of Tom Brady's caliber, that amount of time can feel to opposing defenses like an eternity. Carolina's best hope was to stop New England on downs and force an overtime period. On the ensuing kickoff, Kasay mistakenly and inexplicably booted the ball out of bounds—a penalty. By rule, the ball was placed on New England's 40-yard line, where the Patriots began a final drive with excellent field position. Brady and the Patriots hoped to take advantage of the short field. Three passes for 20 yards moved the first down chains. After two plays went bust, Brady faced a critical third down situation at the Carolina 40-yard line. The Patriots needed three yards for a first down. More important, Brady needed to advance the football another 10 yards at least to get in range for a chance at a game-winning field goal. Brady's pass to Deion Branch picked up 17 big yards. Branch was the top receiver of the game with 10 receptions for 143 yards and a touchdown.

With seven seconds left on the clock, New England's kicking unit hurried onto the field. On the next play, the contest was finally decided for good. Patriots' kicker Adam Vinatieri booted a 41-yard field goal with four seconds left. New England won, 32–29. Vinatieri had now kicked game-winning field goals in the final seconds of *two* Super Bowls. The Patriots were champions for the second time in three years. Tom Brady was named Super Bowl MVP for a second time. He completed 32 of 48 passes for 354 yards and three touchdowns. Not to be outdone, Delhomme completed 16 of 33 passes for 323 passing yards and three touchdowns. Never had two quarterbacks with such dissimilar styles posted such identical statistics. *Sports Illustrated*, which once hailed the

Baltimore Colts' 1958 NFL title game sudden-death victory the *Best Football Game Ever Played*, labeled this the *Greatest Super Bowl of All Time*. Nobody doubted it. The NFL's future as a business looked bright. The Patriots were a slick product easily marketed, and a darn good football team. The Patriots were on the come, the teams were back to playing exciting Super Bowls again, and even the losers were loveable again. Delhomme's Super Bowl showing was by far the greatest performance by an unknown quarterback in a losing effort. He lingered on the field long after the final whistle. "I think it's difficult to ever truly get over losing a Super Bowl," he said. "You understand how hard it is to get there and how hard they are to win. The way we lost, on a field goal, that's even worse. Yet at the same time, we made it to one, and so many people don't."

An exciting game was largely overshadowed by its halftime show. The musical performance by Justin Timberlake and Janet Jackson ended in "The Wardrobe Malfunction," exposing for about half a second Ms. Jackson's naked right breast, ornamented by a star-shaped nipple shield, to 144 million viewers watching on live television. This led to an investigation by the Federal Communications Commission, an immediate review by the House of Representatives on the responsibility of television networks, and a national debate on broadcast decency. Now, networks airing live programming do so with a longer delay. More than one Super Bowl partygoer was heard to shout Jack Buck's famous call when Kirk Gibson homered for the Dodgers to win game one of the 1989 World Series: *I can't believe what I just saw!* A positive development from Nipplegate: a software programmer frustrated by not being able to watch repeated showings of the "nip slip" created what eventually will be YouTube.

A PANTHEON OF HEROES

Bill Belichick

Four rings in six Super Bowls coaching the New England Patriots

THE HOODED GENIUS

Prior to Super Bowl XXXVI, the NFL had given the New England Patriots the choice to introduce either the offense or the defense during pregame festivities. But their coach, Bill Belichick, chose neither option. He had a better idea. He wanted the Patriots to be introduced together, all at once. The NFL initially rejected the request. Belichick stood firm and, in the spirit of team unity, appealed the decision. The NFL finally relented and honored the request. The full team introduction demonstrated solidarity, and in the wake of the September 11 attacks, also struck a chord with the American public watching from home. "When we did that," linebacker Tedy Bruschi recalled, "I could feel the shock in the stadium." Setting precedent, the Super Bowl combatants are now always introduced as a team.

Belichick's career coaching record in fifteen seasons with New England now stands at an eye-popping 175

(AP Photo/David J. Phillip)

wins against just 65 losses, a .729 winning percentage, through the 2014 season. And with his four Super Bowl titles as a head coach (and two more as an assistant with the New York Giants under Bill Parcells), Belichick has clearly earned his place in the pantheon of great modern coaches. No coach has taken a team to the Super Bowl more times than Belichick, whose Patriots have played in six Super Bowls, winning four. And Belichick is threatening to chalk up number five at the end of this season.

The Patriots have never been more popular than they were in 2001. But winning changes everything. Has any hugely successful coach ever been tied to cheating or bending the rules or skirting them as much as Belichick? First there was the Tuck Rule game in 2002, then Spygate in 2007, and Deflategate in 2015. For all his success, the coach in the hooded sweatshirt is nefarious in the eyes of many football fans throughout the nation. Outside of its own New England fan base, the Patriots wear the black hats, and Belichick is seen as a figure willing to bend or break any rule to win. To zealous, die-hard Patriots fans, the criticism is mere squawking from a bunch of sore losers who are upset that Belichick's unorthodox tactics have outfoxed their team yet again.

For the first forty-one years of the team's existence, the Patriots were an NFL laughingstock. It was a franchise defined by bumbling play, lousy coaching, and poor stadium conditions. Somehow, the team managed to play in three championship games—one AFL title game and two Super Bowls—in those forty-one seasons. New England lost all three by a combined score of 132–41. Along the way, with the additions of coach Bill Belichick and quarterback Tom Brady, New England has established itself as the premier franchise in the NFL. The team's first game after their Super Bowl victory was played in brand new, privately funded Gillette Stadium. A second championship banner was hung in that stadium the following year. Players have been known to take pay cuts to perform there. The ownership under Robert Kraft is considered the best in football, perhaps the best in sports. And the New England franchise wasn't done yet.

Patriots' Ring of Honor

In all, 22 players won three Super Bowl rings in four years during the Patriots run. They are: Tom Brady (quarterback); Kevin Faulk, Patrick Pass (running back); Troy Brown, David Patten (wide receiver); Joe Andruzzi, Matt Light, Stephen Neal (offensive line); Tedy Bruschi, Ted Johnson, Willie McGinest, Roman Phifer, Mike Vrabel (linebacker); Richard Seymour (defensive line); Ty Law (defensive back); Tom Ashworth, Matt Chatham, Je'Rod Cherry, Larry Izzo, Lonie Paxton, Adam Vinatieri (special teams). Offensive lineman Adrian Klemm earned three rings but never made an appearance in a postseason game.

Following the 2004 regular season, the Patriots defeated the Philadelphia Eagles, 24–21, in Super Bowl XXXIX. Once again, a Vinatieri field goal in the fourth quarter was the difference maker. The numbers say he is the best clutch kicker in Super Bowl history. Vinatieri won three Super Bowls during the decade for New England by kicking the deciding field goal in all three, twice with time expiring. He has attempted more field goals (10), made more field goals (7), made more extra points (13) and scored more points (34) than any other kicker in Super Bowl history. He owns four rings in all, having won another Super Bowl with the Indianapolis Colts. Once again, linebacker Mike Vrabel contributed on offense and defense. In the first quarter, he recorded a sack of Philadelphia quarterback Donovan McNabb. The Patriots' opening drive of the second half ended with Tom Brady's 2-yard touchdown pass to Vrabel, who had lined up as a tight end, to tie the game. Incredibly, Vrabel is one of 21 players with two touchdown receptions in a Super Bowl career—and the only defensive player on the list!

The Patriots organization is solidifying its status as a dynasty even in a modern era with a salary cap and free agency. With the victory, New England became the first team since the Denver Broncos in 1997 and 1998 to win consecutive Super Bowls. The Patriots also became the second team after the Dallas Cowboys to win three Super Bowls in a four-year window. Brady completed 23 out of 33 passes for 236 yards and two touchdowns. Wide receiver Deion Branch was named Super Bowl MVP based on his performance of 11 receptions totaling 133 receiving yards. Each member of the Patriots received a payment of $68,000 as the winners' share. The Eagles each received $36,500. Adjusted for inflation, the winners' share was actually less than the $15,000 paid to each member of the Green Bay Packers for winning Super Bowl I, in 1967.

The Wardrobe Malfunction prompted a string of half-time shows featuring classic rock acts such as Paul McCartney, Prince, Tom Petty and the Heartbreakers, and The Black Eyed Peas, aiming to prevent a repeat of the incident. These veteran rockers, with hundreds of stadium shows to their credit, acquitted themselves nicely. At halftime in 2009, Bruce Springsteen looked into the camera and shouted, "I want you to step back from the guacamole dip. I want you to put the chicken fingers down and turn your television all the way up." The rock star from New Jersey went on to cheer for the hometown team, the New York Giants, and their aw-shucks young quarterback, Eli Manning.

New York Giants, Super Bowls XLII and XLVI

When the New England Patriots arrived at Super Bowl XLII, they were already billed as the greatest team in NFL history. The Patriots did the improbable by going unbeaten through the 2007 regular season. It marked the first time since the NFL expanded the season to sixteen games that a team went undefeated. The 2007 Patriots left a memorable and historic imprint on the game. The team's leader, quarterback Tom Brady, won his first NFL most valuable player award, throwing for a career-best 4,806 passing yards and an NFL record 50 touchdowns, against just eight interceptions. His passer rating of 117.2 is the second-highest season rating in NFL history. His favorite target, receiver Randy Moss, caught 98 passes for 1,493 receiving yards and an NFL record 23 touchdown catches. As a team, New England scored 589 points—an average of 36.8 point per game—and scored 75 total touchdowns. The Patriots added postseason victories over the Jacksonville Jaguars in the divisional playoff round and over the San Diego Chargers in the AFC Championship Game to run the streak to an amazing 18–0.

Unlike the Patriots, the Giants arrived at the Super Bowl with a just-happy-to-be-here attitude. New York's punter Jeff Feagles would be playing in his first Super Bowl after twenty years in the NFL. After beginning the season with two bad losses, the team recovered to win six straight games, only to split the final eight games and finish the regular season with a 10–6 record. The Giants qualified for the postseason only as a wildcard team. The Giants had lost in the NFC wildcard round the past two years, and the franchise had not won a playoff game in seven seasons. The Giants were looking for their first Super Bowl victory in seventeen years, since beating the Buffalo Bills in Super Bowl XXV.

The Patriots were back in the Super Bowl for the fourth time in seven years. Because the Patriots were undefeated, in pursuit of the mythic 19–0 season, and owners of the most prolific aerial circus in NFL history, while the Giants barely earned a playoff spot and squeaked through the NFC title game (largely because of a Brett Favre interception), the Giants seemed to be just another minor hurdle for New England. Leading up to Super Sunday, almost every midweek story had an angle about how the incumbent Patriots had become a football powerhouse, the NFL's Goliath, and the Giants took their place at the kids' table as the puny, irrelevant David.

Forgotten in all the hype and hoopla is the fact that this Super Bowl was also a rematch of the final game of the regular season, won by New England, 38–35. At the time, the Patriots were 15–0 and on a mission to complete the perfect season. A loss for the Giants meant nothing in terms of the playoff seeding, so the debate raged as to whether coach Tom Coughlin should play his starters or rest them for their first-round encounter with the Tampa Bay Buccaneers. Coughlin told his team to play to win. "There is nothing but positives," he said. "I told the players in playing this game everything would be positives, there would be no negatives and that is how I feel. I don't know any better way to be prepared for the playoffs than to go against a team that was 15–0." Despite the tough loss, the Giants arrived at the Super Bowl, played at University of Phoenix Stadium, in Glendale, Arizona, believing they could beat the Pats. (The satirical newspaper *The Onion* offered a different view, running this headline ahead of the Super Bowl: "Giants: We Almost Beat the Patriots Once, We Can Almost Beat Them Again!")

The Fox network featured an eye-glazing nine hours of pregame coverage prior to kickoff. The official game coverage began at 6:00 p.m. Eastern time, with kickoff at 6:32 p.m.; Fox was on the air at 9:00 a.m., filling airtime with Ryan Seacrest interviewing celebrities arriving for the game and with comedy sketches featuring Frank Caliendo impersonating the former Raiders' coach John Madden. When the game finally began, the Giants showed they too knew how to milk a clock. After calling tails to win the coin toss, the Giants started the game with the longest drive in Super Bowl history, a sixteen-play, 77-yard march that consumed 10 minutes (the Giants also have the second-longest Super Bowl drive: 9:29 against the Buffalo Bills in Super Bowl XXV). But New England stopped the drive on the 14-yard line, forcing the Giants to settle for a Lawrence Tynes 32-yard field goal for a 3–0 lead.

The defenses reigned supreme for 45 minutes; the score was a meager 7–3 in favor of the Patriots entering the fourth quarter. In the final period, Eli Manning stepped into the spotlight. He targeted rookie tight end Kevin Boss on a 45-yard strike on the Giants' first drive of the fourth quarter. The drive extended into a seven-play, 80-yard touchdown march, capped by Manning's scoring pass to little-used receiver David Tyree, putting the Giants ahead, 10–7, four minutes into the fourth quarter. The teams traded possessions over the next eight and a half minutes. The Giants' defensive line, led by Michael Strahan and Osi Umenyiora, harassed Brady all night. They sacked him five times for losses totaling negative 37 yards. However, as advertised, Brady finally did respond with a touchdown march of his own, putting the Pats ahead with a scoring strike to Randy Moss. Manning and the Giants got the ball back at their own 17-yard line with 2 minutes 42 seconds left.

Manning completed two passes to Amani Toomer for 20 yards, and then the Giants' offense stalled out. On fourth down from the 37-yard line, needing less than one yard, Tom Coughlin decided to go for it. Manning handed the ball to the 6'4" 264-pound running back, Brandon Jacobs, who lowered his head and bulled ahead for the necessary first-down yardage. Three plays later, *it* happened. *The play.* On third-and-five from the New York 44-yard line, Manning found himself in trouble. He broke free as the pocket collapsed around him and fired the ball 32 yards downfield to David Tyree, who was surrounded by New England defenders. Tyree out-jumped the coverage and held on for a miracle catch, pinning the ball against his helmet as he fell to the ground. When you consider what was at stake at the time, the Eli Manning to David Tyree

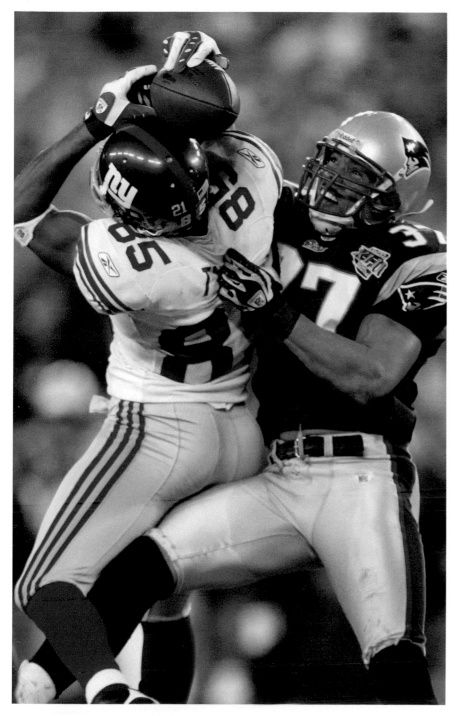

David Tyree makes an amazing catch to keep the Giants' game-winning drive alive in Super Bowl XLII. (AP Photo/Gene Puskar)

third–and–5 is probably the single-greatest play in Super Bowl history.

The New York Giants running back Reuben Droughns could not believe Tyree made the catch. "No, I cannot. It was just an amazing effort by him. Going through practice all week, he was dropping balls, dropping passes in the end zone, and then just all of a sudden, here he is making an amazing catch." Said Tyree: "When I look at it, I don't think that's really something that's humanly possible. I couldn't work hard to do that. I couldn't train. It was like I was kind of the co-star and God was the star in that event." Manning was his usual down-to-earth self. "It was just a great catch by David Tyree. I found a way to get loose, and just really threw it up. He made an unbelievable catch and saved the game."

Tyree's circus catch kept the Giants alive, but they still needed a touchdown. On another key third down snap, needing 11 yards to convert a first down, Manning scrambled free again, and this time zipped a 12-yard pass to Steve Smith, who stepped out of bounds to stop the clock. On the next play, Manning lofted a pass to the left corner of the end zone. After shaking free from his man, wide receiver Plaxico Burress cradled the ball for the winning score. Giants' fans across the nation leaped in celebration. Big Blue had just won its third Super Bowl title. The Patriots had one more possession, but Manning had left them only 35 seconds. Brady could do nothing, and New York won 17–14. When it comes down to it, this game is the greatest Super Bowl of all-time. It's probably the biggest upset, too. It was a seesaw battle. For sheer quality and excitement, the game was outstanding; it had Tyree's catch as a memorable moment for the ages, and the historical significance of spoiling the Patriots' undefeated season can't be topped. And after the game, *The*

Onion's tone had changed, as evidenced by the headline "Eli Manning Wins Biggest Game of Tom Brady's Life."

Four years later, the Giants and Patriots met again in a Super Bowl rematch. Long before the Giants reached Super Bowl XLVI, New York's season got off to an uninspired start. The Giants won six of the first eight games of the 2011 season, but then fell into a funk, losing four straight games to fall to 6–6. After winning two of three, the Giants faced the Dallas Cowboys in the season finale with both teams tied for the division lead with 8–7 records. The Giants won convincingly, 31–14, to clinch the division title and a postseason berth. In the playoffs, the Giants defeated the Atlanta Falcons, Green Bay Packers, and the San Francisco 49ers to win the NFC championship.

The Giants were the first team in NFL history to reach the Super Bowl despite scoring fewer points than their opponents. With a 9–7 record, they were the third team to win fewer than 10 games in a 16-game season and reach the big game. (The previous teams to go 9–7 and reach the Super Bowl were the 1979 Rams and the 2008 Cardinals.) In this Super Bowl rematch, just three Patriots players who appeared in Super Bowl XLII remained—quarterback Tom Brady, defensive tackle Vince Wilfork and place-kicker Stephen Gostkowski—and they had plenty of time to recover from that stinging defeat. "That was a long, long time ago," Gostkowski said. "Obviously, losing in the Super Bowl hurts. But as players, you've got to learn to move on from wins and losses."

The game began on a strange note for the Patriots. After a Giants punt by Steve Weatherford pinned the Pats back near their goal line, Brady took his first snap of the game. Facing a heavy rush from Giants defensive lineman Justin Tuck as he dropped back, Brady threw the ball away with no New England receiver in the area. The referee flagged him for intentional grounding and the Giants were awarded a safety and a 2–0 lead. The Giants then took the free kick and drove 78 yards in nine plays, keyed by Ahmad Bradshaw's 24-yard run, and extended their lead to 9–0 on Manning's two-yard touchdown pass to Victor Cruz. New England added a field goal and then set off on a Super Bowl record-tying 96-yard drive, ending with a Brady to Danny Woodhead score, making it 10–9 New England at the half. Said Giants coach Tom Coughlin: "We had a couple penalties that I thought took points off the board. We got into halftime and I said, 'We can play better than this.' They agreed."

Madonna's performance at halftime was seen by 114 million viewers throughout the world, more than even Michael Jackson's appearance in 1993. The set included an appearance by pop-rap sensation Nicki Minaj and the British hip-hop artist known as M.I.A., who came under controversy for flashing the middle finger during the performance of Madonna's new single "Give Me All Your Luvin'."

When the game resumed, New England carried its momentum into the third quarter. They received the ball to open the second half, and Brady promptly completed a 21-yard pass to Chad Johnson, a.k.a. Chad Ochocinco (to match his jersey No. 85; it was his only catch of the postseason). New England completed its 79-yard drive on the eighth play, a 12-yard touchdown pass to tight end Aaron Hernandez, and there seemed to be no stopping Brady's Patriots. New England had scored 17 unanswered points. It was now 17–9, and the way the Pats were playing it was hard to imagine those would be their last points.

That's when Eli Manning went to work. With the Patriots' secondary dropping back in coverage to prevent the big play, Manning took what the defense gave him. On consecutive

The Giants kept the pressure on Tom Brady during Super Bowl XLVI. (Wikimedia Commons/saboteur)

drives, he marched the Giants downfield. But New England stiffened twice in the red zone, and New York had to settle for field goals. Those kicks would cut the Giants deficit to 17–15 with 35 seconds left in the third quarter. The score remained 17–15, when the Giants got the ball back on their 12-yard line with less than four minutes remaining and one timeout. As Manning said later, there was no rah-rah speech in the huddle. He had succeeded in similar situations, and teammates took their cue from his quiet confidence. As if on cue, Manning quickly made a big play, lofting a perfect strike to receiver Mario Manningham, who made a wondrous tightrope catch for a 38-yard gain at midfield. Thoughts immediately went to the miracle pass to David Tyree four years earlier. Patriots coach Bill Belichick challenged Manningham's catch; replays ruled it was good, and Belichick had to know he was about to witness another Eli Manning drive in the Super Bowl to give him nightmares.

Manning continued to march his team down the field, chewing up the clock and maneuvering the offense back into the red zone. With the Giants facing a 2nd-down-and-goal from the 6-yard line with just over a minute remaining in the game and only needing a field goal to win, Belichick made the decision to just play dead and let them score. Ahmad Bradshaw took the handoff and saw nothing but daylight to the end zone. He realized what New England was trying to do and he tried to stop at the 1-yard line, so as to not give the Patriots any time to mount a comeback, but his momentum carried him forward and he tumbled into the end zone for the score. Even with a failed 2-point conversion, the Giants led 21–17.

New England got the ball back with 57 seconds left, needing a touchdown to win. New England's last-gasp drive didn't get far. Brady got the ball to midfield, and then heaved a long Hail Mary on the game's final play. The pass fell to the turf, and the Giants were again Super Bowl champions, and again had done it versus Brady and the Patriots in stunning fashion with a last-minute touchdown drive. "We've had a bunch of them this year. We've had some fourth-quarter comebacks," said Manning. "We'd been in those situations, and we knew that we had no more time left. We had to go down and score, and guys stepped up and made great plays."

Led, as usual, by Manning himself, coolly and calmly. He opened the game by becoming the first quarterback to complete his first ten attempts in a Super Bowl. And he finished the job by directing the nine-play, 88-yard touchdown drive that put New York ahead with under one minute left. "That was quite a drive that he was able to put together," Giants coach Tom Coughlin said. "He deserves all the credit in the world, because he really has put his team on his shoulders all year." Manning was named Super Bowl MVP for the second time. He completed 30 of 40 passes for 296 yards, one touchdown, and no interceptions. While his numbers weren't spectacular, his play was steady and his leadership solid. Manning rallied the Giants to 12 unanswered points late in the second half. There is no denying that Eli Manning belongs among the league's elite quarterbacks. "Certainly, Eli has had a very good season," acknowledged Tom Brady, who completed 27 of 41 passes for 276 yards, with two touchdowns and one interception. He completed 16 consecutive passes in one stretch, breaking Joe Montana's Super Bowl record of 13. "He made some great throws there in the fourth quarter. We fought to the end, I'm very proud of that. We just came up a little short."

The most significant development of the second half was the way the Giants pressured Tom Brady. The defense, lead by a line of Michael Strahan, Usi Umenyiora, Justin Tuck, and Jason Pierre-Paul, made life miserable for the Pats' quarterback. New York battered Brady, never allowing him to feel at ease in the pocket. The constant harassment took its toll. No player created more trouble than Tuck, whose two second-half sacks set the tone for Big Blue. One of the unsung stars of this game was Giants punter Steve Weatherford. Eli Manning won the Super Bowl MVP award, and rightfully so, but Weatherford was one of the hidden heroes, with three kicks downed inside the 20 and zero returned. We also can't forget about Chase Blackburn, who left a job as a teacher in Ohio to join the Giants in late November—and made a key interception in the fourth quarter

The victory was the Giants' fourth overall championship. The lasting memory of this game was Manning's picture-perfect throw, dropped perfectly over Manningham's shoulder nearly 40 yards downfield. It was a gutsy call on first down, and is the play that history will remember for having won a second ring in four years for Tom Coughlin's Giants.

THE BEST WHO NEVER LOST

Eli Manning

Two rings in two Super Bowls with the New York Giants; MVP of Super Bowls XLII and XLVI

(AP Photo/David J. Phillip)

BIG GAME PLAYER

For most any kid, following in the footsteps of a famous father is overwhelming. Imagine the challenge of also being in the shadow of an older sibling who can do no wrong. Welcome to Eli Manning's world. His father, Archie, is a former New Orleans Saints quarterback. His brother, Peyton, is one of the greatest quarterbacks in NFL history. The Manning brothers are the first brothers to play in Super Bowls as quarterbacks. In the world of pro football, the Manning brothers rule. Both players were first-round NFL draft picks, Super Bowl MVPs, and Super Bowl champs. Peyton led the Indianapolis Colts to a Super Bowl in 2007 and watched his little brother, Eli, lead the New York Giants to a Super Bowl victory in 2008. Eli never dreamed he and his brother would win Super Bowls in back-to-back years. "It's been a fun year, I would say. Watching Peyton win last year and then the Giants winning this year, it's just unbelievable. I'm so proud of the guys on this team. We never had doubt. We had total faith in ourselves and we believed we could win and we earned it."

Eli did a lot of growing up during the second Super Bowl season, in 2011. In the regular season, he threw an NFL-record 15 touchdown passes in the final period. He also led six game-winning drives to bring New York back from fourth-quarter deficits. "He's become confident over time; kind of grew into it," Manning's father, Archie, said. "I always felt like you have to experience those situations before you become confident. He's certainly had his share." That's true. Eli's even done it before in the Super Bowl. In 2008, he took home his first Super Bowl MVP award after a scoring pass to Plaxico Burress with 35 seconds left allowed New York to upset Brady and New England, ruining the Patriots' bid for a perfect season. It was the kind of situation he had dreamed about as kid. Leading his team on a remarkable final drive to win a championship. And he did it again four years later.

The Giants met the Patriots in a Super Bowl rematch in Super Bowl XLVI. The game was being played at Lucas Oil Stadium, in Indianapolis, Indiana. Super Bowl XLVI was inevitably billed as a showdown between Tom Brady and Eli Manning, in the stadium Eli's brother built. The pressure was clearly on, but Eli didn't show a hint of nerves. He controlled the ball masterfully in the first half, as if he was playing a game of two-hand touch with his brothers in the backyard back home in New Orleans. The Giants won, 21–17. Eli Manning, who completed 30 of 40 passes for 296 yards, one touchdown, and no interceptions, was named Super Bowl MVP for the second time in his career. And Manning did it in the House that Peyton Built, the stadium where his Big Bro—a four-time regular-season MVP but owner of only one Super Bowl title—played for the Indianapolis Colts. "It just feels good to win a Super Bowl; doesn't matter where you are," said Eli. Once again, he was at his best in the fourth quarter, completing 10 of 14 passes for 118 yards, when it counted the most.

Eli may be far from a perfect quarterback, but he gives his team a chance to win regardless of the opponent or circumstances. Playing in the pressure cooker of New York, he has handled everything thrown at him by fans and the media and guided his team to a pair of conference championship games and two unforgettable Super Bowl victories. Even though he isn't always pretty, Manning gets the job done. And when it comes to Super Bowl rings, little brother Eli has done big brother Peyton one better. But Eli won't bite on the sibling rivalry angle. "This isn't about bragging rights. This is a lot bigger," Eli said. "This is about a team, an organization being named world champions, and that was the ultimate goal. That's the only thing that's important, is the team finding a way to get a victory. That's the only thing I care about and Peyton and I both know that's what the goal is every year. It's not about anything else."

SECOND QUARTER

AGONY OF DEFEAT

THE BEST WHO NEVER WON

Regular season success is what qualifies teams for the Super Bowl. But is just getting there enough? The greats and near-greats who never earned a ring.

Minnesota Vikings, Super Bowls IV, VIII, IX, and XI

The Minnesota Vikings have a long and storied history, despite having never won a championship. The franchise's most prominent period of success dates from the hiring of coach Bud Grant, in 1967. Grant's hiring was a curious but inspired choice. He played in both the NFL and the NBA. He's the only man to ever do that. He was a first-round draft choice of the Philadelphia Eagles in 1950. But instead Grant chose to focus on basketball, and postpone his NFL debut. He played two seasons with the NBA's Minneapolis Lakers, winning the NBA title in 1950. He then switched to professional football, and joined the Philadelphia Eagles in 1951. He played on defense as a rookie and then on offense, becoming the second-best receiver in the NFL with 56 catches in 1952.

In 1967, Bud Grant replaced Norm Van Brocklin as coach of the Vikings. In addition to having had ten years' experience as a Canadian Football League coach, Grant had played offensive and defensive end, defensive halfback, linebacker, and running back—more positions than most coaches ever play. Gaining a unique perspective of the game from several different positions is what may have led to Grant's unconventional coaching style. For instance, he didn't start training camp until the week before the first preseason game. During the cold Minnesota winters he never allowed the players to have a heater on the sidelines. He never arrived at a game any earlier than one hour before kickoff. He rarely called a full staff meeting of his assistant coaches. He went over game films only a couple of times. He had only a two-hour practice session on a Saturday before a Sunday game.

With the Vikings, Grant built an "all-weather team" that could adapt to various field conditions without domes and sideline heaters. He avoided smaller, faster players, who he felt would be useless on a muddy or icy field. Grant brought the Vikings to the dressing room only one hour before a game in an effort to reduce the players' pregame jitters. He selected his assistant coaches carefully, then let them do the weekly planning and teaching. He felt that six weeks of training camp was an awful way to live, so he cut it to nine days and expected the players to come to camp in shape.

Grant's style worked—up to a point. During his eighteen seasons with the Vikings, he won 158 regular-season games and 10 playoff games, for a career winning percentage of .620. His Vikings won the NFL championship in 1969 and NFC titles in 1973, 1974, and 1976, as well as eleven Central division titles. During the era of 14-game seasons, Minnesota won ten or more regular-season games seven times. The only

Fran Tarkenton faces the formidable Steelers defense during Super Bowl IX. (AP Photo/Phil Sandlin)

game they didn't win was the Super Bowl. But they made it to the big game four times. "Well, it probably bothers other people more than it bothers me," said Grant. "To survive in this business, you can't have a backwards look. You lose a game and then you have to move to the next one. You can't look back and say we could have, would have, should have. When it's over, it's over."

The Minnesota Vikings defense that played in Super Bowl IV was called the "Purple People Eaters," because they wore purple uniforms. The tenacious defense featured a front line that produced two Hall of Famers, Alan Page and Carl Eller. On offense, quarterback Joe Kapp was voted by his teammates as the Vikings MVP for the way he inspired a team-oriented concept throughout the year. In a memorable gesture, Kapp turned down the award and reiterated the team's battle cry that season: "40 for 60"—forty players committed for sixty minutes of football. Players were so confident in the sum total of their talent that they often laughed at opponents when they celebrated touchdowns. Defensive end Jim Marshall said opponents would ask why they were laughing when they had just given up a touchdown. "Yeah," Marshall said, "but you're not going to win the game. We are."

In 1969, the Vikings had an NFL best 12–2 regular-season record. They lost by one point to the New York Giants in the season opener and by a touchdown in the season finale at Atlanta. Both defeats came with starting quarterback Joe Kapp sidelined and backup Gary Cuozzo taking most of the snaps. But in between the Vikes posted 12 straight victories, the longest single-season NFL winning streak in thirty-five years. Leading up to the big game there was a sense of destiny for this Vikings team. Minnesota's

offense led the league in total points scored (379), while Minnesota's defense led the league in fewest points allowed (133). The Vikings had the best record in the league and outscored their opponents by 246 points; the Chiefs hadn't even won their own division.

Super Bowl IV was the fourth and final AFL-NFL World Championship Game before the two leagues merged into one after the season. A lot of folks said the New York Jets' victory in Super Bowl III the previous year was a fluke victory for the AFL. They thought normalcy would be restored when the Vikings won Super Bowl IV at Tulane Stadium, in New Orleans. The Vikings, Joe Kapp, and the Purple People Eaters, were 13-point favorites over Kansas City. In the week leading up to the game, New Orleans had record cold temperatures. The fountain in front of the Chiefs' hotel was frozen solid. The unusual weather persisted. It rained the morning of the game. Scalpers trying to unload tickets for below cost lined the road leading to Tulane Stadium. Pat O'Brien, the film actor best remembered for playing the starring role of the legendary Notre Dame coach in *Knute Rockne: All American*, recited the national anthem. *The Tonight Show* bandleader Doc Severinsen's trumpet drowned him out.

The pre-game show for Super Bowl IV featured two hot-air balloons. One was marked AFL and carried a man dressed as a Kansas City Chief. The other was marked NFL and held a man dressed as a Minnesota Viking. The Vikings balloon failed to gain altitude and was blown into the grandstands. It was a bad sign for the Vikings. When the whistle blew, Minnesota's offense was static and stagnant. The Vikings rushed for only 24 yards in the first half, and failed to convert any third down plays. Kansas City's placekicker Jan Stenerud

The mascots face off before Super Bowl IV. (AP Photo/JS)

of Norway kicked three successful field goals to account for the game's first nine points. When Stenerud was inducted into the Pro Football Hall of Fame in 1991, he became the first player enshrined whose only job was placekicking. The soccer-style kicker booted a then-record long 48-yard field goal, followed by a 32-yarder, and then a 25-yarder. On the ensuing kickoff, the Vikings' returner fumbled the football and the Chiefs recovered it on Minnesota's 19-yard line. "That was a key, key play," said Kansas City quarterback Len Dawson.

The Chiefs' defense, led by 265-pound defensive tackle Curley Culp and the 6'7", 275-pound gigantic tackle Buck

THE BEST WHO NEVER WON

Alan Page, Carl Eller, and Jim Marshall

Four losses in four Super Bowls with the Minnesota Vikings

THE PURPLE PEOPLE EATERS

During the late 1960s and in the 1970s, the Minnesota Vikings played some of the best defense the NFL has ever seen. The defensive line was nicknamed the Purple People Eaters. The name came from the purple color of the Vikings' uniforms and a popular song by Sheb Wooley of the same name. Members of this super front four were defensive tackle Alan Page, defensive end Carl Eller, defensive end Jim Marshall, and defensive tackle Gary Larsen, who was replaced by Doug Sutherland in 1974. Their motto was to "meet at the quarterback."

This unit helped the Vikes to ten postseason appearances in 11 years from 1968 to 1978. At the time, the Purple People Eaters were one of the most identifiable front fours in NFL history, along with the "Fearsome Foursome" of the Los Angeles Rams. Although the front line received the headlines, they benefited from a surrounding cast of talented linebackers such as Roy Winston, Jeff Siemon, and Wally Hilgenberg, and defensive backs Nate Wright, Bobby Bryant, and Paul Krause, a future Hall of Famer whose 81 interceptions are the most in NFL history. "We [didn't] like that nickname," said Marshall. "A one-eyed, one-horned, flying purple people eater? It's a cartoon character. There's no way it takes on the serious-ness of what we accomplished. We always called ourselves The Purple Gang."

The 1969 team gave up a meager 9.5 points per game, the best ever in a 14-game season. That year they became the only defensive line to have all four starters go to the Pro Bowl in the same year! The Vikings were nearly as good over the next two seasons, allowing 10.2 points in 1970 and 9.9 in 1971. "In those days, the offense would get a field goal for a 3–0 lead, and they'd say, 'Okay, we've done our job. Go shut them out the rest of the game,'" said defensive tackle Doug Sutherland. The defense was usually up to the task.

The Minnesota Vikings' defense regularly made history and set records. Alan Page was the first defensive player in NFL history to win the MVP of the league. (No defensive player would win the honor again until New York Giants linebacker Lawrence Taylor, in 1986.) Weighing 240 pounds, Page was relatively small for a lineman, but that didn't stop him from redefining the position of defensive tackle. Previously, defensive tackles depended on pure strength and a savage attack to bring down an opponent. But Page relied on incredible quickness to control the scrimmage line. "A defensive player should think of himself more as an aggressor, not as a defender," he said. Page was an indomitable and durable player. In his fifteen years of pro football, he played in 238 games, all but three of them as a starter. In four Super Bowl losses he recorded 32 tackles and three quarterback sacks.

Carl Eller was a fixture at left defensive end. A remarkably durable player, he missed one game in sixteen NFL seasons. Extremely quick and mobile for his size, he was a superb defender against the run and an excellent pass rusher. Packers quarterback Bart Starr once called Eller the best defensive lineman in football. "He's all the great defensive ends rolled up into one," he said. Eller's height, long arms, and leaping ability made throwing over him about as easy as throwing over a skyscraper. Standing 6 feet, 6 inches tall and weighing 246 pounds, he could take his choice of either tossing blockers aside or specding past them. "[Carl] did some things that were hard to fathom," said teammate Fran Tarkenton. "I saw him literally throw people aside as if they were mannequins." In Minnesota's four Super Bowl losses, Eller recorded 27 tackles.

When their playing days ended, Page and Eller were honored with busts in Canton and enshrined in the Pro Football Hall of Fame. Their teammate and defensive captain Jim Marshall should be. Marshall is often cited as the best player *not* in the Hall of Fame. Though small for his position (6'3", 220 pounds), he had breakneck speed and was keen for getting into the backfield. Marshall was so quick that he sometimes reached the runner before the hand-off did. And when a runner fumbled a ball, it was usually Marshall who recovered it. He holds the NFL record with 29 opponents' fumble recoveries. He also played in 282 consecutive games, more than any other defensive player in NFL history. He started 270 games in a row for the Vikings. Incredibly, in 20 seasons, he never missed a game.

Despite his achievements, Marshall is probably best remembered for his infamous "wrong way run." In 1964, he scooped up a fumble, ran 66 yards into the end zone and then jubilantly tossed the ball into the stands. Trouble was, it was the wrong end zone. "I was so intent on picking the ball up and doing something with it that I wasn't even aware of what I had done until the ball had been whistled dead," he said. "It was the perfect example of a young player using energy without thinking."

The Purple People Eaters devoured offenses, helping the Vikings to three Super Bowls in four years from 1973 to 1976. The 1975 regular season was a historic one for the Vikings defense, as it was the first time ever that a team led the league in total defense, pass defense, and rush defense. (Only one other team, the 1991 Philadelphia Eagles have accomplished that feat.) It's possible that the Vikes would have won a fifth conference championship and played in four straight Super Bowls had the Dallas Cowboys not completed the Hail Mary in the 1975 divisional playoff game.

Buchanan, and linebacker Willie Lanier, completely stifled the Vikings running attack. The Chiefs challenged the Vikings' highly rated defensive front four and ran at them for 151 yards in the game. They found holes in the Minnesota zone defense that few, if any, NFL teams had that season. Chiefs head coach Hank Stram devised an effective game plan against the Vikings. He noticed that Minnesota's cornerbacks liked to play deep and give wide receivers room to work underneath. Kansas City quarterback Len Dawson took advantage and threw quick developing square-outs and slants to his wide receivers. Of the 17 passes Dawson threw, 12 went to his wideouts, accounting for nine of 12 completions. "It's like stealing," Stram said in a famous sideline quote. Dawson became the fourth straight winning quarterback to be Super Bowl MVP.

Kansas City Chiefs coach Hank Stram became the first coach to wear a wireless microphone on the sideline of a Super Bowl game, and the NFL Films' highlights of Super Bowl IV made his sideline routine more legendary than his Super Bowl game plan. "I knew Hank was funny," said NFL Films' owner Steve Sabol. "But I never expected him to be that loose during a championship game. It was like having Henny Youngman coach a football team. Everything was a one-liner." Stram encouraged his team to "just keep matriculating the ball down the field, boys!" In the second quarter, he told everyone on the Chiefs sideline they were about to run the "65 Toss Power Trap" before Mike Garrett took the handoff and ran five yards into the end zone to make it 16–0 before the half. On the scoring run, right guard Mo Moorman filled a crucial blocking role by coming across the middle and employing a pancake block to totally wipe out Minnesota right tackle Alan Page. "He was set up so perfect," said Moorman. "It was like licking the cream off the custard."

For the first time, the Super Bowl halftime show featured a celebrity instead of college marching bands. Carol Channing, a star of stage and screen, led a tribute to Mardi Gras. It was a wild halftime show—if you like wild horses. Since the game was played in New Orleans, the halftime show featured soldiers and horses acting out the Battle of New Orleans. Blanks were fired to sound like gunfire and the noise frightened one of the horses. The horse reared back and almost threw his rider.

In the third quarter, the Vikings finally got on the board when Kapp pulled his teammates together for their only sustained drive of the game, marching 69 yards to score on Dave Osborn's short run. But that was Minnesota's last threat. On the next possession, Dawson threw a short pass that Otis Taylor broke for a 46-yard touchdown, which closed out the scoring at 23–7. Proving that a strong kicking game is a valuable asset, Kansas City punter Jerrel Wilson launched second half punts of 55- and 59-yards to help quash any hopes of a Minnesota comeback. (He had also boomed a 61-yarder in Super Bowl I.) Wilson is the Super Bowl record-holder for highest career punting average, at 46.5 yards per punt (11 punts for 511 yards).

The stunning loss was a crushing disappointment for Minnesota. After the game, referring to his team's three interceptions, three fumbles, and six penalties, Vikings safety Karl Kassulke said, "We made more mental mistakes in one game than we did in one season." The Chiefs did not make a serious mistake all game. It was the Vikings who lost their cool. Near the finish, a brawl nearly broke out after Alan Page was flagged for a 15-yard penalty for a late hit on Dawson.

Mike Garrett celebrates with Otis Taylor after scoring on a 5-yard touchdown run in Super Bowl IV. (AP Photo)

Not only was it a stunning loss for Minnesota, it was also a stunning loss for the entire NFL. Kansas City's surprise victory evened the AFL-NFL portion of the Super Bowl series at two wins each entering the first year of total merger in 1970, and forever quelled any arguments about which league was better or tougher than the other. "We didn't prove that one league was better than the other," said Kansas City defensive back Johnny Robinson. "We simply proved we were a better football team than Minnesota, that we're champions of the world." But the AFC did send a strong message of what's to come; AFC teams would go on to win nine of the next eleven Super Bowls.

Fran Tarkenton began his pro football career with the fledgling Minnesota Vikings in 1961. Both the team and its young quarterback were new to the NFL. In 1967, after a stormy relationship with Vikings coach Norm Van Brocklin, Tarkenton was traded. The New York Giants wanted him, hoping Tarkenton would spark publicity as well as throw touchdowns. The Giants were in hot competition with the New York Jets and their star quarterback, Joe Namath. After five seasons in New York, the future Hall of Famer asked to be traded, and Minnesota took him back.

In 1973, the Vikings advanced to Super Bowl VIII with a 12–2 record and a resounding victory at Dallas in the NFC championship game. Their Super Bowl opponent was the defending champion the Miami Dolphins. The game was played in Houston, in Rice Stadium. This was the first time a Super Bowl game was played at a stadium no current NFL team called home. The facilities were anything but super. The Vikings players complained about the cramped, uncarpeted locker room, and the unreliable showerheads. The practice field, a twenty-minute bus ride from their hotel, had no blocking sleds. "I don't think our players have seen anything like this since junior high school," said coach Bud Grant.

The country was reeling from a gasoline shortage at the time; it was common to see long lines of cars waiting to refuel at overly inflated prices. Most nights the six o'clock news reported on frustrated motorists coming to blows, and even an occasional shooting. Prior to the game, the 52 million viewers watching the CBS broadcast were treated to an interview with New York Jets quarterback Joe Namath, who said, "If Miami gets the kickoff and scores on the opening drive, the game is over." Sure enough, Miami won the coin toss, and Jake Scott returned the kickoff 31 yards to the Dolphins' 38-yard line. The

Dolphins immediately turned to their running attack, eating up yards with runs by Larry Csonka, Jim Kiick, and Mercury Morris. Quarterback Bob Griese completed two passes during the drive, which was capped off by Csonka's five-yard touchdown run. The Dolphins became the first team in Super Bowl history to score on the opening drive, and the rout was on.

Nothing went right for the Vikings. Fran Tarkenton was intercepted once, they lost a fumble, they failed to recover Miami's only fumble on a punt and they had a 65-yard kickoff return and a recovered onside kick nullified by penalties. By the third quarter, the Dolphins were up 24–0 and the Vikings never threatened to make it close. Minnesota blew their best shot to score with less than one minute left in the first half. After driving almost 80 yards, the Vikings were on the Dolphins 6-yard line, facing a 4th-down-and-1. The Vikings chose to go for the first down, rather than kick a field goal. They handed the ball to running back Oscar Reed, who was stuffed by three Dolphins before linebacker Nick Buoniconti forced him to fumble, which Jake Scott recovered. Defending his decision to shun the field goal, Minnesota coach Bud Grant said, "If it's less than a yard, we go for it. We feel we have the players to make it." When it was over, the Dolphins joined the Green Bay Packers as back-to-back Super Bowl champions, proving once again that Broadway Joe Namath was an accurate predictor of the outcomes of these big games.

Tarkenton ran for Minnesota's only touchdown late in the game. He had a good effort statistically with 18 for 28 for 182 yards, but the majority of his passes were short completions to his backs, nothing downfield. Tarkenton and the Vikings were particularly horrid the following year in Super

THE BEST WHO NEVER WON

Fran Tarkenton

Three Super Bowl losses with the Minnesota Vikings

THE MAD SCRAMBLER

Fran Tarkenton played in his first NFL game on September 17, 1961, at Metropolitan Stadium, in Bloomington, Minnesota, against the Chicago Bears. He came off the bench to lead the Vikings to five touchdowns, four passing and one rushing. The Vikings won, 37–13, in a big upset. Why was it such an upset? Not only was it Fran's debut, it was also the Vikings first game ever.

The 6-foot, 185-pounder paved the way for scrambling quarterbacks by being one of the first signal-callers to use his legs to make plays. Instead of dropping straight back in the pocket before passing the football, he would take the snap from center and scramble to the left or right while looking for a receiver. When Tarkenton finally did throw the ball, he usually connected. By the time he retired, in 1978, he had thrown 342 touchdowns—an NFL career record. He also set career records for passing attempts, completions,

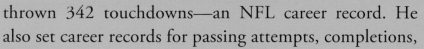

(AP Photo)

and passing yards—records that stood for more than fifteen years.

Starting in 1973, Tarkenton and the Vikings won six straight NFC Central division titles, with a 62–22–2 record, and made it to three Super Bowls, in 1974, 1975, and 1977, but they lost each time. In three Super Bowl appearances he completed 46 of 89 passes for 489 yards, one touchdown, and six interceptions. "We dominated the league in the 1970s," he said. "We did as much as Pittsburgh, the 49ers, or the Miami Dolphins of that era. But I didn't realize then, as I do now, how important it is to win the Super Bowl. We did well, but we never won that last one, so we will never be associated with those great teams of the past."

The future Hall of Fame quarterback was elected to nine Pro Bowls. He suffered a serious leg injury in 1977, but went on to play his best— and last—season in 1978, with 345 completions for 3,468 yards and 25 touchdowns. After an eighteen-year career, Tarkenton's combined rushing and passing total was 50,677 yards—nearly 29 miles, or 500 football fields.

Bowl IX against the Pittsburgh Steelers. The Vikings were down 9–0 in the fourth quarter, and their running game had been stuffed as no team's runners ever had been before—16 of the 20 runs they'd called had picked up two yards or less. And Tarkenton completed just 11 of 26 passes for 102 yards and three interceptions. He was also tackled in the end zone for the first safety in Super Bowl history. He averaged less than 4 yards per pass attempt and failed to lead the Vikings to a single point. He was the first quarterback to lose consecutive Super Bowls.

In 1976, the Vikings won the NFC Central division title for the eighth time in nine years with an impressive 11–2–1 record. The team's two losses came by a total of five points. Minnesota breezed through the playoffs and met the Oakland Raiders in Super Bowl XI, in the Rose Bowl, in Pasadena, California, on January 9, 1977, the earliest calendar date for any Super Bowl. (This was back when the NFL played Super Bowl games with a one-week rest; now there is an entire two-week break between the league championship games and the Super Bowl.)

As expected, a physically superior Raider team manhandled the Vikings in Super Bowl XI, crushing Minnesota by the score of 32–14. Bud Grant's coaching career didn't end until after the 1985 season, but this was the last time he would be humiliated in a Super Bowl. "We just played them on the wrong day," he quipped afterward. "Next time we'll play them on a Wednesday." Tarkenton frequently had Raiders like Otis Sistrunk, John Matuszak, and Ted Hendricks in the pocket with him. Due to constant harassment, he completed only 17 of 35 passes for 205 yards, one touchdown, and two interceptions. "They just totally dominated us," Tarkenton said. Minnesota was held scoreless until the last minute of the third quarter, and by then the Raiders had a commanding 19–0 lead. The Vikings scored a meaningless touchdown with 25 seconds left in the game. Alan Page, one of seven Vikings who started in all four Super Bowls (three others played in each game), wasn't around to see the touchdown. With about a minute and a half remaining and the outcome already decided, Page had headed for the dressing room. "He just walked off and left," said linebacker Jeff Siemon.

The Vikings were at their absolute worst in Super Bowls. Not only did the Vikings lose four times, they never led in any game. In four Super Bowls, the Vikings were outscored 51–10 in the first half and 95–34 overall. Outrushed on average 216 yards to 57 and outgained 324 total yards to 237. Their average time of possession was just less than 25 minutes. Minnesota's leading rusher in any game was Chuck Foreman with 44 yards (in 17 carries) against the Raiders. In the last three Super Bowls, the Vikings allowed Larry Csonka to rush for 145 yards, Franco Harris to rush for 158, and Clarence Davis to rush for 137. In all, the Vikings gained only 227 yards rushing in their four Super Bowl losses combined. This while giving up an *average* of 216 rushing yards a game. "I don't know how you can play in four of these things and lose them all," moaned Minnesota's Hall of Fame offensive tackle Ron Yary after Super Bowl XI. "Not only to lose them all, but to play bad football. I don't know how or why it happened, but for the first time in all the years that I've been playing football, I'm embarrassed."

Bud Grant's Minnesota Vikings reached the Super Bowl four times and lost four times—a record for futility matched only by that of the Buffalo Bills' teams of the 1990s. Minnesota has not returned to the big game since Super Bowl XI, in 1977. Ten Vikings played in all four Super Bowls: Alan Page, Carl Eller, Jim Marshall (defensive line); Ron Yary, Mick Tingelhoff, Ed White (offensive line); Wally Hilgenberg, Roy Winston (linebacker); Paul Krause (defensive back); and Fred Cox (placekicker).

Buffalo Bills, Super Bowls XXV, XXVI, XXVII, and XXVIII

Coach Marv Levy and his AFC champion Buffalo Bills set a new standard for excellence by reaching the Super Bowl four years in a row, after the 1990, 1991, 1992, and 1993 seasons—but the Bills managed to lose every time. First was the 20–19 heartbreaking loss to the New York Giants when Scott Norwood's 47-yard field goal attempt slipped wide right at the end of regulation. Second was the 37–24 whipping by the Washington Redskins. Third was a 52–17 mashing by the Dallas Cowboys, which included nine Buffalo turnovers. Fourth was a 30–13 loss in a Cowboys rematch, when the Bills led 13–6 at halftime but were outscored 24–0 in the second half.

To be sure, the Buffalo Bills of the early Nineties never would have been in position play in four Super Bowls without a roster of marvelous players on offense and defense. Quarterback Jim Kelly, running back Thurman Thomas, and receiver Andre Reed sparked an electrifying offensive unit. Bruce Smith, the NFL's all-time sacks leader, and linebacker Cornelius Bennett commanded the swarming defense. These players might be immediately associated with the all-time greats if only Super Bowl XXV had ended with a slightly different kick. Some may snicker at the Bills for losing four

straight Super Bowls, but consider the dominance it takes for one team to win the AFC title four years in a row. "People always ask, would you rather win one time or go four times and lose? It's a hard question. But to be honest with you, I would rather go four times and lose," said Jim Kelly.

In order to go to the Super Bowl four times and lose, a team needs to do a lot of winning. And the Buffalo Bills under coach Marv Levy did just that. Coach Levy's team finished the 1989 season with a 9–7 record, good enough to win the AFC Eastern division title. It was Buffalo's first winning record in eight years. But their season would end quickly with a 34–30 loss to the Cleveland Browns in a divisional playoff shootout. However, valuable lessons were learned from the game, as the Bills found a new rhythm when they ran a no-huddle offense with quarterback Jim Kelly in a "shotgun" alignment a few yards behind the center. During the offseason, Coach Levy opted to ditch the huddle and play sixty minutes of stop-us-if-you-can, playground style football.

No team used a no-huddle as their regular offense before the 1990s. But coach Levy knew what he was doing. He earned a master's degree in English History from Harvard. And he'd learned to adapt his coaching philosophy from year to year, to best match the skill set of his players, over the years coaching teams in the Canadian Football League, United States Football League, and National Football League. In 1987, his first full season with the Bills, the team returned to respectability with a 7–8 record. The following season they posted a 12–4 record and won the first of six AFC Eastern division titles. He was named NFL Coach of the Year in 1988. From 1988 to 1997, the Bills had the highest winning percentage in the AFC, and second in the entire NFL only to the San Francisco 49ers. Levy, who is the winningest coach in Bills' history, had a 112–70 regular season record and was 11–8 in the playoffs during his eleven seasons in Buffalo.

Chief among many reasons for Buffalo's success was a fast-paced offense that was always in overdrive. In essence, Coach Levy took the Run-and-Shoot offense and shot it with adrenaline. He made it a *no-huddle* Run-and-Shoot offense. He called it the K-Gun. This offense was an up-tempo, attacking offense designed to keep the defense on their heels. After every play, the Bills would line up on the ball and Kelly would make the play calls at the line of scrimmage. The main difference between Buffalo and the rest of the league's no huddle was the Bills ran it as their base offense for most of the game, no matter the situation. This wore out opposing defenders. Levy named the K-Gun after agile tight end Keith McKeller, whose ability to effectively block and catch passes, thereby staying on the field, made the system possible. The K-Gun offense was elegant in its simplicity. In essence, it created numerical mismatches downfield; for instance, four receivers against three defensive backs. The no-huddle offense is common in today's NFL game. "Finally, about twenty years after, that is a style that has finally come into vogue," said Levy.

Kelly took to the K-Gun quickly, and Buffalo got off to a terrific start in 1990. Using the no-huddle offense fulltime, they won nine of their first ten games. The players liked operating in this new, quick-strike attacking style, with the results to prove it. This was best demonstrated in back-to-back home wins in September, when the Bills scored three touchdowns in 77 seconds in a 29–28 win over the Denver Broncos. Then, one week later, Buffalo mounted a furious rally and busted out for 24 points in the fourth quarter to stun the Los Angeles Raiders, 28–24. Using the K-Gun, Kelly found an offensive weapon in which to thrive. He had the single

best quarter of his Hall of Fame career, against the Philadelphia Eagles, on December 2, 1990. He went 8-for-8 passing for 229 yards and three touchdowns. James Lofton, Andre Reed, and Thurman Thomas all caught touchdowns in that first quarter, and a Scott Norwood field goal made it 24–0 after only 15 minutes of play. On the day, Kelly was 19 of 32 for 334 yards, three touchdown passes, and no interceptions. He had three passes over 50 yards, including a 71-yard bomb and a 63-yard score to Lofton. Though the Eagles came back to make a game of it, the Bills won, 30–23, and had seen a glimpse into the bright future.

What made Buffalo's version of a no-huddle offense unique was the addition of their excellent young running back Thurman Thomas. He was a double threat, capable of coming out of the backfield as a pass receiver, and an explosive threat whose jitterbug running style proved elusive against would-be tacklers in the open field. It was the versatility of Thomas that allowed the Bills to attack defenses on the ground more than a typical no-huddle offense. The result was a high-octane, all-cylinders onslaught that wore down opponents and helped Kelly, Thomas, Andre Reed, and James Lofton cement Hall of Fame legacies. Andre Reed was Kelly's primary "go-to" wide receiver. He ranks among the NFL's all-time Top Ten receiving leaders in receptions, receiving yardage, and touchdown catches. Kelly to Reed was a lethal combination, connecting for 65 touchdowns during their career together, trailing only the tandems of Peyton Manning to Marvin Harrison (112), Steve Young to Jerry Rice (85), Peyton Manning to Reggie Wayne (69) and Dan Marino to Mark Clayton (79). Reed is the most prolific receiver in Bills history. His 951 receptions—third on the NFL all-time list at the time of his retirement—are 266 more than the next best Bills receiver. Known for his ability to gain huge chunks of yardage after the catch, he was a big-play receiver, and a reliable possession receiver, too. He amassed 13,198 receiving yards in his 16-year career, and caught 50 or more passes in 13 seasons, a mark exceeded only by Jerry Rice.

In 1989, the Bills beat the Miami Dolphins with a thrilling fourth quarter score on the season's final day to clinch the AFC Eastern title with a 13–3 record. Following the 1989 regular season, the offense continued to be unstoppable in the playoffs, as they beat the Miami Dolphins, 43–34. Smelling a first Super Bowl appearance, the Bills destroyed the Raiders, 51–3, in the AFC title game, played at a raucous Rich Stadium, in Buffalo. The Bills were going to Super Bowl XXV, where the New York Giants would be waiting for them. The first Super Bowl loss to the Giants will forever be remembered for Scott Norwood's failed 47-yard field goal attempt with seconds on the clock. The kick had the distance, just not the necessary accuracy required to make Buffalo the champions of all football. The ball drifted wide to the outside of the right goal post and delivered a second Super Bowl title in five years to the Giants. The negative turn of events following "Wide Right" overshadowed an excellent statistical performance by Thurman Thomas. He rushed for 135 yards, caught five passes for 55 yards, and scored on a 31-yard run in the 20–19 loss. What made his stat line even more impressive was that the Bills had the football for just nine minutes in the second half and 19:27 overall.

The following season, the Bills offense was even stronger. Thurman Thomas was the league's most valuable player, amassing 2,038 all-purpose yards and 12 touchdowns. The

The Giants' Reyna Thompson celebrates the thrill of victory while kicker Scott Norwood (11) and holder Frank Reich suffer the agony of defeat in Super Bowl XXV. (AP Photo/Rusty Kennedy)

THE BEST WHO NEVER WON

Jim Kelly

Four consecutive Super Bowl losses with the Buffalo Bills

(AP Photo/Reinke)

HIS AIM WAS TRUE

When coach Marv Levy turned over the reins on offense to quarterback Jim Kelly and unleashed the K-Gun a generation ago, the Buffalo Bills took the NFL by surprise. Kelly was in his sixth professional season in 1990 when Levy let him take charge of the offense. "He had enough guts back in the day to let [me] call the plays," Kelly said. It probably wasn't that difficult knowing he had Thurman Thomas in the backfield, Andre Reed lining up to his left, and James Lofton and Don Beebe lining up on the right. Kelly had the horses, and he posted a career best 101.2 passer rating. The Bills went to their first Super Bowl after that season.

The hurry-up worked for the Bills because opponents weren't prepared to stop it, in game planning or in conditioning. Jim Kelly said defensive linemen didn't have the endurance to keep lining up and pounding in the trenches every 15 or 20 seconds. "They were not used to going at that pace," he said. This wasn't the first time Kelly orchestrated the no-huddle to tear apart a league. In 1984, while playing with the USFL's Houston Gamblers, he had thrown for 5,219 passing yards and 44 touchdowns. Kelly took home the USFL most valuable player award and earned a reputation as a quarterbacking Texas gunslinger. To be sure, this wasn't the NFL, but Kelly learned to flourish playing in an offensive system that never takes its finger off the trigger.

Kelly was born in Pittsburgh, Pennsylvania. He played quarterback *and* linebacker for his high school team. He was recruited to play linebacker for Penn State University! But Kelly wanted to pass and enrolled at the University of Miami, in Florida, where he broke a school passing record with 5,228 career yards. "Ever since I was a little boy I wanted the ball in my hand, whether it was a basketball, baseball, or football," Kelly said. "I always wanted to be the guy to run the show. I thrived on it." The Buffalo Bills selected Kelly with the 14th pick of the 1983 NFL draft. This draft has been hailed as one of the all-time great quarterback drafts in NFL history, with six quarterbacks taken in the first round besides Kelly, including two other future Hall of Famers, John Elway and Dan Marino. But Kelly decided to join the United States Football League instead. He played with the league's Houston Gamblers before joining the Bills in 1986. (The USFL folded in 1985.)

Kelly was worth the wait, and immediately lived up to his advance billing. He was the top-rated quarterback in the NFL in 1990 and led the league in touchdown passes, with 33, in 1991. He also thrived in pressure-packed situations, bringing the Bills back from fourth quarter deficits to victory 23 times. Kelly reveled in his reputation as a quarterback with a "linebacker's mentality." The image of Kelly diving into the end zone at Joe Robbie Stadium to beat the Dolphins on the game's final play in 1989 to clinch the AFC Eastern division title will remain with Bills fans forever. It was his first rushing touchdown in 45 games in the NFL. "He was a tough guy, he wasn't a prima donna quarterback," said teammate Mark Kelso. "He'd just as soon put his shoulder down and run you over when he could run, not that he was the swiftest guy when he got out of that pocket. But he could certainly take a lot of hits and had a tremendous amount of toughness."

Kelly played 11 seasons in Buffalo during his NFL career, and he passed for more than 3,000 yards in a season eight times. He threw for 35,467 passing yards and 237 touchdowns, all of which are Bills' records. In fact,

he owns every major passing record in franchise history. Kelly's Buffalo career, and his legacy, went beyond personal, individual statistics. Above all, he will be remembered as the spark behind eight playoff appearances in nine seasons by the Bills, from 1988 to 1996, six division titles, and an unprecedented four Super Bowl appearances in a row. Given the current state of the free-agency ridden, high-turnover NFL, the last record may be safe for all time.

Kelly's postseason record is up for debate. He registered a 101–59 regular season won-loss record as a starter, but was 9–8 in the postseason. There is no doubting his AFC divisional playoff and AFC championship game records are formidable. In Super Bowls, however, he completed 81 of 145 passes for 829 passing yards, two touchdowns and seven interceptions, in four games, often playing from behind, when opposing defenses knew he would be passing. He set a record with 58 pass attempts in Super Bowl XXVI against the Redskins. In that game, he completed 28 of 58 passes for 275 yards, two touchdowns, and four interceptions.

Throw away the numbers, close the record book. Jim Kelly's lasting legacy is leading the Buffalo Bills to a record four straight Super Bowl games between 1991 and 1994. Of course, the elephant in the room is that Kelly and the Bills lost all four in a row. Kelly's teammate, center Kent Hull, managed to find some consolation despite suffering a fourth straight Super Bowl loss. "In the immediate future we'll be thought of as losers," he said. "But one day down the road, when I'm no longer playing, they'll say, 'Wow, they won four straight AFC championships. They must have been good.'" It's a sentiment Jim Kelly agrees with. "The further we're removed from those games, the more people appreciate what we were able to do."

Bills offense continued to roll in a 37–14 win over the Kansas City Chiefs in the divisional playoff game. The offense stalled a bit in the AFC championship game, scoring only 10 points. But the Bills defense showed why they too were one of the best units in the NFL. The swarming defense, led by Smith and Bennett, held the Broncos scoreless until the final minutes. The Bills won, 10–7, earning a second straight trip to the Super Bowl. There they faced the NFC champion Washington Redskins.

Bruce Smith was a beast on the defensive line. Drafted out of Virginia Tech with the first overall pick in 1985, he consistently tormented opposing quarterbacks, year after year. He reached double-digit sacks in 13 of his 19 career seasons. He was the league's defensive player of the year twice (1990 and 1996) and was an 11-time Pro Bowl selection. He finished his Hall of Fame career as the NFL's career sacks leader, with 200 quarterback sacks in 279 games. Cornelius Bennett was a distinguished linebacker during his nine seasons with Buffalo. He was the AFC defensive player of the year twice (1988 and 1991) and was a five-time Pro Bowl selection. Known by the nickname Biscuit, he was a member of all four of Buffalo's Super Bowl losing teams, and later, as a member of the Atlanta Falcons, found himself once again on the losing side of a Super Bowl for a record fifth time.

The start of Super Bowl XXVI did not go as planned for Thurman Thomas. He missed the first two offensive plays of the game. He wasn't hurt. He just couldn't locate his helmet! Thomas was preparing to go on the field with the rest of his teammates after the Redskins offense went three-and-out on their first possession of the game. The only problem was Thomas' helmet was not where he had left it prior to the coin toss. "I couldn't find it," Thomas said after the game. "I didn't know where it was. For some reason somebody moved it. I was very upset." It was the start to a miserable day overall for Thomas. He rushed for just 13 yards on 10 carries, as the Bills lost, 37–24, to the Redskins. Previously, only the Minnesota Vikings (VIII, IX) and Denver Broncos (XXI, XXII) had ever lost back-to-back Super Bowl games.

By 1992, the Bills dynamic offense had become a virtual juggernaut during the regular season. On September 13, in a 34–31 shootout victory over the Steve Young-led San Francisco 49ers, Kelly passed for a career-high 403 yards in the first NFL game without a punt. Meanwhile, Thurman Thomas had another stellar season posting 2,113 all-purpose yards (1,487 rushing yards and 626 receiving yards). Reed was the team's leading receiver, with 65 catches for 913 yards. Reed had a spectacular performance in the Bills' extraordinary January 3, 1993 playoff victory over the Houston Oilers in a game that was called The Comeback. Houston held a decisive 35–3 lead during the third quarter, but the Bills recovered to win in overtime, 41–38, in what is still the largest comeback in NFL history. Andre Reed was awesome during the comeback. He caught three touchdowns in the second half. In all, he caught eight passes for 136 yards.

The Bills won their next two postseason matchups against the Pittsburgh Steelers and the Miami Dolphins, advancing to Super Bowl XXVII, against the resurgent Dallas Cowboys franchise. The Bills followed the Miami Dolphins (VI, VII, VIII) as the only team ever to play in three straight Super Bowls. As they prepared to face the Cowboys, in Pasadena, the Bills hoped to learn from the failures of previous seasons. When the Bills jumped on the board first with a two-yard Thomas touchdown run, the Buffalo sideline was brimming with optimism. However, the Bills lead was gone in a flash as two turnovers led to 14 points at the end of the first quarter. An injured Jim Kelly was knocked out of the game midway through the second quarter, limiting him to 4-of-7 passing for 82 yards and two interceptions. Turnovers would continue to pile up for the backup quarterback Frank Reich and the Bills, as the Cowboys went on to win the game in a laugher, 52–17.

The Bills had committed a record nine—yes, that's nine—turnovers. Pardon the despondent blue-clad Bills faithful for feeling a tad disheartened. Said Marv Levy: "I had a call-in show, and after the third (Super Bowl loss), a fan called in and said, 'Please don't go back to the Super Bowl next year. I can't stand it. I get so depressed, I can't go to work the next day.' I said, 'Sir, I understand. But I'm glad that you're not on my team.'"

The Super Bowl XXVII blowout against the Cowboys would have been worse had it not for Don Beebe's hustle and never-say-quit attitude. Beebe attended little known Chadron State (enrollment about 3,000) in Nebraska. He set numerous school football records his senior year and starred on the indoor track team. He ran the 60-yard dash clocked in a time of 6.3 seconds. He somehow managed to get an invitation to the NFL scouting combine, where he

dazzled with a 4.4 seconds clocking in the 40-yard dash, the best among all receivers. The Bills took a chance and drafted the 5-foot-11, 185-pound Beebe with the 82nd pick in 1989. He wound up playing nine years as a receiver and kick returner with the Bills, Panthers and Packers, appearing in a record-tying six Super Bowls (a mark equaled only by Tom Brady and Mike Lodish) and winning once with the Packers.

Beebe is best remembered for his extreme hustle in the fourth quarter of Super Bowl XXVII, with the Bills trailing 52–17. Dallas defensive end Leon Lett recovered a Bills fumble, and was running for a certain touchdown, with no Bills player in front of him. Beebe was chasing from behind, running the length of the field. He came out of nowhere, caught up to Lett just a few yards from the goal line, stripped the ball from Lett's hand, and forced Lett to fumble after a length-of-the-field footrace. The loose ball went through the end zone for a touchback and prevented a Dallas touchdown. Had Lett reached the end zone with the ball, Dallas would have set a Super Bowl record by scoring 59 points in the game. "Don Beebe is the epitome of what the heart of a champion is all about," said Buffalo coach Marv Levy. "Beebe showed what a fighting heart is all about. He gave everything he had all the time."

Besides Beebe, the lone Bill who could walk away proud of his day was wide receiver Andre Reed, who caught eight passes for 152 yards. A consistent scoring threat out of relatively little known Kutztown State University, Reed made most of his career receptions over the middle where linebackers and hard-hitting safeties prowled. "He was really good at running the short route and turning it into a long gain," said teammate Steve Tasker. "Jim (Kelly) loved it because it was an easy throw for a lot of yards. We all loved it because he could turn a nothing five-yard completion into a 65-yard touchdown. That's what Andre's gift was." In his four Super Bowls, Reed caught 27 passes, the second most in Super Bowl history (behind Jerry Rice, 33) and gained 323 receiving yards, third most ever (behind Rice's 604 yards and Lynn Swann's 364). He played 16 NFL seasons and retired following the 2000 season with 951 receptions for 13,198 receiving yards and 87 touchdowns.

In 1993, the Bills won their fifth division title in six years with a 12–4 record. They beat the Raiders, 29–23, to earn a return trip to the AFC championship game. There, Buffalo faced Joe Montana, now quarterback of the Kansas City Chiefs. The Bills knocked out Montana early in the game, and won going away, 30–13, to claim their record fourth straight AFC title. The Bills became the first team ever to play in four straight Super Bowls. Understandably, the Bills were heavy underdogs in Super Bowl XXVIII facing the Cowboys in a rematch in Atlanta.

With the exception of a solid performance in Super Bowl XXV against the Giants (135 rushing yards and a touchdown), Thurman Thomas did not fare well on the game's biggest stage. He wasn't even a factor in the other three Super Bowls—at least not in a positive sense. Once he found his helmet, he rushed for only 13 yards on 10 carries against the Redskins. Then he gained a paltry 19 yards on 11 carries against the Cowboys. His untimely fumble in Super Bowl XXVIII against Dallas broke the Bills' spirit and catapulted the Cowboys to a second straight Super Bowl title.

At first, the picture for Buffalo looked rosy. Through the first half the Bills played solid football and had a 13–6 lead at intermission. But just 55 seconds into the third quarter, Thomas lost a costly fumble that was returned for a game-tying touchdown, and the Cowboys never looked back, winning the game 30–13 to hand the Bills a crushing fourth straight Super Bowl defeat. "It's frustrating, it really is," said Kelly. "We should have won. The Cowboys have a hell of a defense. Take your hats off to them. They come up with 24 unanswered points. That last fumble was once in a million. These things always happen to the Bills. Don't count me out yet. I have a few years left. Our goal is the same. We'll do it until we get it right."

We're not sure which is a more incredible achievement, the fact that the Bills managed to make four straight Super Bowl appearances, or the fact that they failed to win the big game even once. The Bills surrendered an average of 32 points in their four Super Bowl losses. Buffalo's record is arguably one of the weirdest records in NFL history, because we're not sure whether to applaud, laugh, or shake our heads in disbelief. "It's not likely to be repeated," said general manager Bill Polian, the architect of the Bills, in reference to their record four straight Super Bowl appearances. "We were like the Brooklyn Dodgers of the 1950s; a great team that didn't win it all. Except the Dodgers did win one."

ONE SHOT AT GLORY

When an opportunity for greatness finally arrives, these players seize the day, and earn a place in Super Bowl lore.

Phil Simms
Super Bowl XXI
New York Giants 39, Denver Broncos 20
January 25, 1987
Rose Bowl, Pasadena, CA

	1	2	3	4	OT	T
Denver Broncos	10	0	0	10		20
New York Giants	7	2	17	13		39

New York Giants' quarterback Phil Simms was nearly perfect—completing 22 of 25 passes for 268 yards, three touchdowns and no interceptions—as the Giants whupped the Broncos, 39–20, in Super Bowl XXI.

"This might be the best game a quarterback has every played," Giants coach Bill Parcells said.

Simms indeed had the game of his life, putting on a display of precision passing unmatched in Super Bowl history. He completed a record 88 percent of his passes, including 10 for 10 in the second half, when the Giants scored 24 points to flip a 10–9 halftime deficit into a 33–10 lead.

Simms threw touchdown passes to three different receivers: a 6-yard pass to tight end Zeke Mowatt; a 13-yard scoring strike to tight end Mark Bavaro; and a 6-yard pass to wide receiver Phil McConkey.

"I was like a fastball pitcher," Simms said. "I had great location all day. Almost every pass landed exactly where I wanted it to. I've never played better. I told 'em before the game I was smoking."

This was the team's first Super Bowl triumph and the Giants' first NFL title in thirty years. "We buried all the ghosts today," Parcells said. "They're all gone."

Simms, too, buried all the ghosts on this day. In the eight years since being drafted from Morehead State in 1979, he had been benched on occasion, injured frequently, and criticized incessantly. He was taunted mercilessly by skeptics on sports radio call-in shows and booed vociferously inside his home stadium. Now he had silenced the doubters. In Super Bowl XXI Simms was unbelievable. He still holds the all-time record for highest completion percentage (88 percent) and highest quarterback rating (150.92) in a Super Bowl game. He didn't throw an incomplete

Phil Simms was as close to perfect as a quarterback could be in Super Bowl XXI. (AP Photo/Reed Saxon)

pass in three of the four quarters. "In my wildest dreams, I couldn't have hoped it would work out this way," Simms said. "We just had a great game plan and executed it like the coaches wanted us to." In the excitement of the victory celebration, Simms became the first Super Bowl MVP to utter the famous postgame announcement: "I'm going to Disney World!"

With the game decided, linebacker Harry Carson gave Bill Parcells a Gatorade shower, which had become the team's victory trademark. Using a sneak attack, Carson had disguised himself by wearing a security guard's yellow windbreaker and sloshed Parcells from behind. Jim Burt first doused Parcells after a win earlier in the season, but it was Carson who kept it up, bathing Parcells after each of the Giants' postseason wins. Parcells did not mind the dunks. "It's fun. If you have fun, fine. It's not all life and death." However, while Burt and Carson popularized the Gatorade shower, they didn't pull off the first dunking. That honor goes to former Chicago Bears lineman Dan Hampton, who collaborated with teammates Steve McMichael and Mike Singletary to get coach Mike Ditka wet after a regular-season win over the Vikings in 1984.

Reflecting on the game, Giants coach Bill Parcells said: "Winning the Super Bowl represents a great sense of satisfaction. Team satisfaction. Personal satisfaction. You can't deny that. But you know what? Bobby Knight told me two days after the first Super Bowl we won, 'You're gonna want to win the second one more than you wanted to win the first one.' He was right."

"We buried all the ghosts today. They're all gone," said Bill Parcells after Super Bowl XXI. (AP Photo/Eric Risberg)

Doug Williams
Super Bowl XXII
Washington Redskins 42, Denver Broncos 10
January 31, 1988
Jack Murphy Stadium, San Diego, CA

	1	2	3	4	OT	T
Washington Redskins	0	35	0	7		42
Denver Broncos	10	0	0	0		10

The Washington Redskins were trailing the Denver Broncos, 10–0, early in the second quarter of Super XXII when quarterback Doug Williams completed an 80-yard touchdown bomb to wide receiver Ricky Sanders. This ignited the Redskins, who erupted for an NFL postseason record 35 points in the quarter—scoring five touchdowns in 18 plays—to bury the Broncos in a flurry of Super Bowl records.

It is amazing how quickly a game that seemed to be totally in Denver's control completely changed direction on that Williams-to-Sanders connection. The Redskins never lost their momentum, either, en route to a 42–10 victory. There were many standouts for the Redskins, as Williams won MVP honors with 340 passing yards and four touchdowns (all in the second quarter), and rookie running back Timmy Smith set a Super Bowl record with 204 rushing yards.

Seemingly lost in those fireworks is the damage that Sanders inflicted on Denver. He added another 50-yard scoring catch and finished with 9 receptions for 193 yards, a feat topped only by Jerry Rice, who had 215 the following year.

"I would've loved to have won MVP, but I was happy regardless. Doug had a great game. Timmy had a great game. We could've all been co-MVPs," said Sanders.

Doug Williams sets to throw downfield during Super Bowl XXII. (AP Photo/Elise Amendola)

ONE SHOT AT GLORY

These players squandered their opportunity of a lifetime, leaving them to wonder what might have been.

Jackie Smith
Super Bowl XIII
Pittsburgh Steelers 35, Dallas Cowboys 31
January 21, 1979
Orange Bowl, Miami, FL

	1	2	3	4	OT	T
Pittsburgh Steelers	7	14	0	14		35
Dallas Cowboys	7	7	3	14		31

After playing fifteen years on mediocre St. Louis Cardinals teams, Jackie Smith was lured out of retirement by the Cowboys in 1978 due to injuries to Dallas' tight ends. Smith agreed to play one more season with Dallas and then end his career.

That season, as luck would have it, the Cowboys reached Super Bowl XIII. For the thirty-eight-year-old Smith, it was one last shot to become a champion. His defining moment occurred with two minutes thirty seconds left in the third quarter of Super Bowl XIII. The Cowboys, trailing 21–14, had a third down at the Steelers' 10-yard line. Smith somehow slipped unguarded past the Pittsburgh defense and was standing alone in the middle of the end zone. QB Roger Staubach's pass looked like a certain touchdown to tie the score. But the ball bounced off Smith's hands and fell to the ground—incomplete pass, fourth down.

An incredulous gasp shook the stadium; players on both sidelines went berserk; and Smith sat there in the end zone, with shoulders slumped, stunned.

"Oh, bless his heart," said TV announcer Verne Lundquist of Smith's predicament. "He's got to be the sickest man in America."

Heartbreak hit the Cowboys and their fans. Instead of tying the score, Dallas had to settle for a field goal and an eventual 35–31 loss to the Steelers.

"I was wide open and I just missed it," said Smith of the botched play. "It was a little behind me, but not enough that I should have missed the ball."

To his credit, Staubach conceded that his pass to a wide-open receiver was a change-up that floated too low and faded a bit behind Smith, resulting in a slip just as he was about to make the catch.

"I saw him open and I took something off it," said Staubach. "I didn't want to drill it through his hands. The ball was low. It could have been better. Chalk that one up to both of us."

Smith was a Hall of Fame tight end who caught 480 passes in 210 games. But he is forever associated as the player who drops an easy touchdown pass in the end zone, costing Dallas another title and haunting Cowboys fans ever since. Sticking to his original game plan, Smith retired following Super Bowl XIII; he never played in another football game.

"I hate for it to end like this," said Smith. "I hope it won't haunt me, but it probably will."

John Banaszak (76) celebrates and John Fitzgerald recoils after Jackie Smith's third-quarter drop in Super Bowl XIII. A touchdown catch would have tied the score. (AP Photo)

Neil O'Donnell
Super Bowl XXX
Dallas Cowboys 27, Pittsburgh Steelers 17
January 28, 1996
Sun Devil Stadium, Tempe, AZ

	1	2	3	4	OT	T
Dallas Cowboys	10	3	7	7		27
Pittsburgh Steelers	0	7	0	10		17

Neil O'Donnell all but gift-wrapped the Super Bowl XXX Vince Lombardi Trophy for the Dallas Cowboys, in 1996. The Steelers quarterback threw a pair of interceptions right into the arms of cornerback Larry Brown, who simply had to catch the football to win the Super Bowl MVP award. Both times, the Cowboys quickly converted Brown's take-aways into touchdowns, helping the Dallas franchise to its fifth Super Bowl title.

O'Donnell threw his first interception in the third quarter. The Steelers had the ball on their own 48-yard line. It was third and long. Brown was deep in zone coverage. No Steeler ran near him. But O'Donnell threw the ball his way anyway.

Brown intercepted the pass with ease at the Dallas 38-yard line and returned the ball 44 yards to the Pittsburgh 18-yard line. "The ball just slipped out of my hands," said O'Donnell. "It's something that happens." Brown had his own theory. "I think there was some miscommunication between the receiver and O'Donnell. I was reading the quarterback all the way."

On the first play after the interception, Dallas quarterback Troy Aikman completed a 17-yard pass to sure-handed receiver Michael Irvin, down to the 1-yard line. On the next play, Emmitt Smith dove in for a score, increasing Dallas' lead to 20–7. The Steelers responded early in the fourth quarter with a field goal for 20–10. Then Pittsburgh coach Bill Cowher called for a surprise onside kick. The Steelers recovered! A quick Steelers' touchdown cut the deficit to three points.

Remarkably, Pittsburgh battled back to 20–17 with just over four minutes left in the game. O'Donnell wanted badly to orchestrate a scoring drive to tie the score or take the lead. The Steelers had the ball on their own 32-yard line. It was second down and 10. O'Donnell dropped back to pass against another Cowboys blitz—and threw another pass right into Brown's waiting arms! Brown returned the ball 33 yards to the 6-yard line. Two plays after the interception, Emmitt Smith scored again with 3:43 left in the game and Dallas led 27–17.

This was déjà vu all over again. Another Cowboys blitz and another O'Donnell pass went right into the arms of Brown with no Steeler in sight. "He had a bad read on the first one," Brown explained. "The second one, they had been running slants on me all day and I got a jump on it." Brown was the first defensive back to win the MVP trophy since Jake Scott of the Miami Dolphins in Super Bowl VII. "Winning [the Super Bowl MVP] you're thrilled because that's the ultimate, to accomplish something as a team, but it's also one of those things you'll never forget as an individual," he said.

O'Donnell completed 28 of 49 passes for 239 yards, one touchdown and three interceptions. He appeared flustered during the game's most crucial moments. He was sacked four times and often seemed to be throwing under pressure because his passes were inconsistent and off the mark.

Larry Brown (24) after his late-fourth quarter interception of Neil O'Donnell's pass. (AP Photo/Beth Keiser)

The Steelers were seriously let down by his two bad throws. "We're all in this together," O'Donnell said. "You just can't single out one individual and say this is the reason why we lost the football game."

The Cowboys won their third championship in four years. It was a hard-fought win, not like the runaway back-to-back victories over the Buffalo Bills. "I think it's a feeling more of relief than anything else," Troy Aikman said. The Dallas Cowboys began a downward spiral after this Super Bowl triumph. The Cowboys won just one postseason game over the next twelve seasons.

THIRD QUARTER

GAME ACTION

Over the course of fifty years, the Super Bowl has provided some of the most memorable games in sports history. Fans have watched Super Bowls in which the underdog team beat the odds or the favorite team demonstrated its dominance. They've also seen "squeakers" that were decided as regulation ended. A half century's worth of games inevitably produces standouts. See if your favorites are here.

SHOCKING UPSETS

On any given Sunday, any NFL team can beat any other NFL team—especially on Super Bowl Sunday. That's why they play the game. Here are some memorable shockers.

Super Bowl III
New York Jets 16, Baltimore Colts 7
January 12, 1969
Orange Bowl, Miami, FL

	1	2	3	4	OT	T
New York Jets	0	7	6	3		16
Baltimore Colts	0	0	0	7		7

In 1969, the New York Jets needed respect, and so did their football league. They were part of the American Football League, which was only nine years old and wasn't taken seriously. Some people called the AFL the "Mickey Mouse league." Others called the AFL a "scrap heap" because many AFL players were rejects from NFL teams.

The Jets players were aware of all that as they prepared to face the Baltimore Colts in the Super Bowl. The Colts were part of the National Football League, which had been around for 49 years. Like many NFL teams, the Colts thought they were better and stronger than any AFL team. The Colts had crushed many of their opponents that season and were favored to win the Super Bowl by 18 points.

But the Jets' quarterback, Joe Namath, was confident his team would win. Five years earlier, "Broadway Joe" had taken New York City by storm when he elected to sign with the AFL's Jets over the NFL's St. Louis Cardinals for a record $427,000 over three years. (He was the number one pick in the AFL draft. In the NFL draft, the Cardinals had chosen him twelfth overall.) He went on to become the AFL Rookie of the Year in 1965, an AFL All Star in four of his first five seasons, and the league's MVP in 1968 and 1969. He was the first quarterback in either league to throw for 4,000 yards in one season (1967). Remarking on Namath's outsized contract, *New York Daily News* columnist Dick Young wrote, "After a look at Joe Namath in pulsating color, I'm convinced of one thing. The Jets aren't paying him enough."

So, perhaps understandably, Namath wasn't intimidated by the Colts. Responding to a heckler at a pre-game event three days before the Super Bowl, Namath made an outrageous statement. "The Jets will win on Sunday. I guarantee it," he said.

Earl Morrall looks downfield for a Colts receiver. (AP Photo)

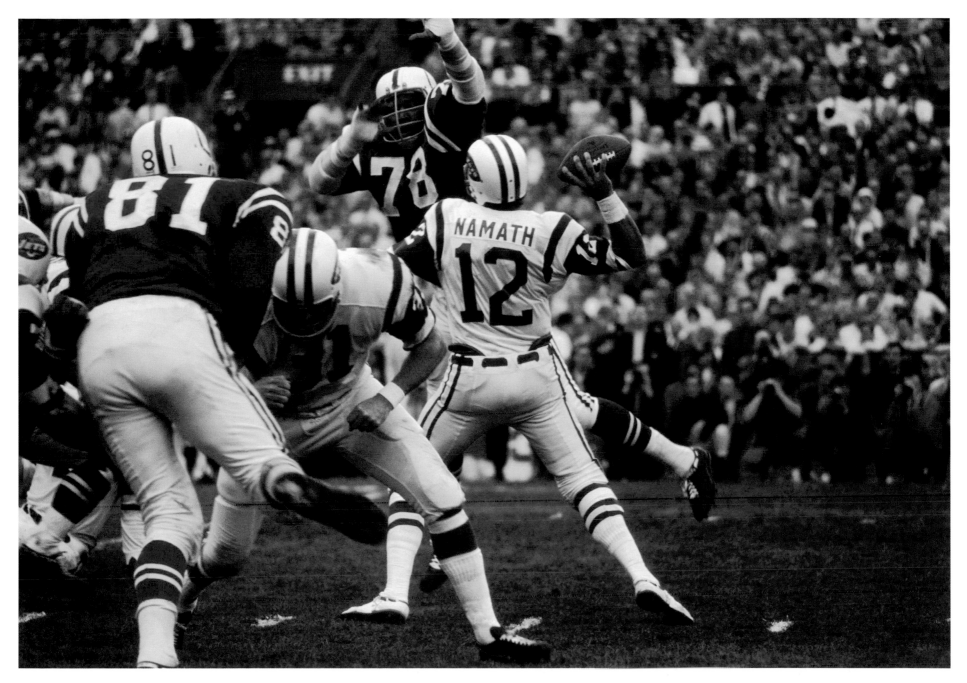

Joe Namath gets off a pass before Bubba Smith closes in during Super Bowl III. (AP Photo)

Still, when game day arrived, Namath admitted to being awestruck. "I remember walking out [for the coin toss] and seeing [Colts QB] Johnny Unitas there. I thought about when I was in high school and guys called me 'Joey U,' and now I'm out on the field with him."

Hobbled by an injury, Unitas returned to the sideline and watched that season's MVP, Earl Morrall, start for the Colts. Namath then shook off any pregame jitters and proceeded to make good on his guarantee: He was 17 of 28 for 206 yards.

"Namath played a great game," said Dave Anderson, who covered the Jets for the *New York Times* that season and later wrote *Countdown to Super Bowl* about the game. "He didn't throw the ball that much, but when he did, he threw to George Sauer, because Don Maynard had a bad hamstring from the [AFL title] game against the Raiders. But the Colts didn't know how bad it was. Probably the game's most important play was [on the Jets' second series] when they sent Maynard deep down the field and Namath overthrew him. That incompletion showed the Colts that Maynard was still a deep threat. The Jets figured they could get one sprint out of Maynard, and then they virtually ignored him for the rest of the game. The Colts had to double-cover Maynard. That left George Sauer to work alone against two aging players, linebacker Don Shinnick and cornerback Lenny Lyles. Maynard didn't catch one ball all game, but Sauer caught eight."

The Jets led for the whole game. In fact, the mighty Colts didn't even score any points until less than four minutes were left in the fourth quarter. By then, it was too late and the Jets won, 16–7. The Jets were not only the first AFL team ever to win a Super Bowl, but their win remains the biggest upset in Super Bowl history.

Namath collected the MVP award and plaudits from the Colts and his teammates. "Namath's quickness took away our blitz," said Colt coach Don Shula after the game. "He beat our blitz more than we beat him." Namath's teammates remarked on his positivism before and during the game. "He never let up all game," said Jets rookie John Dockery. "Every time he'd come to the sidelines after a series he'd pat everybody and keep telling us, 'C'mon, c'mon—today is our day.'"

It was the Jets' day, alright. And Namath's. And the AFL's. The "Mickey Mouse league" had arrived.

The morning after Joe Namath famously guaranteed a win by the Jets, New York coach Weeb Ewbank confronted his quarterback at breakfast. When Namath confirmed what he'd said the night before, Ewbank moaned, "Ah, Joe, Joe, Joe, you know what they're going to do?" referring to the Colts. "They're going to put that [story] up on the locker room wall. Those Colts are gonna want to kill us."

Of course, Super Bowl III didn't quite turn out that way. And the Jets' victory was an especially satisfying win for Ewbank, who'd coached Baltimore to NFL titles in 1958 and 1959, only to be released after the 1962 season. Never did Ewbank publicly gloat about defeating the team owned by the man who had dismissed him six years before, Carroll Rosenbloom.

But who could have blamed him if he had?

Super Bowl XXV
New York Giants 20, Buffalo Bills 19
January 27, 1991
Tampa Stadium, Tampa, FL

	1	2	3	4	OT	T
Buffalo Bills	3	9	0	7		19
New York Giants	3	7	7	3		20

The silver anniversary Super Bowl was one to remember. The Bills had just trounced the Raiders, 51–3, in the AFC title game, the largest margin of victory in a championship game in fifty years. Meanwhile, the Giants with backup quarterback Jeff Hostetler reached the Super Bowl by squeaking past the 49ers on a last-second field goal in a game in which they didn't score a single touchdown. But the Giants, despite an aging defense, toppled the high-powered Buffalo Bills' K-Gun offense by physically pounding the Bills receivers every time they touched the ball. As devised by coach Bill Parcells, it was the perfect game plan, something every underdog needs to pull off a Super Bowl upset.

The NFL's big parties leading up to the big game were cancelled because of the war in the Persian Gulf. Amid these somber overtones, with guard dogs and metal detectors at the entrances to Tampa Stadium, all fans entering the gates were given tiny American flags. There was a jet fighter fly-over and Apache attack helicopters hovering around the stadium to protect the airspace. The atmosphere surrounding Super Bowl XXV was high in patriotism, highlighted by an inspiring rendition of "The Star Spangled Banner" by Whitney Houston during the pregame ceremonies. Her stirring performance was overwhelming. After she sang,

80,000 people began chanting in unison "U-S-A! U-S-A! U-S-A!" Houston's interpretation of the national anthem is the best in Super Bowl history. It clocked in at 1 minute 48 seconds, one of the longest in Super Sunday's history (yes, people keep track of such things). It was released as a single to critical acclaim, reaching No. 20 on the Billboard charts. Only a performer of Ms. Houston's immense talent could turn the national anthem into a pop hit. ABC, the network broadcasting the game, did not televise the live halftime show. Instead, they aired a special *ABC News* report updating events of the Gulf War, anchored by Peter Jennings. The halftime show was a 25-year salute to the Super Bowl, produced by Disney, and featured a performance by boy band New Kids on the Block.

With the troops watching from half a world away on Armed Forces television, the Bills controlled much of the first half and led 12–3 with a shot at putting the game away. They had just tackled New York quarterback Jeff Hostetler in the end zone for a two-point safety. Hostetler was severely shaken up, and had this been a boxing match, the ref might have stopped it. (After the game he still suffered from a severe headache.) But the courageous Giants back-up was game, and at the end of the first half he led the Giants on an 87-yard touchdown drive that got them back in it, and then he led them on a long march after the intermission.

The Giants won the game with ball control, grinding out a record 40:33 of possession time (a 2-to-1 ratio), including the longest drive in Super Bowl history (9:29) to open the third quarter. They wore out the Bills on a humid muggy night. They ran Ottis Anderson behind a smash-mouth offensive line. Anderson rushed for 102 yards and a touchdown and won the MVP award. Buffalo's halfback Thurman Thomas also rushed for over 100 yards. He gained 135 rushing yards on 15 carries and 55 more yards on five catches.

This was the first Super Bowl without a turnover. Buffalo quarterback Jim Kelly completed 18 of his 30 pass attempts for 212 yards. His counterpart, Hostetler, completed 20 of 32 passes for 222 yards and a touchdown. Despite the offensive production, the defenses got the last laugh. Scott Norwood kicked four field goals for the Bills, and Matt Bahr added three for the Giants. But the game wasn't decided until Buffalo's Scott Norwood missed a 47-yard field goal with four seconds left. A 21-yard field goal by New York's Matt Bahr midway through the final quarter provided the decisive points. Norwood, who up to that moment had enjoyed a wonderful six-year career, retired after one more season. "A great, great, great kicker was Scott Norwood," said Jason Elam, kicker for the Denver Broncos in two Super Bowl wins. "And he'll only be remembered for the one that he missed."

SEESAW BATTLES

Lead changes. Momentum swings. Offenses marching up and down the field. These thrilling games boast the most dramatic back-and-forth action.

Super Bowl XXXIV
St. Louis Rams 23, Tennessee Titans 16
January 30, 2000
Georgia Dome, Atlanta, GA

	1	2	3	4	OT	T
St. Louis Rams	3	6	7	7		23
Tennessee Titans	0	0	6	10		16

If you like drama, it's hard to beat the ending that Super Bowl XXXIV gave the stunned audience of 72,625 at the Georgia Dome, in the first Super Bowl of the new millennium. The St. Louis Rams, known as "The Greatest Show on Turf" because of a record-setting offense, built a 16–0 third-quarter lead over the Tennessee Titans. But the Rams' offense was neither great nor much of a show. They had piled up a ton of yards but just one touchdown, three times having to settle for field goals. Soon their 16-point lead would dwindle to nothing as the Titans fought their way back to make this a game—and oh, what a game!

The Tennessee quarterback Steve McNair, with great scrambles and good throws, rallied the resilient Titans to an exciting comeback, tying the game at 16–16, with 2 minutes 12 seconds left, and appeared to be sending the game into overtime. But on St. Louis' very next play, from their 27-yard line, quarterback Kurt Warner dropped back and was looking to pass to one of his speedy receivers running deep down the field. A long play such as this needs time to develop, and Warner's protection was barely good enough. The Tennessee rookie defensive end Jevon "The Freak" Kearse bull-rushed through the line and into Warner's face. Warner lofted the ball toward Isaac Bruce an instant before Kearse knocked him over. "He just got that ball off on time," said Mike Martz, the St. Louis offensive coordinator. "Just a hair later, and the play never happens."

Warner's long spiraling throw came back to earth and into the arms of wide receiver Isaac Bruce in stride for a scorching 73-yard touchdown pass. It was a moment Bruce won't soon forget. "I thought about Marcus Allen and his recollections of his 73-yard touchdown, where he reversed field, how everything went in slow motion for him," said Bruce. "The very

Kevin Dyson stretches for the end zone on the last play of Super Bowl XXXIV as Jeff Zgonina signals "no score." (AP Photo/John Gaps III)

same thing happened for me. I saw the faces in the crowd. I looked up at the Jumbotron during the play. I saw big [offensive lineman] Orlando Pace's paw in the Jumbotron. He was celebrating."

When center Mike Gruttadauria got to the end zone, he hugged Bruce and whomever else he could get his mitts on. He thought they were Super Bowl champions! Then he saw the clock. "Wait a minute," he thought. "Does that say 1 minute and 50-something seconds left? Oh, no." On the sideline, coach Dick Vermeil had a similar thought: "I said, 'I hope it's not too soon.'" It wasn't—but it was darn close.

The Rams were ahead, 23–16, but the Titans still had 1:54 to try to tie the score. The Titans weren't giving up. Starting from their 12-yard line, McNair rallied his team and drove them to the Rams' 10-yard line with six seconds left. The Super Bowl would come down to the game's final play. The Titans had no timeouts left. Tennessee quarterback Steve McNair threw a slant pass to wideout Kevin Dyson, who appeared to be heading toward a touchdown. But St. Louis linebacker Mike Jones saved the Super Bowl with a sure clutch tackle just one yard short of the end zone as the clock ran out, preventing the overtime and giving the Rams the heart-stopping victory. The loss was a tough one for the Titans, especially Bruce Matthews, the most versatile and durable lineman in NFL history. The 14-time Pro Bowler got his lone shot at a Super Bowl ring at age thirty-eight, but he and his teammates came one yard short.

This was a stalwart effort by Steve McNair in defeat. He set a Super Bowl record for rushing yards by a quarterback, gaining 64 yards on eight carries. He also completed 22 out of 36 passes for 214 yards. (In 2009, McNair, 36, was killed in a murder-suicide by his girlfriend.) Lost in the end-of-game drama was the fact that the Titans needed a Music City Miracle to get to the Super Bowl. That's the name given to Tennessee's famous, trick kickoff return play that burned the Buffalo Bills in a wild-card playoff game. After the Bills had taken a 16–15 lead on a field goal with 16 seconds left in the game, Titans tight end Frank Wycheck grabbed the kickoff and threw a lateral pass across the field to Kevin Dyson, who then waltzed 75 yards to score the winning touchdown and earn a 22–16 Tennessee victory.

The winning quarterback on this day was Kurt Warner, whose football career was a rags-to-riches story. Raised in Cedar Rapids, Iowa, he was overlooked by Division I colleges, and in order to stay in football shape during the day, he had to work nights, at one point working the graveyard shift stocking shelves at a supermarket. In 1995, he got a contract with the Iowa Barnstormers of the Arena Football League. There, he set a few league passing records and received notice from the St. Louis Rams, a struggling NFL team. The Rams under coach Dick Vermeil were abysmal in 1997, with a 5–11 record. Vermeil had been the coach of the Philadelphia Eagles team that lost to the Oakland Raiders, 27–10, in Super Bowl XV. A notorious workaholic who made a habit of sleeping in his office, he retired two years later, citing burnout. "I'm physically and mentally drained," Vermeil said. "I just have to get out of coaching for a while. It's as simple as that." Two decades later, he returned to the sidelines as coach of the St. Louis Rams.

When Vermeil signed Warner, he was shipped overseas for seasoning to play in the NFL Europe League, in the spring of 1998. There, his accurate and strong arm continued to earn attention and praise. He led the league in passing yardage and touchdowns. The Rams brought him back as a third-string quarterback. The team took a step backward, finishing the season at 4–12. The following season, Warner's life would change. First, he played well enough in training camp to earn the backup position. Then, in late August, the team's starting quarterback went down with a season-ending knee injury. In his place, the Rams turned to Warner. He went on to throw 41 touchdown passes, only the second quarterback in history to surpass 40. The Rams finished the season with a 13–3 record, one of the biggest single-year turnarounds in NFL history. The setting for the final chapter of the storybook season was the Super Bowl.

Warner went from benchwarmer to Super Bowl quarterback, in 2000. He threw for a Super Bowl-record 414 yards and two touchdowns. The touchdown to Bruce was his only completion of the fourth quarter. He was voted the Super Bowl MVP. Incredibly, the season that began with him fighting for a back-up job ended with him as the NFL MVP and the Super Bowl MVP. "Sure, I had my tough times," he said, "but you don't sit there and say, 'Wow, I was stocking groceries five years ago, and look at me now.' You don't think about it, and when you do achieve something, you know luck has nothing to do with it."

Over the ensuing decade, Warner captained two other teams to the Super Bowl, but he did not win another title. Two years later, he led the Rams to Super Bowl XXXVI but suffered a disappointing last second defeat to New England, 20–17. He threw for 365 yards and brought the Rams back from a 14-point deficit in that game. He then spent the 2004 season with the New York Giants keeping the starting quarterback seat warm for rookie Eli Manning. He joined the Arizona Cardinals in 2005, and proved he had plenty left in the tank. In 2008, he led another prolific offense to its first appearance in the big game. The Cards narrowly lost to the Pittsburgh Steelers, 27–23, in Super Bowl XLIII. On the big stage, Warner shined once again, throwing for 377 yards and three touchdowns.

Warner's teams went just 1–2 in the Super Bowl, but his performances for the St. Louis Rams and Arizona Cardinals established him as one of the top quarterbacks of his era. The top three single-game passing yards performances in Super Bowl history all belong to Warner. In Super Bowl play, he completed 83 of 132 passes for a 62.9 percent completion rate, with 1,156 passing yards (second best), six touchdowns and three interceptions, in three games. Warner enjoyed a sensational 2009 season. In Week 2, he completed 24 of 26 passes to set a single-game record for completion percentage (92.3%). After leading Arizona to the NFC West title, he enjoyed one final hurrah by passing for 379 yards and five touchdowns in a thrilling 51–45 playoff win over the Green Bay Packers.

Super Bowl XLIII
Pittsburgh Steelers 27, Arizona Cardinals 23
February 1, 2009
Raymond James Stadium, Tampa, FL

	1	2	3	4	OT	T
Pittsburgh Steelers	3	14	3	7		27
Arizona Cardinals	0	7	0	16		23

This game was a classic back-and-forth affair, with a breathtaking finish. The Arizona Cardinals mounted one of the greatest comebacks in Super Bowl history—scoring

James Harrison races 100 yards to the end zone after his interception. (AP Photo/John Bazemore)

Santonio Holmes catches the game-winning touchdown in Super Bowl XLIII. (AP Photo/Chris O'Meara)

16 consecutive points in the 4th quarter—but the Steelers answered with an improbable game-winning drive. In this wild finish, the Steelers went from chokers to champions in less than three minutes.

The Steelers led 20–7 in the fourth quarter, only to see Kurt Warner and the Cardinals rally famously to go in front 23–20 with 2:37 remaining. The game's thrilling final minutes were set up by Warner's 65-yard touchdown pass to a streaking Larry Fitzgerald, giving the Cardinals their first lead in the Super Bowl.

"You know you're two minutes away from being world champions," said Warner.

But Ben Roethlisberger had other plans. The Pittsburgh QB (20-for-31, 256 yards) delivered a classic two-minute drive. He went 6-for-8 for 83 yards, the key play a 40-yard pass to Santonio Holmes, giving the Steelers a first down at the 6-yard line. Two plays later, Big Ben found Holmes in the corner of the end zone with 35 seconds left, giving Pittsburgh its second Super Bowl title in four seasons.

Holmes' catch was a thing of beauty. With three Cardinals defenders draping over him, Holmes leapt to snare the ball with both arms stretched fully above his head in the back right corner of the end zone, his toes barely dragging inbounds.

Replays confirmed the call.

"I knew it was a touchdown 100 percent," Holmes said. "My feet never left the ground. All I did was stood up on my toes and extend my hands."

It was a wild ending to a game of improbable swings. The stunning swings overshadowed Pittsburgh linebacker James Harrison's record 100-yard interception return for a touchdown to end the first half. In a memorable scene, Harrison collapsed in the end zone and spent several minutes regaining his breath as his teammates celebrated. It was the longest play in Super Bowl history (since surpassed on a 108-yard kickoff return by Baltimore's Jacoby Jones in Super Bowl XLVII), increasing the Steelers' lead to 17–7 at halftime.

Two plays—one at the end of each half—defined this battle, preventing the upset-minded Cardinals from authoring a Cinderella story against the Steelers.

Harrison's play saved the lead, and Holmes won it all with an incredibly athletic grab on a pinpoint toss from Roethlisberger. Holmes, the MVP, caught 9 passes for 131 yards and that winning touchdown.

Pittsburgh now had six Super Bowl titles and a crowded trophy case, but as team owner Dan Rooney said, "We'll make room for this one."

Super Bowl XLV
Green Bay Packers 31, Pittsburgh Steelers 25
February 6, 2011
Cowboys Stadium, Arlington, TX

	1	2	3	4	OT	T
Pittsburgh Steelers	0	10	7	8		25
Green Bay Packers	14	7	0	10		31

Counterprogramming efforts are not limited to television; for Super Bowl XLV in 2011, a radio station in Green Bay, Wisconsin, announced it would counterprogram the game with dead air, since the hometown Packers were playing in the game! So for shame on the Cheese Head who missed Aaron Rodgers cap off a tremendous postseason with an

James Harrison closes in just as Aaron Rodgers releases a pass in Super Bowl XLV. (AP Photo/Paul Sancya)

incredible performance in the biggest game of his career. Rodgers completed 24 of 39 passes for 304 yards and three touchdowns, leading the franchise to its fifth Super Bowl title.

The Packers dominated most of the first half of Super Bowl XLV, jumping out to a 21–3 lead before Pittsburgh cut it down to 21–10 at halftime. The Steelers scored in the third quarter to pull even closer, 21–17. Then, on the first play of the fourth quarter, with coach Mike Tomlin's team driving for perhaps its first lead of the game, Steelers' running back Rashard Mendenhall had the ball knocked out of his hands by linebacker Clay Matthews's jarring hit. The Packers recovered, and Rodgers soon hit wide receiver Greg Jennings in the end zone for a 28–17 lead.

But the resilient Steelers were far from done. They pulled within 28–25 midway through the fourth quarter with wide receiver Mike Wallace's 25-yard touchdown reception from quarterback Ben Roethlisberger and a two-point conversion. Then the Packers answered with Mason Crosby's 23-yard field goal with 2:07 remaining. Now the Packers tried to hold on for dear life, and prevent the Steelers from scoring on their final drive of the game. Roethlisberger, it turned out, had no more comebacks left in him like the one he staged to win the Super Bowl against Arizona two years earlier. Three passes in the final minute fell incomplete. The Packers were champions again for the first time since 1996, when Brett Favre was the quarterback. Aaron Rodgers was named Super Bowl MVP. The baton had officially been passed.

Nick Collins (36) celebrates with Clay Matthews after returning a Ben Roethlisberger interception for a touchdown. (AP Photo/Paul Sancya)

Super Bowl XLVII
Baltimore Ravens 34, San Francisco 49ers 31
February 3, 2013
Mercedes-Benz Superdome, New Orleans, LA

	1	2	3	4	OT	T
Baltimore Ravens	7	14	7	6		34
San Francisco 49ers	3	3	17	8		31

This game featured two young quarterbacks with polar-opposite styles, a thirty-four-minute power outage, one of the most exciting second halves ever, and a spectacular final stretch. It also featured a faceoff between two head coaches who are brothers.

Three weeks earlier, San Francisco 49ers quarterback Colin Kaepernick made his first postseason start, a 45–31 win over the Packers, and set the NFL single-game record for most rushing yards by a quarterback, 181, breaking Michael Vick's record of 173 in a 2002 regular season game. Meanwhile, Joe Flacco, the classic pocket passer for the Baltimore Ravens, became the first quarterback to defeat both Peyton Manning (Broncos) and Tom Brady (Patriots) in the same postseason.

The Ravens opened Super Bowl XLVII in thrilling fashion as their first drive of the game ended with a touchdown pass from Super Bowl MVP Joe Flacco to wide receiver Anquan Boldin. Flacco threw two 2nd quarter touchdown passes as Baltimore took a 21–6 lead into halftime. After halftime, the Ravens received the kickoff from the 49ers, and Jacoby Jones returned the kickoff for a record setting 108-yard touchdown. Soon after Jones' score, the stadium lights went out.

The restoration of power re-energized the 49ers. They regrouped, regained their composure, and outscored the Ravens 23–3 over a span of 12:23 (including 17 straight points during a four-minute stretch in the third quarter) to cut the lead to 31–29 with just under 10 minutes left in the game. The Ravens responded with another field goal, but you just knew this would be one of those Super Bowls that came down to the very end.

The Niners had a final chance to take the lead late in the game. Trailing 34–29, they drove to the Baltimore 5-yard line with 2 minutes left and a chance to win the franchise's sixth Super Bowl. They made a thrilling charge down the stretch only to come up just short in the end. Four incomplete passes by Kaepernick—all targeted to Michael Crabtree ended the 49ers' bid. The Ravens ran the clock down to four seconds and took an intentional safety, and the game was over. The Ravens won their second Super Bowl since the franchise moved from Cleveland to Baltimore. Flacco completed 22 of 33 passes for 287 yards and three touchdowns.

Kaepernick, making just his tenth career NFL start, continued to impress with his arm and legs. He scrambled seven times for 62 yards and one touchdown. He also completed 16 of 28 passes for 302 yards, one touchdown, and one interception. The interception was by Ed Reed, who finally earned his first Super Bowl ring. Reed's interception was his ninth career postseason interception, tying the NFL record. This loss was a first for the San Francisco 49ers franchise in six Super Bowl appearances. Kaepernick's interception was the first in Super

MVP Joe Flacco and Ray Lewis celebrate the Ravens win over the 49ers in Super Bowl XLVII. (AP Photo/Matt Slocum)

Bowl play for a quarterback wearing a San Francisco 49ers uniform. Joe Montana and Steve Young never threw an interception in the big game.

Ray Lewis, thirty-seven, went out in style, winning his second Super Bowl ring twelve years after the first, when he was MVP of the game against the Giants. He finished the game against the 49ers with seven tackles, including two on the 49ers final drive, to preserve the win. Lewis retired after the game. "I wanted to see [your] faces when that confetti came out of the sky," he told his teammates during the post-game celebration. "And now I get to ride into the sunset with my second ring."

Linebacker Ray Lewis retired after winning his second championship ring with the Ravens. (Wikimedia Commons/Jay Baker, MarylandGovPics, Maryland State Archives)

"THE HARBAUGH BOWL"

Super Bowl XLVII has also been dubbed "The Harbaugh Bowl" as it pit brother against brother. Jim Harbaugh was the 49ers' coach; his brother, John, coached the Ravens. It was the first time brothers opposed each other in the Super Bowl as coaches. The Ravens' defense gave up 468 yards of offense and 31 points to the 49ers. "It wasn't perfect, it wasn't pretty," John Harbaugh said. "But it was us."

Moments after John's Ravens claimed a narrow 34–31 victory over younger brother Jim's 49ers, the elder Harbaugh found himself in an interesting spot. John, who was a year older than Jim, met his little brother at midfield as the confetti was falling for his team. "I love you," John said. "Good job."

BEAT DOWNS

Call it a mismatch, no contest, one-sided, lopsided, or a team's very bad day; the result of these games were never in doubt.

Super Bowl XX
Chicago Bears 46, New England Patriots 10
January 26, 1986
Superdome, New Orleans, LA

	1	2	3	4	OT	T
Chicago Bears	13	10	21	2		46
New England Patriots	3	0	0	7		10

The Bears, who had won both of their playoff games by shut-outs, continued to play brilliant defense, winning their first Super Bowl by 36 points, the biggest blowout in Super Bowl history at the time.

This was no contest. Only one of New England's first 16 plays gained positive yardage. The Patriots didn't pick up a first down until late in the second quarter. As the game went on, the Bears defense kept getting meaner and more suffocating. When it was over, Chicago defenders had set a record for fewest rushing yards allowed (seven—that's *seven*—for the whole game), and 123 total yards (minus-19 at halftime), and recorded seven quarterback sacks. Just how bad was it? Said New England's offensive lineman Ron Wooten: "Before the end, it kind of felt like we were the team that the Globetrotters play all the time."

The pregame hype was more entertaining than the game. Coach Mike Ditka's Bears came into the week with a swagger unmatched in the history of the Super Bowl. They had recorded and released a music video titled "Super Bowl Shuffle," but they were able to back up all that bravado with one of the most intimidating defenses of all time.

Chicago's innovative "46 Defense" had been the hot topic all season as "Da Bears" rolled to a 15–1 record. Never in the history of football had a defense so intimidated opposing quarterbacks. This unique scheme, conceived by Chicago defensive coordinator Buddy Ryan, was committed to an all-out pass rush that was designed to confuse opposing offensive linemen. The genius of the 46 Defense was how it created and disguised the pressure.

This may have been the best blitzing team of all time. The front line was loaded with phenomenal pass-rushing talent, including Hall of Famers right defensive end Richard Dent (the game's MVP with 1½ sacks, three other tackles, two forced fumbles, one pass deflection), left defensive end Dan Hampton (three tackles, one sack, one fumble recovery), and hard-charging middle linebacker Mike Singletary (1½ tackles, two fumble recoveries).

On offense, the Bears' plucky quarterback, Jim McMahon, passed for 256 yards and ran for a pair of touchdowns (all while wearing a homemade headband with "Rozelle" written on it) and Kevin Butler kicked three field goals.

Mercifully, Up With People exited the Super Bowl stage for good with their Super Bowl XX halftime performance titled, "Beat of the Future." After four times headlining, the most of any act in the game's history, the Uppies' cheery message of global understanding through music was finally silenced.

"Some say the 46 (defense) is just an eight-man front. That's like saying Marilyn Monroe is just a girl."—Buddy Ryan

---

Mike Ditka is carried off the field after the Bears trounced the Patriots in Super Bowl XX. (AP Photo/ Phil Sandlin)

IS YOUR REFRIGERATOR RUNNING?

Chicago's 308-pound defensive tackle was so big he was nicknamed the "Refrigerator." Because of his size, strength, and uncanny quickness and agility, the Bears sometimes used him in their goal-line offense. In Super Bowl XX, the Fridge was handed the ball on New England's one-yard line. He knocked the Patriots defenders sideways and rumbled into the end zone! With that, Perry recorded more career Super Bowl touchdowns—one—than team-mate Walter Payton, who ranks second on the NFL's all-time career rushing list.

Not only was Perry the biggest ball carrier ever to score in a Super Bowl, his championship ring is the largest ever—size 25, compared to 10 or 12, the size for an average adult male.

Super Bowl XLVIII
Seattle Seahawks 43, Denver Broncos 8
February 2, 2014
MetLife Stadium, East Rutherford, NJ

	1	2	3	4	OT	T
Seattle Seahawks	8	14	14	7		43
Denver Broncos	0	0	8	0		8

The Seattle Seahawks jumped out to the fastest lead in Super Bowl history on a safety 12 seconds into the game and they never looked back. Seattle absolutely dominated from start to finish. They took a 36–0 advantage before allowing Denver's first score on the final play of the third quarter, and then put up another score for good measure. The Seattle defense stonewalled what had been the most prolific scoring offense in NFL history. The Denver Bronco's high-flying offense, which scored more points than any team ever had in the regular season, mustered only 279 yards, one touchdown, and eight points against the swarming Seattle defense, known as the "Legion of Boom."

The Broncos had the most explosive offense in the NFL, leading the league with 606 points scored—the highest total in NFL history. Theirs was a quick-striking attack, as they scored points on their opening possession in eight straight games leading into the playoffs and a ninth time against the San Diego Chargers in the divisional playoff game. In only five out of 18 games leading into the Super Bowl did the Broncos score fewer than 30 points; with 20 points being the season low. Commanding the offense was the quarterback Peyton Manning, now in his second year with Denver following a successful 14-year stint in Indianapolis. Manning posted one of the best seasons of any quarterback in NFL his-

tory, leading the league in completions, attempts, yards, and touchdown passes. His 5,477 passing yards and 55 touchdown passes both set new NFL records.

Peyton Manning and the Broncos had mile-high hopes for this game, which was Denver's first Super Bowl appearance in 15 years. However, the game quickly turned into a rocky experience for the team from Colorado. Manning threw two interceptions in the first half. The Seahawks linebacker Malcolm Smith, who returned one of Manning's errant throws 69 yards for a touchdown, recovered a fumble and made nine tackles, was named the game's MVP. Denver's crushing defeat marked the fifth time the Broncos have lost a Super Bowl, the most in NFL history. Denver's overall record in the Super Bowl now stands at two wins and five losses. For his part, Manning has been to three Super Bowls—two with the Indianapolis Colts, and one with Denver—with but only one victory to show for it. Fair or not, Manning's penchant for failure in the biggest games prompts discussion about his legacy. "I don't know if you ever get over [losing]," he said. "To finish this way is very disappointing. It's not an easy pill to swallow, but we have to."

Denver coach John Fox lost in the Super Bowl for a second time. He is the sixth coach to lead two teams to the Super Bowl (Don Shula, Dick Vermeil, Bill Parcells, Mike Holmgren, and Dan Reeves are the others, although only Reeves and Fox are winless.) His Carolina Panthers had come up short against the New England Patriots in Super Bowl XXXVIII, losing 32–29 on a last-second field goal by Adam Vinatieri. This time, the complete domination displayed by Seattle against Fox's Broncos caught pretty much everyone off-guard.

The Seattle quarterback, Russell Wilson, 25, delivered a pair of touchdown passes in the lopsided victory, making him

Denver's Knowshon Moreno tries to scoop up the loose ball in the end zone after the snap sailed past Peyton Manning. Cliff Avril (56) closes in for the safety. (AP Photo/Paul Sancya)

Russell Wilson scampers away from Mike Adams during second half action of Super Bowl XLVIII. (AP Photo/Chris O'Meara)

just the fourth quarterback to win a Super Bowl in his second season. "Sometimes I think I'm made for these situations," he said. "I just try to be prepared. When you're prepared, you're never scared. You just go. You trust your teammates, you trust the guys you have around you, you trust the preparation, you trust that the ball's going to bounce your way."

Selected by Seattle in the third round of the 2012 NFL draft, Wilson had a strong college career at Wisconsin, but he was widely considered too small (at 5'11" and 206 pounds) to be an NFL quarterback. Wilson immediately proved the doubters wrong, grabbing the starting job from the very first game of the season and winning fans with his speedy running and strong arm. The Seahawks lost in the second round of the playoffs that year, but Wilson was named the NFL's Rookie of the Year. The next year he took the Seahawks all the way to victory in Super Bowl XLVIII.

The 2014 season offered Wilson and the Seahawks the opportunity to earn a rare achievement: a second straight Super Bowl championship. At Super Bowl XLIX, Wilson and the Seahawks faced off against the New England Patriots, a proven football dynasty hungry for its first championship in ten years. After nearly four full quarters of close, back and forth play, Wilson wound up with one last late game opportunity to secure the win for Seattle. On a crucial goal line play, however, Wilson threw a fatal interception that ensured a Patriot victory and prevented the Seahawks from becoming two-time champions. Wilson said the hardest thing about the loss was walking off the field, knowing he'd let the fans down. "I'm the one that threw the pass, but I know I'll throw another one," Wilson said. "And hopefully I'll be remembered for something different."

Grammy-nominated pop star Katy Perry and her dancing costumed sharks also took a bite out of the history books

Katy Perry performing during the Super Bowl XLIX halftime extravaganza. Some thought the dancing sharks stole the show. (Wikimedia Commons/Huntley Paton)

with a record audience for the performer's halftime show. Perry's colorful pyrotechnic extravaganza attracted 118.5 million viewers to watch her ride in on a giant animatronic lion, making it the most watched halftime show in the Super Bowl's 49-year history. "Super Bowl XLIX delivered for all of our partners, proving once again that the Super Bowl is the most dominant and consistent property on television," said Mark Lazarus, chairman of NBC Sports.

FOURTH QUARTER

POWER PLAYS AND MIND GAMES

PLAYS THAT TURN THE GAME

These plays changed the course of Super Bowl history.

John Riggins' Fourth Down Run
Super Bowl XVII
Washington Redskins 27, Miami Dolphins 17
January 30, 1983
Rose Bowl, Pasadena, CA

	1	2	3	4	OT	T
Miami Dolphins	7	10	0	0		17
Washington Redskins	0	10	3	14		27

A 6'2", 240-pound rusher known as "The Diesel," Redskins' fullback John Riggins could run down the field like a truck. He really made his mark in Super Bowl XVII. The Redskins had lost just one game all season. But the 'Skins trailed by four points with ten minutes remaining, and were facing a

tough decision: 4th-down-and-1 at the Miami 43-yard line. It was too far for a field goal, but why punt when down late? That was when coach Joe Gibbs called the play forever emblazoned in Redskins' lore as "70-chip."

The Redskins went to their horse. Riggins took a handoff, ran left, broke a tackle attempt by Don McNeal, and busted a 43-yard touchdown run—busting open the game. Washington added another touchdown to clinch its first Super Bowl victory, beginning their run of four Super Bowls and three rings in twelve years.

Washington's offensive line, affectionately called "the Hogs," battered the Dolphins' "Killer B's" defense all game, allowing Riggins to run untouched through the first line of defense. A good portion of rushing yardage was directed toward the left side of the line of scrimmage, to take advantage of the punishing blocking force leveled by left guard Russ Grimm and left tackle Joe Jacoby, who teamed to perfect the Redskins' "counter trey" running play. Riggins ran for 166 yards on 38 carries, and was named the game's MVP. No other back had ever run for 100 yards or more in four straight playoff games. No other back had gained more than 158 yards in a Super Bowl.

John Riggins rushed for a record 166 yards in Super Bowl XVII. (AP Photo)

Pittsburgh Gets One for the Thumb
Super Bowl XL
Pittsburgh Steelers 21, Seattle Seahawks 10
February 5, 2006
Ford Field, Detroit, MI

	1	2	3	4	OT	T
Seattle Seahawks	3	0	7	0		10
Pittsburgh Steelers	0	7	7	7		21

Ben Roethlisberger's play at quarterback brought the Pittsburgh Steelers to Super Bowl XL, but it was a pass from one wide receiver to another that was the signature moment of this supremely controversial championship game. Antwaan Randle El threw the first touchdown pass by a wide receiver in Super Bowl history, connecting with Hines Ward on a 43-yard scoring strike to clinch Pittsburgh's 21–10 win over the hard-luck Seattle Seahawks. The highlight play was an end-around-reverse toss pass, and Randle El lofted a beautiful spiraling pass to a wide-open Ward, who took it into the end zone for the Steelers score that finally clinched Pittsburgh's long wait for the franchise's fifth Super Bowl triumph.

At twenty-three, Roethlisberger became the youngest quarterback to start and win a Super Bowl, though he showed every bit of his youth and inexperience. Big Ben completed just 9 of 21 passes for 123 yards and two interceptions. His 22.6 passer rating was the lowest in Super Bowl history by a winning quarterback. He threw two interceptions in the red zone, the second of which was returned for a Super Bowl-record 76 yards by Seattle's Kelly Herndon. Roethlisberger, however, did convert eight third downs in the game, and showed off his improvisational skills in the second quarter,

Steelers wide receiver Antwaan Randle El uncorks a 43-yard touchdown pass to Hines Ward in Super Bowl XL. (AP Photo/David J. Phillip)

completing a 37-yard pass to Hines Ward on a third-and-28 play that set up the Steelers' first touchdown, a 1-yard dive by Big Ben, giving Pittsburgh a 7–3 halftime lead.

The Rolling Stones performed during intermission. Mick Jagger shouted: "This one we could have done for Super Bowl I," as Keith Richards and the boys began to strum the opening riff to "Satisfaction." In the wake of Janet Jackson's "wardrobe malfunction," ABC and the NFL insisted on a five-second live delay and censored sexually explicit lyrics (about a male rooster) to the song "Rough Justice" by briefly turning off Jagger's microphone, which most definitely ruffled his feathers.

The Steelers received the second half kickoff, and just two plays later, running back Willie Parker broke through for a 75-yard touchdown run, giving Pittsburgh the lead, 14–3, and setting a record for the longest run in Super Bowl history, besting Marcus Allen's memorable Super Bowl XVIII run by one yard. The Seahawks scored a touchdown to close the gap, 14–10, and had the ball with 9:06 to play, driving for a go-ahead touchdown. That's when Pittsburgh defensive back Ike Taylor intercepted a Hasselbeck pass at the 5-yard line and returned it 24 yards. A questionable penalty on Hasselbeck for blocking below the waist added another 15 yards to the return, and insult to injury. Three plays later, looking to capitalize, coach Bill Cowher made a bold call. "When we called it, my eyes lit up and I had to try to not give it away," Randle El said.

On a first-and-10, Roethlisberger pitched the ball to running back Willie Parker, who handed the ball back to Randle El on a reverse from the Steelers 43-yard line. Randle El was a college quarterback at Indiana who switched to wide receiver in the NFL. Randle El rolled to his right, suddenly halted his run, and fired a bullet to Hines Ward, wide open

and streaking downfield. Ward corralled the ball and leaped into the end zone on a 43-yard trick play for a touchdown, sending the thousands of Terrible Towel-waving Steelers fans into frenzy. Ward caught five passes for 123 yards and one touchdown, while also rushing for 18 more, and was named the Super Bowl MVP.

The Super Bowl victory was the Steelers' fifth ring—"one for the thumb"—and first title since their glory days of the Seventies. It was also a long time coming for coach Bill Cowher, who promised owner Dan Rooney when he was hired in 1992 that the Vince Lombardi Trophy would come back to Pittsburgh. It took fourteen years, but it was well worth the wait. When Cowher, who bitterly lost Super Bowl XXX to the Cowboys, finally got his hands on the trophy, he promptly handed it to Rooney, saying, "I've been waiting a long time to do this. This is yours, man." It was also a long wait for Steeler running back Jerome "The Bus" Bettis, in his tenth and final year with the Black and Gold. Bettis at last got his Super Bowl ring in his hometown of Detroit. "I'm a champion. I think the Bus' last stop is here in Detroit," said Bettis, who ran for 43 yards on 14 carries.

The Helmet Catch
Super Bowl XLII
New York Giants 17, New England Patriots 14
February 3, 2008
University of Phoenix Stadium, Glendale, AZ

	1	2	3	4	OT	T
New York Giants	3	0	0	14		17
New England Patriots	0	7	0	7		14

This Super Bowl upset is celebrated for the most amazing, game-changing play in the title game's history. The New York Giants were trailing the undefeated New England Patriots by four points with the clock ticking down in the fourth quarter. Facing a crucial third down and 5 situation, from their 44-yard line, Giants quarterback Eli Manning called a play in the huddle. "The play call was 62 Max Y Sail Union," said David Tyree, primarily a special teams player and back-up receiver. "I'm running a post over the top. Steve Smith's running an out cut, a deep out inside, and you've got some in-breaking routes with Amani [Toomer] and Plaxico [Burress]." Tyree got the right coverage to come open on the post. But the pocket collapsed quickly on quarterback Eli Manning, who escaped the grasp of three defenders to extend the play. Manning was nearly sacked, but broke free and heaved a prayer downfield toward the relatively unknown Tyree, who was blanketed by Patriots star safety Rodney Harrison. "It was just kind of like playing backyard football, living in the moment," Tyree said. "Eli's doing his best impression of Michael Vick or something and playing way above the Xs and Os."

So was Tyree, who leaped for the jump ball against Harrison in the middle of the field and briefly pinned it against his helmet with his right hand before securing the ball with his left as he and Harrison crashed to the ground. Tyree somehow held on for a spectacular 32-yard catch and a critical first down to extend the Giants' drive. Four plays later, Manning hit Plaxico Burress for a 13-yard touchdown. The Patriots' last-gasp drive fell short and the Giants were champions with a 17–14 win. Tyree had no idea just how incredible his catch was until he got back to the hotel that night and saw a replay on television. "It stunned me," Tyree said. "For me, it brings on a real sense of humility. I knew my role. I knew what I was capable of as a player and a wide receiver. But obviously, that really exceeds anybody's expectations as far as the timing of the play. I always see it as a gift from God."

Of course, everyone remembers "The Helmet Catch." (It won the ESPY award for Best Play of 2008. While accepting the award, Manning jokingly thanked his offensive line "for giving me zero pass protection.") Manning to Tyree third-and-five is probably the single greatest play in Super Bowl history. Its degree of difficulty is staggering, and it occurred at a decisive moment in the game. It's often forgotten Tyree had also scored a go-ahead touchdown early in the fourth quarter, only for the Patriots to regain the lead. Tyree had a total of three catches for the game, which nearly outdid his four catches during the entire regular season. Tyree never made another NFL catch after "The Helmet Catch." After missing the 2008 season because of injuries, the Giants cut him. He appeared in 10 games with the Baltimore Ravens in 2009, mostly on special teams, and signed a one-day contract to retire a Giant in 2010. Tyree has moved on, but still holds a special place in Super Bowl lore. "There are going to be many people who have played or will continue to play that will have much more decorated careers," Tyree said. "But by the grace of God—and I say that genuinely—I get a chance to be remembered as a part of the game."

DECISIONS THAT TURN THE GAME

These decisions changed the course of Super Bowl history.

The Trick Kick
Super Bowl XLIV
New Orleans Saints 31, Indianapolis Colts 17
February 10, 2007
Sun Life Stadium, Miami, FL

	1	2	3	4	OT	T
New Orleans Saints	0	6	10	15		31
Indianapolis Colts	10	0	7	0		17

The Who were performing a rock 'n' roll halftime show when New Orleans Saints coach Sean Payton walked through his team's dressing room and stopped at Thomas Morstead's locker to deliver an important message. "We're doing it," the coach said. Morstead, the Saints' punter and kickoff specialist, knew exactly what his coach meant. Payton was planning an onside kick, a play the team called Ambush. It was a play the rookie kicker had been practicing less than two weeks, a squib kick he tried to "bend like Beckham." It was a gutsy call. "I wasn't too worried," Morstead said. "Just terrified."

With the Saints trailing 10–6 at halftime, and the Colts set to receive the second half kickoff, Payton was reluctant to give Peyton Manning and the Colts the ball to start the third quarter. So he decided to call for an onside kick in the hopes of gaining momentum in a close contest. "We were going to be aggressive," Payton explained. Aggressive play calling was nothing out of the ordinary for the Saints coach. "He plays to win the game," linebacker Scott Fujita said. "I knew we were going to get it."

When the teams returned to the playing field for warm-ups, Morstead made sure to practice one deep kickoff, just to make sure the Colts wouldn't suspect anything was up. Then he teed it up for real, and squibbed a kick 15 yards toward the left sideline. The ball bounced along the ground, headed toward Indy's Hank Baskett. Suddenly, the pigskin took a quirky hop. The ball ricocheted off Baskett's chest, setting off a mad scramble that took more than a minute to sort out. Finally, after a long scrum, the officials called New Orleans ball. Chris Reis recovered for the Saints. "We felt like the momentum was on our side," said Saints quarterback Drew Brees. The Saints' offense responded with their first touchdown of the game, six plays and 58 yards later, for the go-ahead score.

The Who had finished singing "Won't Get Fooled Again," and a few minutes later, the Colts were fooled. The successful onside kick had given the Saints the edge they needed. "We knew we were going to call it at some point," Payton said. "At halftime I just told them, 'Hey, we're going to open up the second half with this. It's going to be a great play.'"

Onside kicks are expected at the end of the game when the trailing team is running out of time. Morstead, known more for his punting, had never attempted an onside kick in his NFL career. Had the kick failed, it would have put the Saints in a tough spot, giving Peyton Manning and the Colts the ball with a short field. But New Orleans stunned the Indianapolis Colts and the millions of people watching the game by recovering the kickoff to start the second half of Super Bowl XLIV, in Miami.

MVP Drew Brees holds up his son after the Saints beat the Colts, 31–17 in Super Bowl XLIV. (AP Photo/Eric Gay)

No team in Super Bowl history had ever attempted such a daring play so early in a Super Bowl game. Payton made the right call, as it turned out. Thanks to his bravado, the Saints won the first Super Bowl title in franchise history, beating Peyton Manning and the Indianapolis Colts, 31–17.

Payton drew praise from President Barack Obama at the White House ceremony for the first-time champions. "I make some tough decisions every day, but I've never decided on an onside kick in the second half of the Super Bowl. That took some guts," Obama said.

For Pete's Sake, Coach!
Super Bowl XLIX
New England Patriots 28, Seattle Seahawks 24
February 1, 2015
University of Phoenix Stadium, Glendale, AZ

	1	2	3	4	OT	T
New England Patriots	0	14	0	14		28
Seattle Seahawks	0	14	10	0		24

Pete Carroll, the Seattle Seahawks coach, was one yard away from winning the Super Bowl. Though his team trailed the New England Patriots by four points with less than thirty seconds left to play in Super Bowl XLIX, the Seahawks had the ball at the Patriots' 1-yard line. But instead of giving the ball to bruising halfback Marshawn Lynch, Carroll called a pass play instead. The decision famously backfired. The pass thrown by Seahawks quarterback Russell Wilson was intercepted, and a stunned Seattle team fell to New England, 28–24.

"Man, what were they thinking?" the Patriots cornerback Brandon Browner said. The Seahawks had a second-and-goal with two valuable timeouts at their disposal. Two plays earlier, the Patriots had seen the ghost of David Tyree when Jermaine Kearse made an acrobatic 33-yard juggling catch on his back at the Patriots' 5-yard line with a defender draped all over him. Then on first down Marshawn Lynch ran the ball to the doorstep of the goal line. Was there anybody inside University of Phoenix Stadium, or watching on television, or in the Patriots huddle, or on the Seahawks sideline that didn't think Lynch would get the ball? Lynch, the 215-pound bruiser known as Beast Mode, already had 102 rushing yards and the Patriots defense was wearing down from absorbing all his punishment. During the season, in this very same situation, no team had yet found a way to stop Lynch. Yet instead of remaining grounded, Carroll chose to throw.

New England coach Bill Belichick was clearly anticipating the run. His Patriots lined up with an eight-man front and three cornerbacks. But Carroll had already made the decision to pass the ball. He sent three wide receivers into the game. "Make sure we throw it here," Carroll told his coaches and his quarterback as they decided on what play to call, adding, "We'll run on third and fourth down." Those two downs now belong in an alternate universe, one where Carroll keeps his senses and hands the ball to Lynch, the two-legged rushing monster and the team's best player. In a puzzling move, Pete Carroll didn't give Lynch even one shot to gain that final yard, to finish off the reeling Patriots. "We didn't want to waste a running play there," Carroll said.

So with three opportunities to place the football in the sure hands of Marshawn Lynch and let him try to bull his way those final 36 inches, Carroll made the inexplicable deci-

Jermaine Kearse makes an amazing catch late in Super Bowl XLIX. (AP Photo/David J. Phillip)

sion to go a different way. He called on his quarterback Russell Wilson to throw a slant pass over the middle to Ricardo Lockette. The call backfired, as undrafted rookie cornerback Malcolm Butler jumped in front of Lockette and intercepted Wilson's pass at the one-yard line to seal the victory for the Patriots, snuffing out the Seahawks season. "How do you throw the ball when you've got Marshawn Lynch," asked Seahawks cornerback Tharold Simon. "People were screaming and hollering, 'Why not run the ball?' and stuff like that. When you've got Beast Mode, why not run the ball three times down there?"

Jermaine Kearse was one unexplainably bad play call away from being a Super Bowl hero. The Seattle wide receiver had just made an incredible 33-yard catch off a tip by New England's Malcolm Butler, who, ironically, would be the game's hero minutes later. Seahawks quarterback Russell Wilson showcased his trademark touch with a high-arcing deep throw down the sideline. Butler, the first-year cornerback, did what he could to break up the deep pass, and just got his fingertips on it. Yet Kearse had the presence of mind to stay with the play, keeping his eyes fixed on the ball after Butler's deflection, and tipping it to himself several times with his back on the turf before finally grasping it. Kearse's bobbling catch while he lay on the ground set up the Seahawks with a first-and-goal, trailing 28–24. Unfortunately for the Seahawks, two plays later, Wilson threw an interception near the goal line to essentially end the game—and ironically Butler, an undrafted free agent, was the one who came up with the game-sealing pick.

The Patriots rookie defensive back Malcolm Butler, not long ago employed at Popeye's, recognized the pass route from his hours studying the opposition game film. Wilson threw a bullet. Just as he released the pass, Butler veered in front of Lockette to intercept Wilson's pass. Butler made a terrific play jumping the route and outmaneuvering Lockette for the ball. "I thought it was going to be a touchdown when I threw it. I thought it was game over," Wilson said. "The guy just barely cut in front of him. We had a chance to make the play. The guy made a great play. One inch too far."

"Why wouldn't you give it to Beast Mode?" New England linebacker Jamie Collins asked. That was the question on the minds of 70,288 people inside University of Phoenix Stadium, and why the 70 million viewers at home were scratching their heads. "I think all of us are surprised," Seahawks receiver Doug Baldwin said. Carroll had outsmarted himself. "My fault totally," said the coach, explaining that because the Patriots' defensive formation clogged the middle, it seemed prudent to throw the ball in that situation. "That's a play that's supposed to work. I hate that we have to live with that."

Carroll made the worst play call you'll ever see at the worst time possible. He will never be able to explain his horrific decision to anyone's satisfaction. It rendered Kearse's catch an interesting footnote, nothing more. Of course, give credit to Butler, who made a title-saving play for the ages. Of course, credit Tom Brady, four Super Bowl titles to his credit, and Bill Belichick, whose own baffling decision to keep the clock running at the end will be forgotten. Credit the Pats; they made a miraculous goal line stand to transform a sure defeat into an inspiring victory. After two disappointing Super Bowl failures against the New York Giants, they were the champs again. Tom Brady, Super Bowl MVP—for a third time—with four touchdowns (although he had two costly interceptions), threw his arms up in the air on the bench. The Patriots had won their fourth title of the Brady-Belichick era.

Strong safety Malcolm Butler made a goal line interception that sealed the win for the New England Patriots. (AP Photo/David J. Phillip)

Even a comprehensive book such as this one can't include all the thrilling games, spectacular plays, inspiring players, and boneheaded blunders of the past forty-nine years that make the Super Bowl a spectacle that people talk about for years afterward.

No book would be complete without a mention of Super Bowl XLI, when the Indianapolis Colts defeated the Chicago Bears, 29-17, on February 4, 2007. This game is notable as Peyton Manning's one Super Bowl title in three tries, to date. The Colts quarterback was named the game's MVP, completing 25 of 38 passes for 247 yards and one touchdown, a 53-yard toss to Reggie Wayne. The Colts coach Tony Dungy became the first American-American head coach to win a Super Bowl. Dungy has two Super Bowl rings: one as a defensive back with the Steelers in 1979, and one as the Colts' coach in 2007. He joined Mike Ditka and Tom Flores as the only men to win Super Bowl rings as both a player and head coach. The musical performance by Prince was a classic; perhaps the best of all the halftime shows. Wielding a purple guitar in the shape of his unpronounceable symbol, the highlight is a face-melting guitar solo during "Let's Go Crazy" followed by his biggest hit, "Purple Rain"—which he performed in a driving rainstorm.

Another great game with stirring performances occurred in Super Bowl XXXI, when the Green Bay Packers defeated the New England Patriots, 35-21, on January 26, 1997. This was truly a seesaw battle. On Green Bay's second play of the game, the Packers quarterback Brett Favre—a three-time league MVP who also won just one Super Bowl—fired a 54-yard bomb to Andre Rison for a touchdown. Later in the game, he threw an 81-yard touchdown pass to Antonio Freeman (then a Super Bowl record). He also ran for a touchdown. Another Green Bay star of the game was defensive lineman Reggie White, who set a Super Bowl record with three sacks, including back-to-back takedowns in the third quarter. (Arizona's Darnell Dockett equaled White's sack record in Super Bowl XLIII). But the biggest star of the game was Desmond Howard, the former Heisman Trophy winner from the University of Michigan. There have been ten kickoff return touchdowns in Super Bowl history, but only one kick returner has been the Super Bowl most valuable player: Desmond Howard. And in doing so he is the fourth player to win both the Heisman Trophy and Super Bowl MVP: Roger Staubach, Jim Plunkett, and Marcus Allen are the others. Howard was the difference maker in the game by setting Super Bowl records for kickoff return yards (154), punt return yards (90), and all-purpose return yardage (244). Favre's sharp passing and White's defensive prowess propelled the Packers to another Super Bowl appearance in 1998, but the Packers lost to the Denver Broncos. Favre completed 39 of 69 passes for 502 yards and five touchdowns (plus one rushing) in two Super Bowl games.

One of the worst Super Bowl performances ever by a quarterback belongs to Rich Gannon, when the Oakland Raiders were trounced by the Tampa Bay Buccaneers, 48-21, in Super Bowl XXXVII, on January 26, 2003. In the biggest game of his career, Gannon had a historically catastrophic performance, throwing a Super Bowl-record five interceptions—three of which are returned for touchdowns. "Just absolutely terrible," said Gannon, who was also sacked five times. "A nightmarish performance," he called it.

Kerry Collins can certainly relate. His New York Giants were overmatched by the Baltimore Ravens in Super Bowl XXXV, on January 28, 2001. In his lone Super Bowl appearance, Collins was intercepted four times in the 34-7 shellacking. He completed 15 of 39 passes for 112 yards and was sacked four times for a dismal passer rating of 7.1—the lowest of any quarterback in Super Bowl history. New York's lone points came on a Ron Dixon kickoff return. That was part of a fluke sequence in the third quarter when the teams traded touchdowns on three consecutive plays (an interception return and back-to-back kickoff returns). In a strange quirk, the Ravens received important contributions on offense, defense, and special team from players named Lewis. The top rusher was Jamal Lewis, who gained 103 yards and scored a touchdown in the Super Bowl, becoming the second rookie ever to rush for over 100 yards in the big game, and at twenty-one, he is the youngest player to score a touchdown in a Super Bowl. Jermaine Lewis returned a kickoff for a touchdown, and Ray Lewis was the Super Bowl MVP. Fittingly, the coach in charge of the defense, considered among the best ever, was Marvin Lewis. Another side note from this game: Glenn Parker, an offensive lineman for the Giants who also played for the Buffalo Bills, lost a fifth Super Bowl, tying him with Cornelius Bennett for most Super Bowl losses.

It is not possible to recognize all the players who earned Super Bowl rings or accomplished impressive Big Game feats. One such player is Preston Pearson, who won two rings in five Super Bowls as a running back with the Baltimore Colts, Pittsburgh Steelers, and Dallas Cowboys—the most storied NFL teams of his era. Pearson was the first player to participate in five Super Bowls, doing so with three different teams. He won rings with the Steelers in Super Bowl IX and the Cowboys in Super Bowl XII. His teams came up short in the big game with the Colts (III) and Cowboys (X, XIII). Pearson holds the distinction of playing for three of the greatest coaches in NFL history: Don Shula, Chuck Noll, and Tom Landry, with eight Super Bowl titles between them. And don't think we forgot about kicker Matt Stover. In the Colts' 31-17 loss to the Saints in Super Bowl XLIV, Stover made a 38-yard field goal. At forty-two years old, Stover became the oldest person to play in a Super Bowl.

So many fascinating Super Bowl tidbits, so little time, and so few pages! Bob Griese and his son, Brian, are the only father and son quarterback combination in NFL history to both win Super Bowl titles. The younger Griese earned his Super Bowl ring with the Denver Broncos in Super Bowl XXXIII, in 1999. In all, there have been five father-and-son combinations to play in a Super Bowl. The others are: Julius Adams and his son Keith; Frank Cornish and his son Frank Jr.; Tony Dorsett and his son Anthony; and Manu Tuiasosopo and his son Marques. Another Super family is the Hilgenbergs. They have been part of five Super Bowls. Uncle Wally played linebacker for the Minnesota Vikings in Super Bowls IV, VIII, IX and XI. Nephew Jay played center for the Chicago Bears in Super Bowl XX.

Reporting on half a century of Super Bowl games has been a pleasure. As stated in the introduction, I hope to be around to write the next book in fifty years. By then, perhaps, the four active franchises without a Super Bowl appearance—the Cleveland Browns, Jacksonville Jaguars, Detroit Lions, and Houston Texans—will have written their own new chapters for the history books.

RECORDS AND STATISTICS

I	Jan. 15, 1967	Los Angeles Memorial Coliseum	Green Bay 35, Kansas City 10
II	Jan. 14, 1968	Orange Bowl (Miami)	Green Bay 33, Oakland 14
III	Jan. 12, 1969	Orange Bowl (Miami)	New York Jets 16, Baltimore 7
IV	Jan. 11, 1970	Tulane Stadium (New Orleans)	Kansas City 23, Minnesota 7
V	Jan. 17, 1971	Orange Bowl (Miami)	Baltimore 16, Dallas 13
VI	Jan. 16, 1972	Tulane Stadium (New Orleans)	Dallas 24, Miami 3
VII	Jan. 14, 1973	Los Angeles Memorial Coliseum	Miami 14, Washington 7
VIII	Jan. 13, 1974	Rice Stadium (Houston)	Miami 24, Minnesota 7
IX	Jan. 12, 1975	Tulane Stadium (New Orleans)	Pittsburgh 16, Minnesota 6
X	Jan. 18, 1976	Orange Bowl (Miami)	Pittsburgh 21, Dallas 17
XI	Jan. 9, 1977	Rose Bowl (Pasadena, Calif.)	Oakland 32, Minnesota 14
XII	Jan. 15, 1978	Superdome (New Orleans)	Dallas 27, Denver 10
XIII	Jan. 21, 1979	Orange Bowl (Miami)	Pittsburgh 35, Dallas 31
XIV	Jan. 20, 1980	Rose Bowl (Pasadena, Calif.)	Pittsburgh 31, Los Angeles 19
XV	Jan. 25, 1981	Superdome (New Orleans)	Oakland 27, Philadelphia 10
XVI	Jan. 24, 1982	Silverdome (Pontiac, Mich.)	San Francisco 26, Cincinnati 21
XVII	Jan. 30, 1983	Rose Bowl (Pasadena, Calif.)	Washington 27, Miami 17
XVIII	Jan. 22, 1984	Tampa (Fla.) Stadium	Los Angeles 38, Washington 9
XIX	Jan. 20, 1985	Stanford (Calif.) Stadium	San Francisco 38, Miami 16
XX	Jan. 26, 1986	Superdome (New Orleans)	Chicago 46, New England 10
XXI	Jan. 25, 1987	Rose Bowl (Pasadena, Calif.)	New York Giants 39, Denver 20
XXII	Jan. 31, 1988	Jack Murphy Stadium (San Diego)	Washington 42, Denver 10
XXIII	Jan. 22, 1989	Joe Robbie Stadium (Miami)	San Francisco 20, Cincinnati 16
XXIV	Jan. 28, 1990	Superdome (New Orleans)	San Francisco 55, Denver 10
XXV	Jan. 27, 1991	Tampa (Fla.) Stadium	New York Giants 20, Buffalo 19

XXVI	Jan. 26, 1992	Metrodome (Minneapolis)	Washington 37, Buffalo 24
XXVII	Jan. 31, 1993	Rose Bowl (Pasadena, Calif.)	Dallas 52, Buffalo 17
XXVIII	Jan. 30, 1994	Georgia Dome (Atlanta)	Dallas 30, Buffalo 13
XXIX	Jan. 29, 1995	Joe Robbie Stadium (Miami)	San Francisco 49, San Diego 26
XXX	Jan. 28, 1996	Sun Devil Stadium (Tempe, Ariz.)	Dallas 27, Pittsburgh 17
XXXI	Jan. 26, 1997	Superdome (New Orleans)	Green Bay 35, New England 21
XXXII	Jan. 25, 1998	Qualcomm Stadium (San Diego)	Denver 31, Green Bay 24
XXXIII	Jan. 31, 1999	Pro Player Stadium (Miami)	Denver 34, Atlanta 19
XXXIV	Jan. 30, 2000	Georgia Dome (Atlanta)	St. Louis 23, Tennessee 16
XXXV	Jan. 28, 2001	Raymond James Stadium (Tampa, Fla.)	Baltimore 34, New York Giants 7
XXXVI	Feb. 3, 2002	Superdome (New Orleans)	New England 20, St. Louis 17
XXXVII	Jan. 26, 2003	Qualcomm Stadium (San Diego)	Tampa Bay 48, Oakland 21
XXXVIII	Feb. 1, 2004	Reliant Stadium (Houston)	New England 32, Carolina 29
XXXIX	Feb. 6, 2005	Alltel Stadium (Jacksonville, Fla.)	New England 24, Philadelphia 21
XL	Feb. 5, 2006	Ford Field (Detroit)	Pittsburgh 21, Seattle 10
XLI	Feb. 4, 2007	Dolphin Stadium (Miami)	Indianapolis 29, Chicago 17
XLII	Feb. 3, 2008	University of Phoenix Stadium (Glendale, Ariz.)	New York Giants 17, New England 14
XLIII	Feb. 1, 2009	Raymond James Stadium (Tampa, Fla.)	Pittsburgh Steelers 27, Arizona Cardinals 23
XLIV	Feb. 7, 2010	Sun Life Stadium (Miami)	New Orleans Saints 31, Indianapolis Colts 17
XLV	Feb. 6, 2011	Cowboys Stadium (Arlington, Texas)	Green Bay Packers 31, Pittsburgh Steelers 25
XLVI	Feb. 5, 2012	Lucas Oil Stadium (Indianapolis)	New York Giants 21, New England Patriots 17
XLVII	Feb. 3, 2013	Mercedes-Benz Superdome (New Orleans)	Baltimore Ravens 34, San Francisco 49ers 31
XLVIII	Feb. 2, 2014	MetLife Stadium (East Rutherford, N.J.)	Seattle Seahawks 43, Denver Broncos 8
XLIX	Feb. 1, 2015	University of Phoenix Stadium (Glendale, Ariz.)	New England Patriots 28, Seattle Seahawks 24

SUPER BOWL TEAM AND PLAYER STANDINGS

Super Bowl Standings Team	Games	Win	Loss
Pittsburgh Steelers	8	6	2
San Francisco 49ers	6	5	1
Dallas Cowboys	8	5	3
Green Bay Packers	5	4	1
New York Giants	5	4	1
New England Patriots	8	4	4
Oakland Raiders	5	3	2
Washington Redskins	5	3	2
Baltimore Ravens	2	2	0
Indianapolis/Baltimore Colts	4	2	2
Miami Dolphins	5	2	3
Denver Broncos	7	2	5
New Orleans Saints	1	1	0
New York Jets	1	1	0
Tampa Bay Buccaneers	1	1	0
Chicago Bears	2	1	1
Kansas City Chiefs	2	1	1
St. Louis Rams	3	1	2
Seattle Seahawks	3	1	2
Buffalo Bills	4	0	4
Minnesota Vikings	4	0	4
Cincinnati Bengals	2	0	2
Philadelphia Eagles	2	0	2
Atlanta Falcons	1	0	1
Carolina Panthers	1	0	1
Arizona Cardinals	1	0	1
Tennessee Titans	1	0	1
San Diego Chargers	1	0	1

Highest Passer Rating Super Bowl Game Player (Team)	Rating	Game
Phil Simms (New York Giants)	150.92	SB XXI
Joe Montana (San Francisco 49ers)	147.56	SB XXIV
Jim Plunkett (Oakland Raiders)	145.04	SB XV
Troy Aikman (Dallas Cowboys)	140.69	SB XXVII
Steve Young (San Francisco 49ers)	134.84	SB XXIX
Doug Williams (Washington Redskins)	127.87	SB XXII
Joe Montana (San Francisco 49ers)	127.2	SB XIX
Joe Flacco (Baltimore Ravens)	124.18	SB XLVII
Russell Wilson (Seattle Seahawks)	123.08	SB XLVIII
Terry Bradshaw (Pittsburgh Steelers)	119.17	SB XIII

Highest Passer Rating Super Bowl Career		
Player (Team)	Rating	Super Bowls
Joe Montana (San Francisco 49ers)	127.83	4
Jim Plunkett (Oakland/L.A. Raiders)	122.83	2
Russell Wilson (Seattle Seahawks)	117.39	2
Terry Bradshaw (Pittsburgh Steelers)	112.8	4
Troy Aikman (Dallas Cowboys)	111.93	3
Bart Starr (Green Bay Packers)	105.98	2
Brett Favre (Green Bay Packers)	97.61	2
Kurt Warner (St. Louis Rams, Arizona Cardinals)	96.65	3
Eli Manning (New York Giants)	96.17	2
Roger Staubach (Dallas Cowboys)	95.37	4

Most Pass Attempts Super Bowl Game		
Player (Team)	Attempts	Game
Jim Kelly (Buffalo Bills)	58	SB XXVI
Donovan McNabb (Philadelphia Eagles)	51	SB XXXIX
Tom Brady (New England Patriots)	50	SB XLIX
Jim Kelly (Buffalo Bills)	50	SB XXVIII
Dan Marino (Miami Dolphins)	50	SB XIX
Peyton Manning (Denver Broncos)	49	SB XLVIII
Matt Hasselbeck (Seattle Seahawks)	49	SB XL
Neil O'Donnell (Pittsburgh Steelers)	49	SB XXX
Stan Humphries (San Diego Chargers)	49	SB XXIX
Tom Brady (New England Patriots)	48	SB XLII
Tom Brady (New England Patriots)	48	SB XXXVIII
Drew Bledsoe (New England Patriots)	48	SB XXXI

Most Pass Attempts Super Bowl Career		
Player (Team)	Attempts	Super Bowls
Tom Brady (New England Patriots)	247	6
John Elway (Denver Broncos)	152	5
Jim Kelly (Buffalo Bills)	145	4
Kurt Warner (St. Louis Rams, Arizona Cardinals)	132	3
Peyton Manning (Indianapolis Colts, Denver Broncos)	132	3
Joe Montana (San Francisco 49ers)	122	4
Roger Staubach (Dallas Cowboys)	98	4
Ben Roethlisberger (Pittsburgh Steelers)	91	3
Fran Tarkenton (Minnesota Vikings)	89	3
Terry Bradshaw (Pittsburgh Steelers)	84	4

Most Pass Completions Super Bowl Game		
Player (Team)	Completions	Game
Tom Brady (New England Patriots)	37	SB XLIX
Peyton Manning (Denver Broncos)	34	SB XLVIII
Drew Brees (New Orleans Saints)	32	SB XLIV
Tom Brady (New England Patriots)	32	SB XXXVIII
Peyton Manning (Indianapolis Colts)	31	SB XLIV
Kurt Warner (Arizona Cardinals)	31	SB XLIII
Jim Kelly (Buffalo Bills)	31	SB XXVIII
Eli Manning (New York Giants)	30	SB XLVI
Donovan McNabb (Philadelphia Eagles)	30	SB XXXIX
Tom Brady (New England Patriots)	29	SB XLII
Dan Marino (Miami Dolphins)	29	SB XIX

Most Pass Completions Super Bowl Career		
Player (Team)	Completions	Super Bowls
Tom Brady (New England Patriots)	164	6
Peyton Manning (Indianapolis Colts, Denver Broncos)	90	3
Kurt Warner (St. Louis Rams, Arizona Cardinals)	83	3
Joe Montana (San Francisco 49ers)	83	4
Jim Kelly (Buffalo Bills)	81	4
John Elway (Denver Broncos)	76	5
Roger Staubach (Dallas Cowboys)	61	4
Troy Aikman (Dallas Cowboys)	56	3
Ben Roethlisberger (Pittsburgh Steelers)	55	3
Terry Bradshaw (Pittsburgh Steelers)	49	4
Eli Manning (New York Giants)	49	2

Highest Completion Percentage Super Bowl Game		
Player (Team)	Pct.	Game
Phil Simms (New York Giants)	88.00	SB XXI
Drew Brees (New Orleans Saints)	82.05	SB XLIV
Joe Montana (San Francisco 49ers)	75.86	SB XXIV
Eli Manning (New York Giants)	75.00	SB XLVI
Tom Brady (New England Patriots)	74.00	SB XLIX
Ken Anderson (Cincinnati Bengals)	73.53	SB XVI
Troy Aikman (Dallas Cowboys)	73.33	SB XXVII
Kurt Warner (Arizona Cardinals)	72.09	SB XLIII
Russell Wilson (Seattle Seahawks)	72.00	SB XLVIII
Rex Grossman (Chicago Bears)	71.43	SB XLI

Highest Completion Percentage Super Bowl Career		
Player (Team)	**Pct.**	**Super Bowls**
Troy Aikman (Dallas Cowboys)	70.00	3
Peyton Manning (Indianapolis Colts, Denver Broncos)	68.18	3
Joe Montana (San Francisco 49ers)	68.03	4
Tom Brady (New England Patriots)	66.40	6
Eli Manning (New York Giants)	66.22	2
Russell Wilson (Seattle Seahawks)	65.22	2
Len Dawson (Kansas City Chiefs)	63.64	2
Bob Griese (Miami Dolphins)	63.41	3
Jim Plunkett (Oakland/L.A. Raiders)	63.04	2
Kurt Warner (St. Louis Rams, Arizona Cardinals)	62.88	3

Most Passing Yards Super Bowl Game		
Player (Team)	**Yards**	**Game**
Kurt Warner (St. Louis Rams)	414	SB XXXIV
Kurt Warner (Arizona Cardinals)	377	SB XLIII
Kurt Warner (St. Louis Rams)	365	SB XXXVI
Donovan McNabb (Philadelphia Eagles)	357	SB XXXIX
Joe Montana (San Francisco 49ers)	357	SB XXIII
Tom Brady (New England Patriots)	354	SB XXXVIII
Doug Williams (Washington Redskins)	340	SB XXII
John Elway (Denver Broncos)	336	SB XXXIII
Peyton Manning (Indianapolis Colts)	333	SB XLIV
Joe Montana (San Francisco 49ers)	331	SB XIX

Most Passing Yards Super Bowl Career		
Player (Team)	Yards	Super Bowls
Tom Brady (New England Patriots)	1,605	6
Kurt Warner (St. Louis Rams, Arizona Cardinals)	1,156	3
Joe Montana (San Francisco 49ers)	1,142	4
John Elway (Denver Broncos)	1,128	5
Terry Bradshaw (Pittsburgh Steelers)	932	4
Peyton Manning (Indianapolis Colts, Denver Broncos)	860	3
Jim Kelly (Buffalo Bills)	829	4
Roger Staubach (Dallas Cowboys)	734	4
Troy Aikman (Dallas Cowboys)	689	3
Ben Roethlisberger (Pittsburgh Steelers)	642	3

Longest Pass From Scrimmage		
Player (Team)	Yards	Game
Jake Delhomme (Carolina Panthers)	85 (TD)	SB XXXVIII
Brett Favre (Green Bay Packers)	81 (TD)	SB XXXI
John Elway (Denver Broncos)	80 (TD)	SB XXXIII
Doug Williams (Washington Redskins)	80 (TD)	SB XXII
Jim Plunkett (Oakland Raiders)	80 (TD)	SB XV
David Woodley (Miami Dolphins)	76 (TD)	SB XVII
Terry Bradshaw (Pittsburgh Steelers)	75 (TD)	SB XIII
Johnny Unitas (Baltimore Colts)	75 (TD)	SB V
Kurt Warner (St. Louis Rams)	73 (TD)	SB XXXIV
Terry Bradshaw (Pittsburgh Steelers)	73 (TD)	SB XIV

Highest Yards Per Pass Average Super Bowl Game		
Player (Team)	Yds/Game	Game
Terry Bradshaw (Pittsburgh Steelers)	14.71	SB XIV
Jim McMahon (Chicago Bears)	12.80	SB XX
Jim Plunkett (Oakland Raiders)	12.43	SB XV
Russell Wilson (Seattle Seahawks)	11.76	SB XLIX
Doug Williams (Washington Redskins)	11.72	SB XXII
John Elway (Denver Broncos)	11.59	SB XXXIII
Bart Starr (Green Bay Packers)	10.87	SB I
Colin Kaepernick (San Francisco 49ers)	10.79	SB XLVII
Phil Simms (New York Giants)	10.72	SB XXI
Terry Bradshaw (Pittsburgh Steelers)	10.60	SB XIII

Highest Yards Per Pass Average Super Bowl Career		
Player (Team)	Yds/Game	Super Bowls
Terry Bradshaw (Pittsburgh Steelers)	11.1	4
Russell Wilson (Seattle Seahawks)	9.85	2
Bart Starr (Green Bay Packers)	9.62	2
Jim Plunkett (Oakland/L.A. Raiders)	9.41	2
Joe Montana (San Francisco 49ers)	9.36	4
Kurt Warner (St. Louis Rams, Arizona Cardinals)	8.76	3
Troy Aikman (Dallas Cowboys)	8.61	3
Len Dawson (Kansas City Chiefs)	8.02	2
Roger Staubach (Dallas Cowboys)	7.49	4
Eli Manning (New York Giants)	7.45	2

Most Passing Touchdowns Super Bowl Game		
Player (Team)	**TDs**	**Game**
Steve Young (San Francisco 49ers)	6	SB XXIX
Joe Montana (San Francisco 49ers)	5	SB XXIV
Tom Brady (New England Patriots)	4	SB XLIX
Troy Aikman (Dallas Cowboys)	4	SB XXVII
Doug Williams (Washington Redskins)	4	SB XXII
Terry Bradshaw (Pittsburgh Steelers)	4	SB XIII
Joe Flacco (Baltimore Ravens)	3	SB XLVII
Aaron Rodgers (Green Bay Packers)	3	SB XLV
Kurt Warner (Arizona Cardinals)	3	SB XLIII
Donovan McNabb (Philadelphia Eagles)	3	SB XXXIX
Tom Brady (New England Patriots)	3	SB XXXVIII
Jake Delhomme (Carolina Panthers)	3	SB XXXVIII
Brett Favre (Green Bay Packers)	3	SB XXXII
Phil Simms (New York Giants)	3	SB XXI
Joe Montana (San Francisco 49ers)	3	SB XIX
Jim Plunkett (Oakland Raiders)	3	SB XV
Roger Staubach (Dallas Cowboys)	3	SB XIII

Most Passing Touchdowns Super Bowl Career		
Player (Team)	**TDs**	**Super Bowls**
Tom Brady (New England Patriots)	13	6
Joe Montana (San Francisco 49ers)	11	4
Terry Bradshaw (Pittsburgh Steelers)	9	4
Roger Staubach (Dallas Cowboys)	8	4
Kurt Warner (St. Louis Rams, Arizona Cardinals)	6	3
Steve Young (San Francisco 49ers)	6	2
Brett Favre (Green Bay Packers)	5	2
Troy Aikman (Dallas Cowboys)	5	3
Russell Wilson (Seattle Seahawks)	4	2
Doug Williams (Washington Redskins)	4	1
Jim Plunkett (Oakland/L.A. Raiders)	4	2

Most Interceptions Thrown Super Bowl Game		
Player (Team)	**INTs**	**Game**
Rich Gannon (Oakland Raiders)	5	SB XXXVII
Kerry Collins (New York Giants)	4	SB XXXV
Drew Bledsoe (New England Patriots)	4	SB XXXI
Jim Kelly (Buffalo Bills)	4	SB XXVI
Craig Morton (Denver Broncos)	4	SB XII
Donovan McNabb (Philadelphia Eagles)	3	SB XXXIX
Chris Chandler (Atlanta Falcons)	3	SB XXXIII
Neil O'Donnell (Pittsburgh Steelers)	3	SB XXX
John Elway (Denver Broncos)	3	SB XXII
Ron Jaworski (Philadelphia Eagles)	3	SB XV
Terry Bradshaw (Pittsburgh Steelers)	3	SB XIV
Roger Staubach (Dallas Cowboys)	3	SB X
Fran Tarkenton (Minnesota Vikings)	3	SB IX
Billy Kilmer (Washington Redskins)	3	SB VII
Craig Morton (Dallas Cowboys)	3	SB V
Earl Morrall (Baltimore Colts)	3	SB III

Most Passes Interceptions Thrown Super Bowl Career		
Player (Team)	**INTs**	**Super Bowls**
John Elway (Denver Broncos)	8	5
Craig Morton (Dallas Cowboys, Denver Broncos)	7	2
Jim Kelly (Buffalo Bills)	7	4
Fran Tarkenton (Minnesota Vikings)	6	3
Rich Gannon (Oakland Raiders)	5	1
Ben Roethlisberger (Pittsburgh Steelers)	5	3
Roger Staubach (Dallas Cowboys)	4	4
Drew Bledsoe (New England Patriots)	4	1
Terry Bradshaw (Pittsburgh Steelers)	4	4
Earl Morrall (Baltimore Colts)	4	4
Kerry Collins (New York Giants)	4	1
Peyton Manning (Indianapolis Colts, Denver Broncos)	4	3
Joe Theismann (Washington Redskins)	4	2
Tom Brady (New England Patriots)	4	6

Most Rushing Attempts Super Bowl Game		
Player (Team)	Attempts	Game
John Riggins (Washington Redskins)	38	SB XVII
Franco Harris (Pittsburgh Steelers)	34	SB IX
Larry Csonka (Miami Dolphins)	33	SB VIII
Ray Rice (Baltimore Ravens)	30	SB XLVII
Terrell Davis (Denver Broncos)	30	SB XXXII
Emmitt Smith (Dallas Cowboys)	30	SB XXVIII
Matt Snell (New York Jets)	30	SB III
Michael Pittman (Tampa Bay Buccaneers)	29	SB XXXVII
Eddie George (Tennessee Titans)	28	SB XXXIV
Jamal Lewis (Baltimore Ravens)	27	SB XXXV
Franco Harris (Pittsburgh Steelers)	27	SB X

Most Rushing Attempts Super Bowl Career		
Player (Team)	Attempts	Super Bowls
Franco Harris (Pittsburgh Steelers	101	4
Emmitt Smith (Dallas Cowboys)	70	3
John Riggins (Washington Redskins)	64	2
Larry Csonka (Miami Dolphins)	57	3
Terrell Davis (Denver Broncos)	55	2
Thurman Thomas (Buffalo Bills)	52	4
Roger Craig (San Francisco 49ers)	52	3
Antowain Smith (New England Patriots)	44	2
Rocky Bleier (Pittsburgh Steelers)	44	4
Marshawn Lynch (Seattle Seahawks)	39	2

Most Rushing Yards Super Bowl Game				Most Rushing Yards Super Bowl Career		
Player (Team)	**Yards**	**Game**		**Player (Team)**	**Yards**	**Super Bowls**
Timmy Smith (Washington Redskins)	204	SB XXII		Franco Harris (Pittsburgh Steelers)	354	4
Marcus Allen (Los Angeles Raiders)	191	SB XVIII		Larry Csonka (Miami Dolphins)	297	3
John Riggins (Washington Redskins)	166	SB XVII		Emmitt Smith (Dallas Cowboys)	289	3
Franco Harris (Pittsburgh Steelers)	158	SB IX		Terrell Davis (New England Patriots)	259	2
Terrell Davis (Denver Broncos)	157	SB XXXII		John Riggins (Washington Redskins)	230	2
Larry Csonka (Miami Dolphins)	145	SB VIII		Thurman Thomas (Buffalo Bills)	204	4
Clarence Davis (Oakland Raiders)	137	SB XI		Timmy Smith (Washington Redskins)	204	1
Thurman Thomas (Buffalo Bills)	135	SB XXV		Roger Craig (San Francisco 49ers)	198	3
Emmitt Smith (Dallas Cowboys)	132	SB XXVIII		Marcus Allen (Los Angeles Raiders)	191	1
Michael Pittman (Tampa Bay Buccaneers)	124	SB XXXVII		Antowain Smith (New England Patriots)	175	2

Longest Rush From Scrimmage		
Player (Team)	Yards	Game
Willie Parker (Pittsburgh Steelers)	75 (TD)	SB XL
Marcus Allen (Los Angeles Raiders)	74 (TD)	SB XVIII
Timmy Smith (Washington Redskins)	58 (TD)	SB XXII
Tom Matte (Baltimore Colts)	58	SB III
Thomas Jones (Chicago Bears)	52	SB XLI
Larry Csonka (Miami Dolphins)	49	SB VII
Alvin Garrett (Washington Redskins)	44	SB XVII
Timmy Smith (Washington Redskins)	43	SB XXII
John Riggins (Washington Redskins)	43 (TD)	SB XVII
Marcus Allen (Los Angeles Raiders)	39	SB XVIII
Wendell Tyler (Los Angeles Rams)	39	SB XIV

Highest Yards per Carry Average Super Bowl Game		
Player (Team)	Yds/Carry	Game
Tom Matte (Baltimore Colts)	10.55	SB III
Marcus Allen (Los Angeles Raiders)	9.55	SB XVIII
Willie Parker (Pittsburgh Steelers)	9.30	SB XL
Timmy Smith (Washington Redskins)	9.27	SB XXII
Thurman Thomas (Buffalo Bills)	9.0	SB XXV
Clarence Davis (Oakland Raiders)	8.56	SB XI
Thomas Jones (Chicago Bears)	7.47	SB XLI
Larry Csonka (Miami Dolphins)	7.47	SB VII
Tony Dorsett (Dallas Cowboys)	6.0	SB XIII
Joseph Addai (Indianapolis Colts)	5.92	SB XLIV

Highest Yards per Carry Average Super Bowl Career		
Player (Team)	Yds/Carry	Super Bowls
Marcus Allen (Los Angeles Raiders)	9.55	1
Timmy Smith (Washington Redskins)	9.27	1
Dominic Rhodes (Indianapolis Colts)	5.38	1
Walt Garrison (Dallas Cowboys)	5.35	2
Tony Dorsett (Dallas Cowboys)	5.23	2
Larry Csonka (Miami Dolphins)	5.21	3
Willie Parker (Pittsburgh Steelers)	5.03	2
Kenneth Davis (Buffalo Bills)	4.83	4
Joseph Addai (Indianapolis Colts)	4.81	2
Shaun Alexander (Seattle Seahawks)	4.75	1

Most Rushing Touchdowns Super Bowl Game		
Player (Team)	TDs	Game
Terrell Davis (Denver Broncos)	3	SB XXXII
Eddie George (Tennessee Titans)	2	SB XXXIV
Howard Griffith (Denver Broncos)	2	SB XXXIII
Emmitt Smith (Dallas Cowboys)	2	SB XXX
Emmitt Smith (Dallas Cowboys)	2	SB XXVIII
Gerald Riggs (Washington Redskins)	2	SB XXVI
Tom Rathman (San Francisco 49ers)	2	SB XXIV
Timmy Smith (Washington Redskins)	2	SB XXII
Jim McMahon (Chicago Bears)	2	SB XX
Marcus Allen (Los Angeles Raiders)	2	SB XVIII
Franco Harris (Pittsburgh Steelers)	2	SB XIV
Pete Banaszak (Oakland Raiders)	2	SB XI
Larry Csonka (Miami Dolphins)	2	SB VIII
Elijah Pitts (Green Bay Packers)	2	SB I

Most Rushing Touchdowns Super Bowl Career		
Player (Team)	TDs	Super Bowls
Emmitt Smith (Dallas Cowboys)	5	3
Thurman Thomas (Buffalo Bills)	4	4
John Elway (Denver Broncos)	4	5
Franco Harris (Pittsburgh Steelers)	4	4
Terrell Davis (Denver Broncos)	3	2
Marcus Allen (Los Angeles Raiders)	2	1
Ottis Anderson (New York Giants)	2	2
Marshawn Lynch (Seattle Seahawks)	2	2
Eddie George (Tennessee Titans)	2	1
Howard Griffith (Denver Broncos)	2	2
Elijah Pitts (Green Bay Packers)	2	1
John Riggins (Washington Redskins)	2	2
Jim Kiick (Miami Dolphins)	2	3
Timmy Smith (Washington Redskins)	2	1
Pete Banaszak (Oakland Raiders)	2	2
Jim McMahon (Chicago Bears)	2	1
Joe Montana (San Francisco 49ers)	2	4
Tom Rathman (San Francisco 49ers)	2	2
Gerald Riggs (Washington Redskins)	2	1
Roger Craig (San Francisco 49ers)	2	3
Larry Csonka (Miami Dolphins)	2	3

Most Receptions Super Bowl Game		
Player (Team)	Receptions	Game
Demaryius Thomas (Denver Broncos)	13	SB XLVIII
Shane Vereen (New England Patriots)	11	SB XLIX
Wes Welker (New England Patriots)	11	SB XLII
Deion Branch (New England Patriots)	11	SB XXXIX
Jerry Rice (San Francisco 49ers)	11	SB XXIII
Dan Ross (Cincinnati Bengals)	11	SB XVI
Hakeem Nicks (New York Giants)	10	SB XLVI
Joseph Addai (Indianapolis Colts)	10	SB XLI
Deion Branch (New England Patriots)	10	SB XXXVIII
Andre Hastings (Pittsburgh Steelers)	10	SB XXX
Jerry Rice (San Francisco 49ers)	10	SB XXIX
Tony Nathan (Miami Dolphins)	10	SB XIX

Most Receptions Super Bowl Career Player (Team)	Receptions	Super Bowls
Jerry Rice (San Francisco 49ers)	33	4
Andre Reed (Buffalo Bills)	27	4
Wes Welker (New England Patriots, Denver Broncos)	26	3
Deion Branch (New England Patriots)	24	3
Thurman Thomas (Buffalo Bills)	20	4
Roger Craig (San Francisco 49ers)	20	3
Joseph Addai (Indianapolis Colts)	17	2
Jay Novacek (Dallas Cowboys)	17	3
Troy Brown (New England Patriots)	16	3
Lynn Swann (Pittsburgh Steelers)	16	4
Michael Irvin (Dallas Cowboys)	16	3

Most Receiving Yards Super Bowl Game Player (Team)	Yards	Game
Jerry Rice (San Francisco 49ers)	215	SB XXIII
Ricky Sanders (Washington Redskins)	193	SB XXII
Isaac Bruce (St. Louis Rams)	162	SB XXXIV
Lynn Swann (Pittsburgh Steelers)	161	SB X
Rod Smith (Denver Broncos)	152	SB XXXIII
Andre Reed (Buffalo Bills)	152	SB XXVII
Jerry Rice (San Francisco 49ers)	149	SB XXIX
Jerry Rice (San Francisco 49ers)	148	SB XXIV
Deion Branch (New England Patriots)	143	SB XXXVIII
Jordy Nelson (Green Bay Packers)	140	SB XLV
Muhsin Muhammad (Carolina Panthers)	140	SB XXXVIII

Most Receiving Yards Super Bowl Career		
Player (Team)	Yards	Super Bowls
Jerry Rice (San Francisco 49ers, Oakland Raiders)	589	4
Lynn Swann (Pittsburgh Steelers)	364	4
Andre Reed (Buffalo Bills)	323	4
Deion Branch (New England Patriots)	321	3
John Stallworth (Pittsburgh Steelers)	268	4
Michael Irvin (Dallas Cowboys)	256	3
Wes Welker (New England Patriots, Denver Broncos)	247	3
Hines Ward (Pittsburgh Steelers)	244	3
Ricky Sanders (Washington Redskins)	234	2
Antonio Freeman (Green Bay Packers)	231	2

Longest Reception From Scrimmage		
Player (Team)	Yards	Game
Muhsin Muhammad (Carolina Panthers)	85 (TD)	SB XXXVIII
Antonio Freeman (Green Bay Packers)	81 (TD)	SB XXXI
Rod Smith (Denver Broncos)	80 (TD)	SB XXXIII
Ricky Sanders (Washington Redskins)	80 (TD)	SB XXII
Kenny King (Oakland Raiders)	80 (TD)	SB XV
Jimmy Cefalo (Miami Dolphins)	76 (TD)	SB XVII
John Stallworth (Pittsburgh Steelers)	75 (TD)	SB XIII
John Mackey (Baltimore Colts)	75 (TD)	SB V
Isaac Bruce (St. Louis Rams)	73 (TD)	SB XXXIV
John Stallworth (Pittsburgh Steelers)	73 (TD)	SB XIV

Highest Yards per Catch Average Super Bowl Game		
Player (Team)	**Yds/Catch**	**Game**
John Stallworth (Pittsburgh Steelers)	40.33	SB XIV
Lynn Swann (Pittsburgh Steelers)	40.25	SB X
John Stallworth (Pittsburgh Steelers)	38.33	SB XIII
Muhsin Muhammad (Carolina Panthers)	35.00	SB XXXVIII
Antonio Freeman (Green Bay Packers)	35.00	SB XXXI
Willie Gault (Chicago Bears)	32.25	SB XX
Charlie Brown (Washington Redskins)	31.00	SB XVIII
Rod Smith (Denver Broncos)	30.40	SB XXXIII
Chris Matthews (Seattle Seahawks)	27.25	SB XLIX
Isaac Bruce (St. Louis Rams)	27.00	SB XXXIV

Highest Yards per Catch Average Super Bowl Career		
Player (Team)	**Yds/Catch**	**Super Bowls**
John Stallworth (Pittsburgh Steelers)	24.36	4
Ricky Sanders (Washington Redskins)	23.40	2
Lynn Swann (Pittsburgh Steelers)	22.75	4
Max McGee (Green Bay Packers)	21.62	2
Art Monk (Washington Redskins)	19.89	3
Isaac Bruce (St. Louis Rams)	19.82	2
Antonio Freeman (Green Bay Packers)	19.25	2
James Lofton (Buffalo Bills)	19.12	3
Ricky Proehl (St. Louis Rams, Carolina Panthers)	19.12	3
Joe Jurevicius (New York Giants, Tampa Bay Buccaneers, Seattle Seahawks)	19.00	3

Most Receiving Touchdowns Super Bowl Game		
Player (Team)	TDs	Game
Jerry Rice (San Francisco 49ers)	3	SB XXIX
Jerry Rice (San Francisco 49ers)	3	SB XXIV
Greg Jennings (Green Bay Packers)	2	SB XLV
Larry Fitzgerald (Arizona Cardinals)	2	SB XLIII
Keenan McCardell (Tampa Bay Buccaneers)	2	SB XXXVII
Antonio Freeman (Green Bay Packers)	2	SB XXXII
Ricky Watters (San Francisco 49ers)	2	SB XXIX
Michael Irvin (Dallas Cowboys)	2	SB XXVII
Ricky Sanders (Washington Redskins)	2	SB XXII
Roger Craig (San Francisco 49ers)	2	SB XIX
Dan Ross (Cincinnati Bengals)	2	SB XVI
Cliff Branch (Oakland Raiders)	2	SB XV
John Stallworth (Pittsburgh Steelers)	2	SB XIII
Bill Miller (Oakland Raiders)	2	SB II
Max McGee (Green Bay Packers)	2	SB I

Most Receiving Touchdowns Super Bowl Career		
Player (Team)	TDs	Super Bowls
Jerry Rice (San Francisco 49ers)	8	4
John Stallworth (Pittsburgh Steelers)	3	4
Antonio Freeman (Green Bay Packers)	3	2
Lynn Swann (Pittsburgh Steelers)	3	4
Cliff Branch (Oakland/L.A. Raiders)	3	3
Larry Fitzgerald (Arizona Cardinals)	2	1
Doug Baldwin (Seattle Seahawks)	2	2
John Taylor (San Francisco 49ers)	2	3
Mike Vrabel (New England Patriots)	2	4
Hines Ward (Pittsburgh Steelers)	2	3
Muhsin Muhammad (Carolina Panthers)	2	2
Ricky Watters (San Francisco 49ers)	2	1
Ricky Proehl (St. Louis Rams, Carolina Panthers)	2	3
Dan Ross (Cincinnati Bengals)	2	1
Ricky Sanders (Washington Redskins)	2	2
Keenan McCardell (Tampa Bay Buccaneers)	2	1
David Givens (New England Patriots)	2	2
Max McGee (Green Bay Packers)	2	2
Don Beebe (Buffalo Bills)	2	4
Bill Miller (Oakland Raiders)	2	1
Jay Novacek (Dallas Cowboys)	2	3
Michael Irvin (Dallas Cowboys)	2	3
Gary Clark (Washington Redskins)	2	2
Greg Jennings (Green Bay Packers)	2	1
Butch Johnson (Dallas Cowboys)	2	2
Roger Craig (San Francisco 49ers)	2	3

Most Interceptions Super Bowl Game Player (Team)	INTs	Game
Rod Martin (Oakland Raiders)	3	SB XV
Rodney Harrison (New England Patriots)	2	SB XXXIX
Dexter Jackson (Tampa Bay Buccaneers)	2	SB XXXVII
Dwight Smith (Tampa Bay Buccaneers)	2	SB XXXVII
Darrien Gordon (Denver Broncos)	2	SB XXXIII
Larry Brown (Dallas Cowboys)	2	SB XXX
Thomas Everett (Dallas Cowboys)	2	SB XXVII
Brad Edwards (Washington Redskins)	2	SB XXVI
Barry Wilburn (Washington Redskins)	2	SB XXII
Jake Scott (Miami Dolphins)	2	SB VII
Chuck Howley (Dallas Cowboys)	2	SB V
Randy Beverly (New York Jets)	2	SB III

Most Interceptions Super Bowl Career Player (Team)	INTs	Super Bowls
Rod Martin (Oakland/L.A. Raiders)	3	2
Larry Brown (Dallas Cowboys)	3	3
Chuck Howley (Dallas Cowboys)	3	2
Darrien Gordon (Denver Broncos)	2	4
Mel Blount (Pittsburgh Steelers)	2	4
Mike Wagner (Pittsburgh Steelers)	2	3
James Washington (Dallas Cowboys)	2	2
Rodney Harrison (New England Patriots)	2	4
Dexter Jackson (Tampa Bay Buccaneers)	2	1
Jake Scott (Miami Dolphins)	2	3
Brad Edwards (Washington Redskins)	2	1
Thomas Everett (Dallas Cowboys)	2	2
Dwight Smith (Tampa Bay Buccaneers)	2	1
Randy Beverly (New York Jets)	2	1
Barry Wilburn (Washington Redskins)	2	1
Eric Wright (San Francisco 49ers)	2	4

REFERENCES

Books

Chastain, Bill, *Steel Dynasty: The Team That Changed the NFL*. Triumph Books, 2005.

Didinger, Ray, *The Super Bowl: Celebrating a Quarter-Century of America's Greatest Game*. Simon & Schuster, 1990.

Felser, Larry, *The Birth of the New NFL*. The Lyons Press, 2008.

Freeman, Mike, *Undefeated: Inside the 1972 Miami Dolphins' Perfect Season*. It Books, 2012.

Garner, Joe, *100 Yards of Glory: The Greatest Moments in NFL History*. Houghton Mifflin Harcourt, 2011.

Golenbock, Peter, *Landry's Boys: An Oral History of a Team and an Era*. Triumph Books, 2005.

Green, Jerry, *Super Bowl Chronicles: A Sportswriter Reflects on the First 30 Years of America's Game*. Masters Press, 1995.

Halberstam, David, *The Education of a Coach*. Hachette Books, 2006.

King, Peter, *Football: A History of the Professional Game*. Oxmoor House, 1993.

Koppett, Leonard, *The New York Times at the Super Bowl*. Quadrangle Books, 1974.

McDonell, Chris, *The Football Game I'll Never Forget: 100 NFL Stars' Stories*. Firefly Books, 2004.

McGinn, Bob, foreword by Michael MacCambridge, *The Ultimate Super Bowl Book: A Complete Reference to the Stats, Stars, and Stories Behind Football's Biggest Game—and Why The Best Team Won*, Second Edition. MVP Books, 2012.

Pearlman, Jeff, *Boys Will Be Boys: The Glory Days and Party Nights of the Dallas Cowboys Dynasty*. Harper Perennial, 2009.

Peary, Danny, *Super Bowl: The Game of Their Lives*. Diane Publishing Company, 1997.

The Sporting News Complete Super Bowl Book. The Sporting News, 1995.

Zimmerman, Paul, *Dr. Z's 25 Years of Super Bowl Memories*. Time, Inc., 1991.

Historical and Biographical Information

www.abcnews.com

www.cbsnews.com

www.bleacherreport.com

www.forbes.com

www.money.cnn.com

www.pophistorydig.com

www.profootballhof.com

www.superbowl.com

Super Bowl Game Reporting

www.latimes.com

www.nydailynews.com

www.nytimes.com

www.si.com

www.sportingnews.com

www.washingtonpost.com